the structure of political thought

A *study in the history of political ideas*

the structure
of political thought

*A Study in the History
of Political Ideas*

Charles N. R. McCoy

*Head, Department of Politics
The Catholic University of America*

GREENWOOD PRESS, PUBLISHERS
WESTPORT, CONNECTICUT

Library of Congress Cataloging in Publication Data

McCoy, Charles Nicholas Reiten, 1911–
    The structure of political thought.

    Reprint of the ed. published by McGraw-Hill,
New York.
    Bibliography: p.
    Includes index.
    1. Political science—History. I. Title.
[JA81.M24 1975]   320'.09   74–25996
ISBN 0–8371–7880–0

Reprinted with the permission of McGraw-Hill Book Company

Reprinted from an original copy in the collections of
the New York Public Library

Reprinted in 1978 by Greenwood Press, Inc.,
51 Riverside Avenue, Westport, Conn. 06880

Printed in the United States of America

10 9 8 7 6 5 4 3 2 1

the structure
of political thought

*A Study in the History
of Political Ideas*

Charles N. R. McCoy

*Head, Department of Politics
The Catholic University of America*

McGraw-Hill Book Company, Inc.

New York   San Francisco   Toronto   London

preface

A glance at the Table of Contents of this book will give the reader a rapid and cursory idea of what is meant by "the structure of political thought." It will reveal a relation of order between logic and reality, between theoretic science and practical science, between art and prudence. Concealed in the bare outline is a story—indeed, a mystery story, whose solution will make up the construction of this book.

In *The Evolution of Physics*, Albert Einstein has compared the reader of a good mystery story to the scientist who seeks answers to the mysteries written in the book of nature. In drawing out the comparison, he observes that in all good mystery stories it is not the wealth of facts that contributes materially to the solution; rather a time arrives when the investigator has gathered all the facts necessary for at least some part of his problem. The facts frequently appear incoherent, contradictory, and unrelated. But the ideal detective knows exactly when the moment is reached at which further investigation of facts is unnecessary; he knows that "only pure thinking will lead to a correlation of the facts collected. So he plays his violin, or lounges in his arm-chair enjoying a pipe, when suddenly, by Jove, he has it." He has, suddenly, the key to the facts at hand, and indeed he now knows that certain other events must have taken place. He may then, if he wishes, go ahead and collect additional confirmation of his theory, for in the light of his discovered principle he now knows exactly where to look.

It is our purpose in the following pages to assume for the social scientist a role that corresponds to the pure thinking of the investigator. But a caution even more exigent is imposed upon the social scientist than upon the physicist: Einstein goes on to call attention to the fact that the comparison between the reader of a mystery story and the scientist seeking solutions to the mysteries of nature is not a good one all the way. For if the physicist, as he says, is somewhat like a man who tries to comprehend the mechanism of a closed watch, he will nonetheless never be able to compare his image with the real mechanism. Now the mystery that confronts the investigator into the world of culture and civilization is of a directly opposite sort; for here rather it is precisely the familiar world—corresponding to the closed watch of Einstein's simile—that has largely disappeared. That world itself—as Mr. David Riesman has suggested—is found by "radar." The experimental social scientist can as yet not even begin where the experimental natural scientist begins—from the common notions and values of the familiar world, from the closed watch, "visible to my eyes and tangible to my grasp." The state of contemporary culture is such that in his job of investigator the social scientist has to make *his* suppositions about precisely the things that ought to be evident or demonstrable—the watch-case, the tick-tock, the movement of the hands of the watch. Hence, the social scientist is himself a curious case. By the strangest turn of events the ancient truths—self-evident or demonstrable—are able today to serve as "hypotheses," as it were, by which increasingly to explain the world of shadows that we know by radar. In this curious new role the ancient truths will allow us to see why it is that, as Ernst Cassirer observed, in the twentieth century, the age of man's highest technical competence, the elements of myth and magic have for the first time in the history of civilization taken possession of the purely secular sphere.

In this story of political ideas we shall attempt at least a partial solution of the mystery hinted at. All the essential clues that will allow the reader to form his own theory of the case will be presented. And if he follows the plot carefully, he will be brought—as in all good mystery stories—to acknowledge the solution to be inevitable, terrifying and timely.

The author is grateful to Rand McNally & Company for permission to use material from chapters he has contributed to *A History of Political Philosophy*, edited by Joseph Cropsey, and to the editors of the *American Political Science Review* and *Laval Théologique et Philosophique* for use of material from articles that he has contributed to these journals.

The author also wishes to acknowledge with gratitude the help he has received in the preparation of the manuscript from Jerome G. Kerwin, the Rev. Paul A. Woelfl, S.J., and Robert J. McKenna.

Charles N. R. McCoy

contents

Introduction

In *An Essay on Man* Ernst Cassirer observed that our modern theory of man has lost its intellectual center. The reason which he assigns for this loss is very simple and clear: It is not merely that science today is specialized; it is the uniqueness of this specialization. Intellectual history begins indeed with distinguishing the sciences, and with the recognition of general and specialized sciences. The Greeks distinguished mathematics from physics and physics from politics, and within each of these there were specialized studies: *The Parts of Animals* represents an early kind of experimental extension of the general science of physics; *The Constitution of Athens* is a detailed, circumstantial study employing the general principles of political science. But today's specialization is different, and the difference is this: From the time of the great scientific revolution of the seventeenth century, experimental or specialized science has claimed for itself an autonomy that had hitherto never been accorded it. This has meant that whereas formerly every experimental study had been related to scientific truths of a general nature, the new scientific developments have been marked by a scrupulous indifference to what Sir Arthur Eddington has called the "familiar world." In many respects this procedure is proper enough, but it involves a serious danger—that of supposing that the "familiar world" is not as real as the "scientific world." The situation of modern physics in this regard is excellently brought out by Eddington:

I have settled down to the task of writing . . . and have drawn up my chairs to my two tables. Yes: there are duplicates of every object about me—two tables, two chairs, two pens. . . .

One of (my two tables) has been familiar to me from earliest years. . . . How shall I describe it? It has extension; it is comparatively permanent; it is coloured; above all it is *substantial*. . . .

Table No. 2 is my scientific table. It is a more recent acquaintance, and I do not feel so familiar with it. It does not belong to the world previously mentioned. . . . My scientific table is mostly emptiness. Sparsely scattered in that emptiness are numerous electric charges rushing about with great speed; but their combined bulk amounts to less than a billionth of the bulk of the table itself.

I need not tell you that modern physics has by delicate test and remorseless logic assured me that my second scientific table is the only one which is really there—wherever "there" may be. On the other hand I need not tell you that modern physics will never succeed in exorcising that first table . . . which lies visible to my eyes and tangible to my grasp. . . . No doubt they are ultimately to be identified in some fashion. But the process by which the external world of physics is transformed into a world of familiar acquaintance . . . is outside the scope of physics. The frank realization that physical science is concerned with a world of shadows is one of the most significant of recent advances.[1]

We must now observe a matter that lies first at the very origin and then at the climactic center of the history of political thought: In the first great beginnings of human speculation we quite understandably find a tendency to suppose that the world of reality is constructed on the model of human reason. Plato observed that

[1] Sir Arthur Eddington, *The Nature of Physical World*, Cambridge University Press, New York, 1946, pp. ix–xv.

a certain similitude must exist between the world that is known and the mind that knows it; and he was led to suppose that this meant that the real existence of things is exactly the same as their existence in the mind. He thus supposed the "logical universal"— e.g., "man" as predicable of Paul and John, "community" as predicable of family and village—to be a principle of existence; he was in this way led to credit the most universal community, the State, with a richer and more real existence than the family and even than the individual. It was this fundamental doctrine of Plato that was responsible for the strongly "idealistic" construction of his Republic, "laid away in the heavens." Between the time of Plato and the sixteenth century, philosophy succeeded in distinguishing the logical order from the real order. But suppose—and it is indeed rather a fact than a supposition—that the autonomy of modern experimental science should issue in a "scientific" world whose image can never even be compared with the familiar world and can suggest nothing whatsoever of necessity (as Plato's philosophy could) in the familiar world. Do we not see how a great temptation—similar indeed to Plato's but not the same—would arise to look upon this "scientific" world as the "real" world, constructed by human reason? Plato did not commit this absurdity. Plato merely imagined that the world's real existence was essentially an immaterial one and patterned on the order of the human mind. But beginning with the great scientific revolution of the sixteenth and seventeenth centuries the "given" and "familiar" world disappears.

Now there had always been present in Western thought a tendency to revolt against the "givenness" of things; but until the seventeenth century when science asserted its autonomy, this element of revolt had been reduced to bounds by the prevalent teleological view of nature. This teleological view consisted essentially in seeing in nature a purpose, an end, a "reason," similar to, indeed, but not as properly comprehensive, as the purpose explicitly engaged in by man himself. For the Greek mind the government of a political community found a prototype in the laws by which the whole universe is governed; man, indeed, was considered, alone among natural things, to be capable of self-government and of freedom because he was thought to possess the intellectual principle for himself. The principle of the autonomy of nature, asserted by the scientific revolution, meant that, contrary to the classical view, human reason came to be looked upon as not essentially different from the rest of nature, considered now as an original, formative principle. The new, the crucial, the revolutionary factor affecting the whole modern effort, affecting the whole "human condition" has been this reversal in the relationship between man and nature brought about by the autonomy of modern science. Where man had in the past "projected," if you will, the teleology characteristic of human nature on to the rest of nature, this process is now reversed.

In order to understand the implications of this reversal, it is necessary to advert again to the error of Plato. Against Plato's error of supposing that the real world existed essentially in an immaterial fashion and on the pattern of the human mind (the order of logic), Aristotle showed that the first object of the human mind is some material thing under a predicate most indeterminate and confused (the "being" of common predication); and therefore what we first apprehend is not anything according to the proper actuality of its being, according to the order of nature (i.e., as "given").[2] And secondly, that when the human mind comes to know things as they actually are in nature, it does not know them according to the order of causality (i.e., as making them). Plato had projected the logical order on to the real, and he remained caught in this order, never quite descending to the real world. Aristotle not only distinguished the logical order from the real, but within the real order he distinguished between practical science (concerned with some kind of making) and purely theoretic science (concerned with knowledge only). Now modern experimental science differs from philosophical science in that it investigates the real world not as it is "given" but as it is simply "formable" by Him who made it. Nature in the line of its autonomy is

[2] Thus, for example, it is only in the logical order that "animal" is imposed on "man" and "dog" as though it were a determining form. There is no animal apart from the man who is an animal and the dog which is an animal, etc.

thus the same as nature in the line of pure formability; and the "teleology" of nature in this perspective appears as infinite potentiality. We can see, then, that when the teleology of nature in the line of its autonomy is projected on to human nature, man's nature becomes something that is simply and essentially "formable." We have come in view of a world as unreal as Plato's but infinitely more dangerous. And it is infinitely more dangerous because the connection between the scientific world and the familiar world is broken. There is now no limit to what the modern politician may do with human nature—he may "brainwash" it if he has the power: This is Jean Jacques Rousseau's infinitely malleable man; it is Machiavelli's Prince who is half-man, half-beast-lion-and-fox; it is Marx's "generic man"; it is the Kinsey Report's "democratic pluralism of sexuality"; it is Freud's "polymorphous pervert"; it is Riesman's autonomous man; it is George Orwell's world of 1984.

If we are to appreciate this extraordinary outcome of Western political thought we must attend first to an insight of Aristotle's which will throw great light on the matter. As I have said, to the Greek mind, man alone among natural things was thought to be capable of freedom and self-government; but in Book XII of the *Metaphysics*, Aristotle observes that the whole of human nature is in some sense enslaved. Man is the least among intelligent beings.[3] The contrariety of sense and reason in man makes it extremely difficult for him to achieve the freedom of which he is basically capable. And this condition of inferiority as compared with higher intellectual natures produces in man a tendency to revolt against his condition, against the "givenness" of things. This is the reason why, throughout the history of political thought and political practice, we observe a twofold effort toward the conquest of liberty: one, a genuine effort springing from man's genuine and unique capacity for self-government; but the second is a spurious effort, often insinuating itself into the first, confusing itself with it and expressing itself as an "emancipation" from the basic human condition, indeed, from basic natural right. This kind of emancipation makes its first appearance with the early

[3] We have mentioned the fact that man's knowledge is neither according to the order of nature nor according to the order of causality.

Stoic and other "philosophies of conduct" that followed the death of Aristotle. These, however, remained no more than mere philosophies of "escape" and "revolt" and (as Marx himself observed) issued in a "frustrated state of half-contemplation and half-action." The *political* and public character of this spirit of revolt had to await the autonomy of modern science. Speaking broadly, but nonetheless accurately, totalitarianism, modern liberalism, and modern conservatism all have their roots in the reversal of the relation between man and nature; all of them, if in quite different ways, attribute to social processes the kind of intelligence that lurks in the kind of stupidity that defines nature in its pure autonomy as a *substitute intelligence*.[4] Nature was thought of, in the tradition of Aristotle, as a "substitute intelligence" because it acts always or for the most part in the same way and without knowledge of the end, because it does not intend the individual as such but only for the sake of the species, and lastly because it does not extend to the diversity of the species of things—all these characteristics are found once again, on the human level, in modern political movements—in liberalism, in conservatism, and in totalitarianism. The paradox then that we will observe in the history of political thought is that in moving away from the givenness of things toward the condition of "creator," man has moved toward the condition of the substitute intelligence which is nature. This appears as the true meaning of man having lost his intellectual center.

The situation in which modern philosophy finds itself has been well expressed by Max Scheler: "In no other period has man ever become more problematic to himself than in our own days . . . we no longer possess any clear and consistent idea of man. The ever-growing multiplicity of the particular sciences . . . has much more confused and obscured than elucidated our concept of man." [5] And yet no previous age was ever in possession of as many facts and of the technical instruments for research as is our

---

[4] See St. Thomas Aquinas, Commentary, *In II Physics* lect.14.

[5] *Die Stellung des Menschen im Kosmos*, Darmstadt, Reichl, 1928, pp. 13ff. Cited in Ernst Cassirer, *Essay on Man*, Yale University Press, New Haven, Conn., 1944, p. 22.

own age. "But," as Cassirer wisely pointed out, "our wealth of facts is not necessarily a wealth of thoughts. Unless we succeed in finding a clue of Ariadne to lead us out of this labyrinth, we can have no real insight into the general character of human culture. . . ." [6]

The clue of Ariadne to lead us out of this labyrinth, I suggest, is a scrupulous care for the thread of tradition in political philosophy. We must assume, to begin with, that the great writers in the field had a certain competence in handling the terms proper to it. In politics (as in any science) the development of the science is possible because fundamental concepts are employed which serve as a basis for exploration into specialized fields of investigation. The acknowledgment of the need for basic concepts does not require an a priori acceptance of any principle of truth; but it does require a scrupulous fidelity to the factor of tradition in the history of political thought. By the factor of tradition is meant nothing more than is necessarily implied in any intellectual history. Concepts, principles, judgments are handed down in the course of such history, and these concepts, principles, and judgments are either retained or lost, altered or added to. The acknowledgment of the factor of tradition is of primary importance, and from that acknowledgment follows the obligation to understand (not necessarily to accept) the construction of political thought at its beginnings. Only then can the subsequent narration take on significance. Only then can a more nearly genuine reading of the history of political thought be hoped for. And this reading will, I suggest, show the central reason for the central fact of our time: which is, as Cassirer has observed, that in the twentieth century, the age of man's highest technical competence, the elements of magic and myth have for the first time taken possession of the purely secular sphere:

The modern politicians have had to solve a problem that in many respects resembles squaring the circle. The historians of human civilization have told us that mankind in its development had to pass through two different phases. Man began as a *homo magus;* but from the age

---

[6] Cassirer, *Essay on Man*, p. 22.

of magic he passed to the age of technics. The *homo magus* of former times and of primitive civilization became a *homo faber,* a craftsman and artisan. If we admit such an historical distinction our modern political myths appear indeed as a very strange and paradoxical thing. For what we find in them is the blending of two activities that seem to exclude each other. The modern politician has had to combine in himself two entirely different and even incompatible functions. He has to act, at the same time, as both a *homo magus* and a *homo faber.* He is the priest of a new, entirely irrational and mysterious religion.[7]

A careful tracing of the thread of tradition in political philosophy will lead us to see that "brainwashing," the bewildering spectacle of twentieth-century political trials with their curious "confessions," the "radar" guided "other-directed" social character, the "democratic pluralism of sexuality"—all these symptoms of magic in the secular sphere—are expressions of man's having moved toward the condition of creator by having moved toward the condition of "substitute intelligence" of nature. They are expressions of an exorcism possible indeed in the world of culture and civilization as it is not possible in the world of physics. It will also lead us to see that the recovery of man's intellectual center depends on understanding that the very notion of self-government comes from the fact that the human intellect occupies a center position between the condition of creator and the condition of nature: that its capacity to *know* the proper human good is precisely the guarantee of man's independence both from any blind necessity of nature and from any political "art."

[7] Ernst Cassirer, *The Myth of the State,* Yale University Press, New Haven, Conn., 1946, pp. 281–282.

part one

the Classical-Christian tradition

In things relating to perfection . . . intensity is in proportion to the approach to one first principle; to which the nearer a thing approaches, the more intense it is. Thus the intensity of a thing possessed of light depends on its approach to something endowed with light in a supreme degree, to which the nearer a thing approaches, the more light it possesses.

St. Thomas Aquinas

I

Plato: logic and political reality

Logic has been described as an instrument of thought to guide man in an orderly way, with ease and without error, in the construction of science. It is reasonable to suppose, then, that the art of thinking should not at its beginning have benefited by the perfection of its instruments. And this is indeed the case. If we agree—and it is commonly agreed—to fix the beginning of systematic philosophic speculation in the Western world at the seventh century B.C. in Greece, we then find that for two centuries the human mind grappled with the most difficult matters without the aid of adequate instruments of thought. And yet, because one cannot disassociate the object of science from the way in which that object is thought about, it was natural that the early philosophers should have touched to some extent upon problems of logic. As Aristotle remarks, in speaking of the first principles of thought, "some natural philosophers indeed [have treated of these matters] and their procedure was intelligible enough; for they thought that they were alone inquiring about the whole of nature and about being." [1] But since, as Aristotle points out, the rules of thought are applicable in every science ("and all men use them"), "no one who is conducting a

[1] *Metaph.* IV.1005a.31.

11

special inquiry tries to say anything about their truth or falsity—neither the geometrician nor the arithmetician." [2] Indeed, the students of particular sciences, he goes on to observe, "should know these things (the rules of logic) already when they come to a special study, and not be inquiring into them while they are listening to lectures on [their special study]." [3]

Now Greek philosophy took its beginnings with the special study of the physical universe. We need merely advert here to the fact that, because of the failure to make prior investigation into the nature and conditions of human knowledge, this opening period of Greek philosophy (known as the Cosmological Period), extending from the seventh to fifth centuries, ended in a condition of complete intellectual paralysis. The impasse reached in the fifth century is perhaps best reflected in the conflicting theories of two of the greatest of the early thinkers, Heraclitus and Parmenides. It was the teaching of Heraclitus that the only reality is change; there is no underlying substratum that may be said to undergo change, and therefore Heraclitus was saying that science is impossible, for science ought to be necessary and certain, at least in part. Parmenides of Elea had succeeded in transcending the world of physical bodies and even that of mathematical forms, and had attained the notion of *being* as such. But since, according to Parmenides, *that which is*, is, and *that which is not*, is not, there is only one science possible: the science of being. The distinction of things is an illusion because the only difference between two beings must necessarily be non-being, and non-being is not; hence all things are one, without distinction and without change. The philosophy of Parmenides found its most brilliant apologist in Zeno, and the arguments of Zeno appeared to his opponents to be unanswerable. The paradoxes of Zeno became famous; they were designed to show the impossibility of change and plurality. He argued, for example, that motion cannot possibly begin because a body in motion cannot arrive at

[2] *Ibid.*
[3] *Ibid.*

another place until it has passed half the distance between its point of departure and its goal; but the number of intermediate points is not just one but is infinite; for half the space must be transversed, and half of that and half of that, and so on ad infinitum. Since an infinite space cannot be traversed in a finite time, motion is obviously an illusion of the senses.

In discussing the notions of these men, who were his predecessors, Aristotle adverts to the logical problems (among others) inherent in their dilemmas. Heraclitus was in effect saying that it is possible for the same thing to be and not to be at the same time and in the same respect; though, as Aristotle shrewdly observes, "what a man says, he does not necessarily believe." [4] Nonetheless, this was what Heraclitus was *saying;* and indeed, "this belief . . . blossomed in the most extreme (view) . . . such as was held by Cratylus, who finally did not think it right to say anything, but only moved his finger, and criticized Heraclitus for saying that it is impossible to step twice into the same river; for *he* thought one could not do it even once." [5] Parmenides, on the other hand, had maintained that all things are one. Fastening on that which is *one in definition,* he held that *one* is used in this single sense only and concluded that "being" has the same meaning, of whatever it is predicated, and that it means both just *what is* and *what is one.*[6]

The sophists

The difficulties attendant upon the theories of the Greek physicists were indeed insurmountable until such time as the principles of thought should themselves be established. The result was an impasse and a crisis in Greek philosophy. Despairing of reaching truth in the field of physics, men turned toward what appeared

[4] *Metaph.* IV.1005b.24.
[5] *Ibid.* 1010a.10ff.
[6] *Physics* I.186a.33ff.; *Metaph.* I.986b.18ff.

to them to be the more easily accessible field of human behavior.[7]
The new emphasis on humanistic studies was carried out, toward
the middle of the fifth century, by the itinerant teachers in Athens,
known as sophists.[8] The new humanism of the sophists did not,
however, entirely set aside the ways of thinking followed by the
older philosophers of nature. The Greeks of the fifth century had
found in the "flux" of Heraclitus the analogue of changing custom
and convention in human affairs; and their inquiry was addressed,
similarly to that of the early physicists, to the possible existence
of some underlying principle of permanence in human life. At
the middle of the fifth century, Protagoras of Abdera, taking account of the teachings of Heraclitus and Parmenides, drew the
skeptical inference from their doctrine: If, as Heraclitus had maintained, all things are in flux, or if, as Parmenides had held, the
multiplicity of things is the subject matter for opinion but not
knowledge, then "Man is the measure of all things, of what is, that
it is, and what is not that it is not." In a similar way, the sophist
Gorgias of Leontini, called the Nihilist, deriving inspiration from
Parmenides, maintained that the destruction of the popular belief
in the existence of the multiplicity of things led not to the existence of the one (as Parmenides had taught) but to the proposition that nothing must *be*, since nothing is: That if anything
were, it could not be known; and that if anything could be known
it could not be communicated. Gorgias in fact availed himself of
the arguments which Zeno had used, but to prove, contrary to
Zeno's demonstration, that it is just non-being that *is and is one.*
Thus where Protagoras had held that truth is relative to the

---

[7] "But at this period men gave up inquiring into the works of nature, and
philosophers diverted their attention to political science and to the virtues
which benefit mankind." (Aristotle, *On the Parts of Animals* I.642a.30)

[8] The term "sophist" originally signified a man of wisdom. Thus the his-
torian Herodotus calls Solon and Pythagoras sophists. Plato gave it the
limited meaning which signified the paid teachers of Athens during the last
half of the fifth century. Its contemporary connotation—an impostrous pre-
tender to knowledge who employs even fallacy for the purpose of gaining
his argument and his money—was given by Aristotle. (*Rhetoric* I.48.)

individual and that all opinions are equally true, Gorgias held that because nothing is, all opinions are equally false. Those among the sophists who were inclined to suppose that there is some underlying principle in human affairs—something "natural" to all men—were no more successful in escaping the skepticism and subjectivism that were the legacy of earlier physicists. The sophist Callicles, as Plato presents his position in the dialogue called *Gorgias*, finds that "to suffer (rather than to do) injustice is the greater disgrace because the greater evil; but conventionally to do evil is the more disgraceful; . . . whereas nature herself . . . in many ways (shows), among men as well as among animals, and indeed among whole cities and races that justice consists in the superior ruling over and having more than the inferior." [9] It follows then, that the conventional "justice" of a state represents either (1) an attempt to thwart nature by setting up a barrier for the protection of the multitude of weaklings, or (2) conventional justice is simply the conventional expression of the natural strength of the strong. This position is defended at some length by the sophist Thrasymachus, whose views are reported for us by Plato in the *Republic*:

Each government has its laws framed to suit its own interests; a democracy making democratical laws; an autocrat despotic laws; and so on. Now by this procedure these governments have pronounced that what is for the interest of themselves is just for their subjects; and whoever deviates from this, is chastised by them as guilty of illegality and injustice. Therefore, my good sir, my meaning is, that in all cities the same thing, namely, the interest of the established government, is just. And superior strength, I presume, is to be found on the side of government. So that the conclusion of right reasoning is that the same thing, namely, the interest of the stronger, is everywhere just.[10]

[9] Jowett translation, pp. 483–484. In *The Dialogues of Plato*, Random House, New York, 1937.

[10] *Republic*, pp. 338–339.

Socrates and Plato

The sophists had indeed effected a transition from philosophy as cosmology to philosophy as concerning itself with man as a thinking subject; but the character of their pursuit was hardly suited to the task of finding a scientific basis for a theory of knowledge and a science of morals. It was, however, as a catalytic that they served to precipitate a genuine inquiry into the conditions of knowledge, and thus negatively to advance philosophy to the point where the problems left by Parmenides and Heraclitus could be solved. The man who was to rescue Greek philosophy from its parlous state was Socrates (b. 469 B.C.). Although a devoted student of one of the more distinguished sophists, Prodicus, Socrates dedicated his life to eradicating the deadly disease of sophistry from Greek life. Socrates committed none of his doctrine to writing; he led, in fact, very much the same sort of life as his opponents, the sophists, spending his time in discussion with the young men of Athens. Our knowledge of his teaching comes from the accounts of Xenophon, one of his students, and above all from Plato, his great disciple. It is from Aristotle, however, that we have the most valuable information on the teaching of Socrates, and in Book XIII of his *Metaphysics* he tells us that Socrates was the first of the Greek thinkers to raise the problem of universal definition. "For of the physicists," Aristotle writes, "Democritus only touched on the subject to a small extent. . . ." [11] "But it was natural," continues Aristotle, "that Socrates should be seeking the essence, for he was seeking to syllogize, and 'what a thing is' is the starting point of syllogisms; . . . for two things may be fairly ascribed to Socrates—inductive argument and universal definition, both of which are concerned with the starting point of science." [12] The method which Socrates employed, called "maieutic," the art of intellectual midwifery, sought to aid the intellect in bringing forth its proper object by seeking the essences

[11] *Metaph.* XIII.1078b.20.
[12] *Ibid.* 1078b.24.

of things and expressing them in definitions. Philosophy had now advanced beyond the stage where it sought some one universal nature—water, air, fire, numbers, or even absolute being—as the ultimate substance of everything. Socrates had, on the contrary, engaged it in the task of determining and defining the essence of each thing by genus and difference, by a concept proper to itself alone. If we wish to see the Socratic method in operation, we have only to study the masterly use of it in the great dialogues of Plato. Consider, for example, Plato's reply to the very powerful objections made by the sophists against the possibility of the existence of scientific truth in moral matters: The sophists plausibly maintained that if there were anything universally right in morals it would be everywhere the same; but there is obviously nothing so right in human affairs that it obtains force everywhere. In Carthage the sacrifice of human beings was considered a holy and lawful thing, while in Athens it was condemned by law. "What else can law be," the sophist asks, "if not (merely) the things established by law?" To this question Plato replies, through the mouth of Socrates:

If I asked instead what is gold, you would not inquire, what kind of gold. For gold cannot differ from gold, so far as it *is* gold. Nor can law differ from law, in so far as they really are law. Law, therefore, cannot be merely the sum of existing legal rules, for some decrees are good and some evil, but law cannot be evil. Hence all decrees cannot be law, but those only that are good and consonant to law in its true sense. Law, then, is the discovery of a good that exists, it can be discovered only by those who are wise, and such above all are statesmen and kings, whose writings relating to the state men generally call laws. But it is the decree only of the good and the wise that we may *rightly* call laws, and one that is not right we shall no longer call lawful; it becomes "unlawful." [13]

[13] *Minos* cap.IX.137. This dialogue is generally regarded as not being authentic. Nonetheless, "it is among those that are probably contemporary fourth-century work, not deliberate forgeries . . . ; and [may] be taken . . . as contributing to our knowledge of the conception of Socrates current in the fourth century." (Frederich Coppleston, *A History of Philosophy*, The Newman Press, Westminster, Md., 1948, vol. I, p. 134.)

It is by analogy with the distinct natures found in the universe, and with the arts that Plato attempts to establish the universal in moral matters. If the physician's work is the health of the body, if the shepherd's work is the care of his flock, and if the navigator's work is the welfare of his ship, it is reasonable to suppose that man himself, being a supreme work of nature and art (divine), must have a good which is proper to him. And this good Plato calls justice; for "each of us . . . if his inward faculties do severally their proper work, will, in virtue of that, be a just man, and a doer of his proper work." [14]

But it was the very merit and value of the Socratic discovery that contained a latent danger: The discovery of definition involved the possibility of identifying the real order with the logical order, of identifying the real existence of things with their existence in the mind. It was to this error that Plato, by an understandable inadvertence, succumbed. Having observed that knowledge takes place through some kind of similitude, and that the things understood in the mind are understood under conditions of immateriality and immobility, Plato was led to suppose that things existed in themselves under such conditions. Plato's theory that the essences of things were necessarily immaterial—the Doctrine of Ideas—was further determined by his Heraclitean discipleship. As Aristotle tells us:

For having in his youth first become familiar with . . . the Heraclitean doctrines (that all sensible things are ever in a state of flux and there is no knowledge about them), these views Plato held even in later years. Socrates, however, was busying himself about ethical matters and neglecting the world of nature as a whole, but seeking the universal in these ethical matters, and fixed thought for the first time on definitions; Plato accepted his teaching, but held that the problem applied not to sensible things but to entities of another kind—for this reason, that the common definition could not be a definition of any sensible thing, as they were always changing. Things of this other sort, then, he called Ideas, and sensible things, he said, were all named

[14] *Republic*, p. 441.

after these, and in virtue of a relation to these; for the many existed by participation in the Ideas that have the same name as they.[15]

The philosophy of Plato, including his political philosophy, was formed, then, by the confluence of two streams of thought: the speculations of Heraclitus on the problem of being and becoming, and the discovery by Socrates of inductive argument and definition. The solution which Plato worked out, the Doctrine of Ideas, enabled him to account for the nature of science in a better way, however inadequate, than had hitherto been possible. Its inadequacy lay exactly in its achievement: It had found the possibility of defining and classifying things—a task initial and indispensable to science—but it could not distinguish the real existence of things defined from their mode of existence in the logical order. The outcome (as we find it in Plato's writings) of Socrates' seeking the universal in ethical matters and fixing thought for the first time on definitions, was the famous doctrine that virtue is knowledge.

The doctrine that virtue is knowledge

The understanding of virtue as simply a form of scientific knowledge, i.e., that the theoretic understanding of the nature of virtue entails the moral habit itself, was with Plato the immediate result of abstracting from the material conditions and concomitants of virtue: It was in this sense a "logical" and not a real or natural definition. It was indeed the immediate consequence of maintaining that the essences of sensible things subsist under conditions of immateriality and immobility. But since, in fact, human actions and habits proceed from certain natural and material bases, namely, the passions and powers of man's nature as a rational animal, something at the very least more adequate than a purely "logical" definition of virtue was required.[16] Socrates and Plato

---

[15] *Metaph.* I.987a.31–987b.10.

[16] I say "at the very least" because there is also in Plato's doctrine a failure

were constrained, indeed, to go counter to observed facts and to maintain that men never act contrary to the knowledge that they have, and that every virtue is a kind of knowledge and every evil a kind of ignorance. In this, as Aristotle was later to point out, they were partly right and partly wrong. It is not enough to have knowledge of the good in order to pursue it; the latter requires a right desire, and this desire can be hindered by passion so that a person may fail to consider in particular what he knows in general. Now general or universal knowledge does not hold the foremost place in actions, but rather particular knowledge, since actions are about particular or singular things. Plato's error was to suppose virtue to be a form of scientific knowledge, therefore once a person *knows what,* for example, temperance is, he can never again become intemperate. But as Aristotle will later point out, the inclination toward passion can itself prompt a universal proposition contrary to the universal proposition suggested by the reason, and it is under the former that the reason of the unvirtuous man proceeds. In considering the doctrine of Socrates, St. Thomas Aquinas, the greatest of the commentators on the philosophy of Aristotle, explains the matter as follows:

He that has knowledge in the universal is hindered, because of a passion, from reasoning in the light of that universal, so as to draw the conclusion; but he reasons in the light of another universal proposition suggested by the inclination of the passion, and draws his conclusion accordingly. Hence the Philosopher [Aristotle] says that the syllogism of an incontinent man has four propositions, including *two* universals, of which one comes from the reason, e.g. No fornication is lawful, and the other, from passion, e.g. Pleasure is to be pursued. Hence passion fetters the reason, and hinders it from thinking and concluding under the first proposition; so that while the passion lasts, the reason argues and concludes under the second.[17]

---

to distinguish theoretic knowledge from practical knowledge, but this failure itself was preceded and caused by the basic confusion of the logical order and the real. We shall speak of the distinction between theoretic and practical knowledge—introduced by Aristotle—in the following chapter.

[17] *Summa Theol.* I.II.Q.77 a.2 ad 4.

It was this doctrine of Plato's—that virtue is a form of scientific knowledge—that was responsible for his failure to admit the rule of law in the ideal State and for his exclusive reliance on education. Before saying more about this aspect of Plato's teaching, it is necessary to examine a consequence of the doctrine of ideas that was even more crucial in affecting the construction of the ideal republic.

The State—"the individual writ large"

We must observe that the logical universal, insofar as it is predicable of many—as, for example, "man" is predicable of John, James, and Paul—is neither a principle of existence nor a substance. That is to say, "man" is not something apart from John, James, and Paul, who are men. But Plato supposed this universal to be a principle of existence, and he gave to this universal a separate existence. For Plato the universal "man" exists, and the individual men whom we know through our senses are merely weak participations in the idea Man. Now in the logical order the more universal concept is imposed on the less universal as if it were a form determining matter. Thus, in "man is an animal" and "dog is an animal," the terms "man" and "dog" are as variable matter with respect to the imposition of the determining form "animal." But actually, in the real order, "animal" is not the determining form of "man" and "dog"; in the real order "animal" is an indeterminate and confused concept compared with "man" and "dog." For there is no animal in general: There is no animal except dog which is an animal and man who is an animal, etc. Following Aristotle's correction of Plato's error on this point St. Thomas, in the thirteenth century, explained it very clearly:

That which is common to many is not something besides those many except . . . logically: thus animal is not something besides Socrates and Plato and other animals except as considered by the mind, which apprehends the form of animal as divested of all that specifies and individualizes it: for man is that which is truly animal, else it would follow that in Socrates and Plato there are several animals, namely, animal in general, man in general, and Plato himself.[18]

For Plato, on the contrary, the more universal concept in the logical order was looked upon as more real, more determinate, more "rich," and it was thought by him to contain actually, and not merely potentially, its subjective parts. If this were the case, if the subjective parts "man" and "dog" were in the genus "animal" actually and not merely potentially, it would follow that these parts would have no determinate, specific existence; they would be absorbed in the genus. Thus it was that Plato supposed John Smith and Paul Jones to be almost nothing, nothing but weak participations in the idea Man.

It was this identification of the logical order with the real order that was responsible for the absorption, in Plato's political philosophy, of the real parts of political society in the whole.[19] "But what?" Plato asks, "the nature of a large house and that of a small city, are they different with regard to government? Not at all." [20] Indeed, he tells us that the State is nothing but the individual writ large. The mistake of identifying the logical order with the real accounts for the extreme unity that Plato seeks to achieve for the ideal republic. The "justice" that may be perceived in the individual whose "inward faculties do severally their proper work" is perceived only very dimly there, and "in small letters": The State is the individual writ large, for the actions of the individual man are, in Plato's view, principally actions of the whole State. Thus the activity of the individual is absorbed in that of the State, much as man's own nature is itself considered a mere shadow of the archetypal idea Man. The three faculties of the soul, whose harmonious action constitutes the virtue of justice, are the rational, with its proper virtue of wisdom; the spirited, whose virtue is courage; and the appetitive, perfected by the virtue of temper-

[18] *Contra Gentiles* I.chap.26.

[19] See Jacques De Monléon, "Petites notes autour de la famille et de la cité," *Laval Théologique et Philosophique*, vol. 3, no. 2, pp. 262–289, 1947.

[20] *The Statesman* 258E–259D.

ance. These faculties are directly projected by Plato on to the State in terms of its three classes: the rulers, who exercise wisdom for the State; the warriors, who provide the needed courage; and the workers, whose appetites are tempered by the education they receive.

We can now understand the full political implications of Plato's doctrine that virtue is knowledge. The doctrine means, as we have seen, that the rule of reason over the sense appetites is absolute and without contradiction. The appetitive soul is considered in no sense to be free, but immediately and totally subject to the rule of the rational soul. And since the acts of the individual are principally those of the whole State, the artisan and warrior classes are under the despotic rule of the guardians—or of the "philosopher-king," if one best man should be found. An elaborate, State-controlled system of education is designed to fix men in their appointed places in the community. There is no provision for law in the ideal republic; and there can be none, because law derives its effectiveness for commanding obedience from habit, and habit depends on the internal natural liberty of the subject—which in Plato's doctrine of virtue is absent. Here again the Platonic teaching is corrected by Aristotle and very precisely explained in the following passage of St. Thomas:

Reason is the first principle of all human acts, and whatever other principles of human acts may be found, they obey reason in some way, but diversely. For some obey reason instantaneously and without any contradiction whatever. Such are the members of the body, provided they be in a healthy condition, for as soon as reason commands, the hand or the foot proceeds to action. Hence, the Philosopher [Aristotle] says that *the soul rules the body with a despotic rule,* i.e., as a master rules his slave, who has no right to rebel. Accordingly, some held that all the active principles in man are subordinate to reason in this way. If this were true, for a man to act well it would suffice that his reason be perfect. Consequently, since virtue is a habit perfecting man in view of his doing good actions, it would follow that virtue existed only in the reason, so that there would be none but intellectual virtues. This was the opinion of Socrates, who said *every virtue is a kind of pru-*

dence. . . . Hence he maintained that as long as a man was in possession of knowledge, he could not sin, and that every one who sinned did so through ignorance.

Now this is based on a false supposition. For the appetitive part obeys the reason, not instantaneously, but with a certain power of opposition; and so the Philosopher says that *reason commands the appetitive part by a political rule,* whereby a man rules over subjects that are free, having a certain right of opposition.[21]

It is this "right of opposition" based on the free nature of the political subject that Plato's philosophical principles could make no provision for. That is why it is true to say that "the ideal state of the *Republic* was simply a denial of the political faith of the city-state, with its ideal of free citizenship and its hope that every man, within the limits of his powers, might be made a sharer in the duties and privileges of government," and "for this reason Plato's omission of law from his ideal state cannot be interpreted otherwise than as a failure to perceive a striking moral aspect of the very society which he desired to perfect." [22]

Property and the family

Curiously, it is the members of the highest class, the rulers, who are the more seriously deprived of the rights belonging to them as men; for the rulers are to have neither property nor families of their own. As Aristotle says, Plato "deprives the Guardians even of happiness, and says that the legislator ought to make the whole state happy. But the whole cannot be happy unless most, or all, or some of its parts enjoy happiness. . . . And if the Guardians are not happy, who are? Surely not the artisans or the common people." [23] Plato is conscious of this objection and thinks it sufficiently answered by saying "that our aim in founding the State was not

[21] *Summa Theol.* I.II.Q.58 a.2c.

[22] George H. Sabine, *A History of Political Theory,* Holt, Rinehart and Winston, Inc., New York, 1937, p. 65.

[23] *Politics* II.1264b.16–25.

the disproportionate happiness of any one class, but the greatest happiness of the whole." [24] But it is precisely the "whole" that Plato has misconceived by failing to see that, as Aristotle will point out, "the nature of a state is to be a plurality and in tending to the greatest unity, from being a state it becomes a family, and from being a family, an individual; for the family may be said to be more one than the State, and the individual than the family. So that we ought not to attain this greatest unity even if we could, for it would be the destruction of the state." [25] But Plato thinks that loyalty to the common good is hindered by loyalty to one's family and by interest in one's property; he supposes that family affection is incompatible with the affection that should obtain in that larger "family" which is the whole society of the State, where all children are sons of all, and all men are brothers, "all men saying mine and not mine at the same instant of time." He does not see what Aristotle will point out, that

This is not the way in which people would speak who had their wives and children in common; they would say "all" but not "each." In like manner their property would be described as belonging to them, not severally but collectively. . . . That all persons call the same thing mine in the sense in which each does so may be a fine thing, but it is an impracticable one; or if the words are taken in the other sense, such a unity in no way conduces to harmony.[26]

We may note that in opposing the unity based on the alleged real priority of the logical universal, Aristotle makes two things clear: (1) the logical universal—"man" or "community"—insofar as it is predicable of many, has no being outside of the reason; (2) that the logical universal is, nonetheless, quite essential to our knowledge of the real nature of things. The logical universal does not, it is true, exist as such outside of the reason; but it is a universal verily rooted in individual things, as is clear from the fact that what we say of "animal" in general is true of every

---

[24] *Republic,* pp. 420–421.
[25] *Politics* II.1261a.18–23.
[26] *Ibid.* 1261b.23–33.

animal in particular, and what we say of "community" in general is true of every community in particular. It is, for example, true that every man has sense knowledge, but this is true of a cat and dog and every other animal as well. The general definition of "animal" expresses at least that which the different species of animal have in common. In speaking of the general definition of "soul," Aristotle makes the matter clear:

> It is now evident that a general notion can be given of soul only in the same sense as one can be given of figure. For, as in that case there is no figure distinguishable and apart from triangle, etc., so here there is no soul apart from the forms of soul just enumerated. It is true that a highly general definition can be given for figure which will fit all figures without expressing the peculiar nature of any figure. So here in the case of soul and its specific forms. Hence it is absurd in this and similar cases to seek a common definition which will fail to express the peculiar nature of anything that *is*. . . . The cases of figure and soul are exactly parallel; for the particulars subsumed under the common name in both cases—figures and living beings—constitute a series, each successive term of which potentially contains its predecessor, e.g., the square the triangle, and the sensory power the self-nutritive. Hence we must ask in the case of each class of living things, What is its soul, i.e., What is the soul of plant, animal, man? [27]

Just as there is little profit in seeking a common definition of soul, there is little profit in attempting to find a general definition of community which will fail to express the peculiar nature of any community that *is*. "As in other departments of science, so in politics, the compound should always be resolved into the simple elements or least parts of the whole." [28] And in accordance with this method Aristotle will proceed to distinguish the kinds of community that do exist and the different kinds of rule that they imply.

In his later years, Plato had an adumbration of this method. The *Statesman* and the *Laws* attempted to take account of the role of habit and custom in society and introduced the instrument

[27] *De Anima* II.414b–415a.
[28] *Politics* 1252a.7.

of law. But indeed this modification "called for a complete reconstruction of his psychology . . . and of his theory of knowledge. . . ." [29] It was Aristotle who undertook this revision, and it is therefore to Aristotle that we must now turn; for "Aristotle successfully took to pieces Plato's system, adapted to the exigencies of reality the formal principles he had discovered and misapplied, reduced his sweeping perspectives within the limits imposed by a sublime common sense, and thus saved everything vital in his master's thought." [30]

[29] Sabine, *op. cit.*, p. 86.
[30] From Jacques Maritain, *An Introduction to Philosophy*, Sheed & Ward, Inc., New York, 1933, pp. 82–83.

II

Aristotle: political science and the real world

Plato's failure to distinguish clearly the logical order from the real made it impossible for him to construct a truly practical science of politics. For to be practical, we must know how things really are. We have observed that the mode in which things exist in the mind is not the mode of their real existence: the universal, "man," which I know, does not really exist as a universal but exists only in the individuals—John Smith and Paul Jones—who are men. We saw that Plato was prompted to hold the Doctrine of Ideas because he had observed that all knowledge takes place through some kind of similitude, and that since it is a fact that things understood in the intellect are understood under conditions of immateriality and immobility, it seemed to him that things must similarly exist in themselves. The consequence of this view was that all knowledge was reduced to a kind of metaphysics, which itself bore the imprint of purely logical being. Now the contribution of Aristotle was to show that while it is true that all knowledge takes place through some kind of similitude, the conditions of immateriality and immobility under which the intellect receives the species of material and movable bodies does not imply that these latter are themselves with-

29

out matter: for what is received by the knower is received *according to the mode of the recipient.* This is very clear to us in the case of sense knowledge: The color green is not in the eye in the same way in which it is in the colored surface which is seen. The intellect, whose act of knowing is universal and characterized by a certain necessity—as Plato well understood—receives *according to its own mode* the species of material and movable things. According to Aristotle's correction of Plato, the power of the intellect, although not the act of an organ, is a power of a soul which is substantially united to a body, and for this reason it is capable of knowing a universal existing in corporeal matter—i.e., of knowing "man," which is a universal predicable of many individuals, and of knowing it precisely as common to many. The universal which constitutes the formal principle of the singular (that which makes John and Paul to be *the same animal,* namely, *man*) has no separate existence as a universal; "man," *taken as a universal,* belongs to the logical order; as such, it is a universal of predication, it is not a universal "in act." The only thing that is in act is the real singular individual, John Smith, who *has* the nature man; and this universal (which constitutes the formal principle of the individual) really contains matter: flesh and bones.[1] Thus did

---

[1] Aristotle distinguishes three degrees of intellectual abstraction from matter, and these are summarily set forth in the following passage from St. Thomas Aquinas: "*First degree* of abstraction. There are certain objects of speculation which are dependent upon matter as to their existence, since they cannot exist except in matter, and these are distinguished because they depend on matter both really and logically, such as things whose definition posits sensible matter. Hence, they cannot be understood without sensible matter, as, for example, in the definition of man it is necessary to include flesh and bones; and with things of this kind physics, or natural science, is concerned. *Second degree* of abstraction. But certain other things, although they depend upon matter as to their existence, do not so depend as far as the intellect is concerned; because in a definition of them sensible matter is not included, as in the case of lines and numbers with which mathematics deals. *Third degree* of abstraction. But there are still other objects of speculation that do not depend upon matter for existence, because they can exist without matter: either they are never found in matter, as God . . . or they are sometimes in matter and in other cases not, as substance, quality, potency, act, one, and many, and things of this sort. With these things theology treats,

Aristotle reduce Plato's logical absolute to the real man and fix logic in its authentic role as an "organon" or instrument to guide man in an orderly way in the construction of true science. Logic of itself is inadequate to attain reality.

Having disengaged the logical order from the real, Aristotle was in position to distinguish the various kinds of knowledge within the real order: theoretic, practical, and productive. This threefold order is conveniently classified for us, again, by St. Thomas Aquinas in the first lesson of his Commentary on Aristotle's *Ethics*. He describes them as follows:

There is first an order which the reason does not make but only considers, and such is the order of natural things. . . . There is another order which the reason, in the act of reflection, produces in voluntary action, in human behavior. Lastly there is an order which reason by considering makes in external things, as in the making of a house.

And because the consideration made by reason is perfected through habit, the sciences are diversified according to the diverse orders which reason considers. For it pertains to natural science to consider the order of things which reason considers but does not make; and here we include metaphysics also. . . . The order of human acts pertains to moral (ethical and political) science. Lastly, the order which reason produces in external things pertains to the productive arts.[2]

Art and prudence

In the theoretical sciences truth depends solely on conformity of the intellect with *what is*. In practical and productive sciences, however, the human intellect is in a measure the cause of its knowledge, for these sciences are directed to some action to be

. . . because the most important of its objects is God. By another name, it is called metaphysics. . . ." (In *The Trinity and the Unicity of the Intellect,* translated by Sister Rose Emmanuella Brennan, S.H.N., B. Herder Book Co., St. Louis, 1946, pp. 135–136.)

[2] *In I Ethics* lect.1. *In decem libros Ethicorum Aristotelis ad Nicomachum expositio,* A. M. Pirotta, (ed.), Marietti, Turin, 1934.

accomplished and not merely to the knowledge of *what is*. But reason can be engaged in action either (1) by *making* things (in which case its action passes into external matter, as we see in the case of the architect or shoemaker), or (2) by *doing* (in which case the action remains intrinsic to the agent, as we see in one who deliberates, or chooses, or wills). Although in both "making" and "doing" the intellect is in a measure the cause of what it produces, there is a difference of the profoundest import between "making"—the task of art—and "doing"—the sphere of prudence. In art it is the excellence of the *thing made* that is the criterion of truth. The truth of an artistic judgment depends simply on the conformity of the intellect with the work that the artist intends to make. In this, we may observe, art very much resembles the habits of the theoretic intellect, because both are concerned simply with the disposition of the things considered by them and not with the disposition of the will toward these objects: "As long as the geometrician demonstrates the truth, it matters not how his appetite is disposed, whether he be joyful or angry, neither does it matter in a craftsman so long as he turn out a good piece of work." [3] The situation is quite different in the case of action intrinsic to the agent—in "doing," or human behavior. For here the good is in the man himself: He has to be joyful and sad about the right things, about the things which ought to please or displease him. Truth here depends primarily on the rectitude of the man's will. To be a good man it is necessary not merely to know but to desire the proper human good and to desire it in the right way. Indeed we find evidence of this profound difference between "art" and "prudence" in the fact that, as St. Thomas remarks, "more praise is given to the craftsman who is at fault willingly, than to one who is unwillingly; whereas it is more contrary to prudence to sin willingly than unwillingly, since rightness of the will is essential to prudence, but not to art." [4] We readily forgive a moral inadvertence, but we will not pay to hear a violinist who plays off pitch no matter how inadevertently.

[3] *Summa Theol.* I.II.Q.57a.3,4.
[4] *Ibid.* a.4.

This distinction between art and prudence entails other most important consequences for political science. Since practical truth (as distinct from artistic truth and from the truth of theoretic science) depends primarily on the disposition of the will, the intellect is not obeyed in these matters without a certain power of opposition on the part of the appetites which have a certain independence of action. Hence it is that "reason [is said to command] the appetitive part of the soul by a political rule whereby a man rules over subjects that are free." [5] No man is like matter in the hands of a political "artist." The statesman is concerned with the character of his subjects as members of the political community; but the habits, customs, manners, and institutions of a people are the concrete manifestations of character, and unlike works of art, neither can nor may be readily changed or set aside; to do so would violate the internal natural liberty of a people. The kind of total planning that Plato envisaged is simply not in accord with realities.

There is another reason, marking the difference between art and prudence, why the habits, manners, customs, and institutions of a people cannot be readily "devised," executed, set aside. Prudence, unlike art, does not proceed by fixed and clear rules. Art does so proceed and need not deliberate about its means. [6] "Deliberation is concerned with things which happen in a certain way for the most part, but in which the event is obscure, and with things in which it is indeterminate." [7] For Plato, as we have seen, the "operables" of prudence were conceived to be of the same

[5] *Ibid.* I.II.Q.58 a.2c.

[6] ". . . it is clear that art does not deliberate. For an artist does not deliberate in so far as he has art, but in so far as he lacks the certitude of his art: whence it is that the most certain arts do not deliberate. Thus the writer does not deliberate as to how he will form his letters. And even those artists who deliberate, once they have found the certain principle of their art, do not deliberate in executing it; whence it is that the cithar player, if he were to deliberate which string to pluck, would appear most unskilled. Whence it is evident that it is not because he doesn't act for an end that an agent doesn't deliberate, but because he has determinate means for reaching it." (*In II Physics* lect.14.)

[7] *Ethics* III.1112b.9–10.

sort as the "operables" of the art of logic. The theoretic intellect, insofar as it "makes" certain things (such as syllogisms and the proposition), fulfills the definition of art with the respect to the notion of "making," and it proceeds according to determinate and certain rules. But the "art" of politics does not proceed in most certain and determinate ways; the means to its end are infinitely variable and hence require the greatest deliberation. Therefore, granted (as we shall presently see) that there are fixed ends in the nature of man as well as in the natural associations that guarantee the ends of human life, the task of the statesman is infinitely complicated by the contingency and obscurity of the means for attaining the end—for these are found in the concrete circumstances, contingent and variable, of a community. An awareness of this fact is the first step in the "art" of politics.

Finally, the freedom of prudence does not, like the freedom of art, extend to the end itself of action. If we wish—as we legitimately may—to use the term "art" in a broad sense to include moral action, then it must be understood that the "art" of politics does not aim at any good other than that of man's nature. For we must notice that art, taken in the strict sense, bears on contraries: We cannot, morally, brainwash men, but we have all learned that there is an art of doing it. The art of medicine is just as effective in killing as curing an individual—or a whole community, as we know from the threat of biological warfare. That art be put to right *use* requires a moral virtue. This is why, after speaking of art as a virtue (an intellectual virtue), Aristotle says that there is also a virtue of art, meaning, as St. Thomas clearly puts it, that "in order that a man make good use of the art he has, he needs a good will, which is perfected by moral virtue; and for this reason the Philosopher says that there is a *virtue* of art, namely a moral virtue, insofar as the good use of art requires a moral virtue." [8]

Since, then, practical truth depends on the rectitude of man's will, it does not, like art, bear on contraries. If it did, then the judgment of the morally corrupt man would be just as valid as that of the morally good man. To be sure, man is free to become

[8] *Summa Theol.* I.II.Q.57 a.3 ad 2.

either virtuous or vicious, but this liberty of contrariety is not a
mark of the perfection of human nature. Indeed this liberty of
contrariety is not found in the perfect intellectual substances—
the "separate substances"—compared with which Aristotle says
(and for this very reason) that all of human nature is in many
ways enslaved.[9] The "art" of living, for an individual as for a community, does not extend to the first principles of man's nature. As
Aristotle observes—and it is an observation that stands as a barrier
to every form of totalitarianism—"the state does not make men,
but taking them from nature, perfects them." [10]

The reason why man's self-government and liberty are "limited"
in the way just described, is that man himself as such belongs to
the order of things that reason considers but does not make.[11]
The "self" of which man is the cause in "self-government" is the
"self" of man's "second nature," constituted by the political virtues
(the nature which Aristotle treats in the *Ethics* and *Politics*).
This essential and elemental meaning of the limited character of
man's government over himself is brought out by Aristotle in the
treatises on natural science as well as in the *Ethics* and *Politics*.
It is done most strikingly by comparing the first principle in practical science (derived from a consideration of man's "first" or substantial nature) not with the final causes in nature, but with
mathematical axioms. "For virtue and vice respectively," Aristotle
observes, "preserve and destroy the first principle, and in actions
the final cause is the first principle, as the hypotheses are in mathematics." [12] Even though moral reasoning proceeds from final
causes for the sake of which we act, and not from antecedent hy-

[9] *Metaph.* I.982b.29.

[10] *Politics* I.I1258a.21.

[11] See above, p. 31. In Book II of the *Physics* Aristotle shows that the
terminus of the considerations of natural science is reached with those forms
which are in some manner separable from matter—namely, human souls:
"and the concern of the physicist reaches to those things whose forms are
separable indeed, but do not exist apart from matter. Man is begotten by
man and by the sun as well. The mode of existence and essence of the
separable it is the business of the primary type of philosophy (metaphysics)
to define." (*Physics* II.94b.10–15.)

[12] *Ethics* VII.1151a.15.

potheses, the method of politics is compared to that of mathematics in the role played by its principles. A comparison between the final causes in nature and in human action is unsuitable because the necessity that is in the world of nature is a hypothetical necessity, for it depends ultimately on the freedom of the Divine Intellect.[13] But the ends of human life do not depend on the freedom of the human intellect: Prudence does not bear on the contraries of good and evil. It is precisely because Aristotle wants to show that the ends of human life are unchangeable starting points for all the infinitely variable judgments of political prudence that he compares them with the antecedent hypotheses of mathematics; he does not compare them with the final causes in

---

[13] It is to be noted that in the *Physics,* where Aristotle is treating the most general principles of natural science, he regards the whole of natural science as a theoretic science—for the world of nature is knowable by man but not, certainly, made by him. But in the more specialized treatises, such as *On the Parts of Animals,* which investigate in concretion the construction of nature, Aristotle opposes natural science as *practical* to mathematics and metaphysics as theoretic. The reason for this is that the experimental scientist sees the physical universe as something having been made—made of course by the divine art. Aristotle observes: "The causes concerned in the generation of the works of nature are, as we see, more than one. . . . Plainly, however, that cause is first which we call the final one. For this is the Reason and the Reason forms the starting point, alike in the works of art and in the works of nature. For consider how the physician, or how the builder sets about his work. He starts by forming for himself a definite picture . . . of his end—the physician of health, the builder of a house—and this he holds forward as the reason and explanation of each subsequent step that he takes. . . . Now in the works of nature the . . . final cause is still more dominant than in works of art such as these, nor is necessity a factor with the same significance in them all. . . . For there is absolute necessity manifested in eternal phenomena; and there is hypothetical necessity manifested in everything that is generated by nature as in everything that is produced by art, be it a house or what it may. For *if* a house or other such final object is to be realized, it is necessary that such and such material should exist. . . . As with these productions of art, so also it is with the productions of nature. The mode of necessity, however, and the mode of ratiocination are different in natural science from what they are in theoretical sciences. . . . For in the latter, the starting point is that which is; in the former, that which is to be." (*On the Parts of Animals* I.639b.13–640a.2.)

nature because "as with productions of art, so . . . is it with the productions of nature"—the artist is free to determine the end. But the ends of human life do not depend on our simple will, as, in the things of nature the end depends on the simple will of God ultimately, and in the things of art on the simple will of the artist. It is with respect, then, to the fixedness of mathematical hypotheses as antecedents that Aristotle compares the final ends of human life and thus safeguards the fundamental requirements of man's nature by withdrawing such matters from the political art.

Ethics—fundamental principles of self-government

If Plato's notion of the practical was at fault in supposing art and virtue to be identical in essence and definition, this error had its source, as we have suggested, in his failure to distinguish the logical order of things from the natural order. Art imitates nature, as Aristotle teaches in the second book of the *Physics*, and nature, St. Thomas observes, "proceeds in its operations from the simple to the complex; and among things which result from natural agency that which is more complex is the more perfect and constitutes the integration and purpose of the others." [14] Aristotle says, therefore, that "as in other departments of science, so in politics, the compound should always be resolved into the simple elements or least parts of the whole." [15] Plato, on the contrary, because he begins with the logical whole and the logical modalities which are only in the mind, suppresses the natural parts which make up the whole of a thing in its reality as a thing—the government of a large household is the same as that of a small state, and indeed, the State is the individual writ large.[16] Plato's art of government imitates not nature, but the logical modalities by which

[14] *In VIII Libros Politicorum Expositio, seu de Rebus Civilibus.* vol. 21 of the Parma *Opera Omnia*, pp. 364–466, Musurgia Publishers, New York, 1949, Prologue.

[15] *Politics* I.1252a.20.

[16] For a full discussion of the distinction between "logical whole" and "integral whole," see Charles DeKoninck, "Introduction à l'étude de l'âme," *Laval Theologique et Philosophique*, vol. 3, no. 1, especially pp. 25ff., 1947.

we know nature. But it is with the natural parts, the elements of which the State is composed, that Aristotle begins his study of politics "in order that we may see in what the different kinds of rule differ from one another." [17]

Beginning, then, with the elements of which the state is composed, Aristotle considers human actions in terms first of the capacities and potentialities of individual men as such—of what is involved in the regulation of their own individual behavior, of their individual self-government. The treatise on *Ethics,* as St. Thomas observes in his Commentary, contains the very elements of political science because it deals with human actions as they are ordered to the end of man as such. In pursuing this inquiry into the end of human life, Aristotle characteristically opens the discussion by setting forth the popular opinion on the matter. "Verbally," he observes, "there is general agreement; for both the general run of men and people of superior refinement say that [the end of human life] is happiness, and identify living well and doing well with being happy; but with regard to what happiness is, they differ, and the many do not give the same account as the wise." [18] On the principle that such as a man is, so the end in life appears to him to be, he observes that there are three prominent types of life—the life of pleasure, the political life, and the contemplative life, devoted to the pursuit of science and speculative wisdom. He does indeed mention hesitantly—so little claim does it appear to have—a fourth kind of life, the life of the pursuit of money. For reasons that we shall presently mention, Aristotle dismisses both the life of money and the life of pleasure, but we must not overlook the fact that in so doing he acknowledges that those who identify happiness with pleasure or with money are "not without some ground" in doing so; for pleasure has the nature of an end, and he who achieves pleasure rests satisfied in it and seeks nothing beyond it. Pleasure, however, cannot be the answer we are looking for simply because it does not answer the question raised, namely, what is the *specifically* human end proper

[17] *Politics* I.1252a.23.
[18] *Ethics* I.1095a.168ff.

to man: Since the life of pleasure is shared by man and brute animals, it cannot constitute the proper or specific end for man. As for money, the reason why some men pursue it for its own sake is that it is a universal medium of exchange for all temporal goods, and thus men are deluded into supposing it to be the end itself. We see, then, that the claims of the life of pleasure and the life of money, rejected for different reasons (for one, while having the nature of an end is not proper to man, while the other, though proper enough to man has not the nature of an end), bring to light two attributes that must characterize happiness (whatever it turns out to be): It must be something proper to man's nature and it must be something not merely useful but an end in itself.

Of the political life Aristotle confines himself at this point to remarking that the reasons persuading most men to go into politics are insufficient, namely, honor and even the virtue for which they are honored. The end of man and his chief good and happiness ought to be something very proper to him and not accidentally gained nor easily lost, uncertain and adventitious. But honor is a most uncertain thing and is indeed rather more in him who renders it than in the one who receives it. And virtue itself "appears somewhat incomplete; for the possession of virtue seems actually compatible with being asleep, or with lifelong inactivity . . . ; but a man who was living so no one would call happy, unless he were maintaining a thesis at any cost." [19] From this consideration Aristotle derives another attribute of happiness: Whatever happiness turns out to be it must be a certain activity.

The prefatory examination of the common opinion on the nature of happiness completed, Aristotle shows the proper way of seeking the answer to the inquiry. He writes:

Presumably, however, to say that happiness is the chief good seems a platitude, and a clearer account of what it is is still desired. This

---

[19] *Ethics* I.1096a. Virtue being a habit and therefore not always in actual use, is in a man who is asleep; for upon arising he finds that he has the same habit—say, of speaking grammatically—that he had upon retiring. Hence virtue as such can scarcely constitute happiness since it is actually compatible with being asleep.

might, perhaps, be given if we could first ascertain the function of man. For just as for a flute-player, a sculptor, or any artist, and in general, for all things that have a function or activity, the good and the "well" is thought to reside in the function, so it would seem to be for man, if he has a function. Have the carpenter, then, and the tanner certain functions or activities, and man has none? Is he born without a function? Or as eye, hand, foot, and in general each of the parts evidently has a function, may one lay it down that man similarly has a function apart from all these? What then can this be? Life seems to be common even to plants, but we are seeking what is peculiar to man. Let us exclude, therefore, the life of nutrition and growth. Next there would be a life of perception, but *it* also seems to be common even to the horse, the ox and every animal. There remains, then, an active life of the element that has a rational principle; of this, one part has such a principle in the sense of being obedient to one, the other in the sense of possessing one and exercising thought. And, as "life of the rational element" also has two meanings, we must state that life in the sense of activity is what we mean; for this seems to be the more proper sense of the terms. Now if the function of man is an activity of the soul which follows or implies a rational principle, and if we say "a so-and-so" and "a good so-and-so" have a function which is the same in kind, e.g., a lyre-player and a good lyre-player, and so without qualification in all cases, eminence in respect of goodness being added to the name of the function (for the function of a lyre-player is to play the lyre, and that of a good lyre-player is to do so well): if this is the case, [and we state the function of man to be a certain kind of life, and this to be an activity or actions of the soul implying a rational principle, and the function of a good man to be the good and noble performance of these, and if any action is well performed when it is performed in accordance with the appropriate excellence: If this is the case] human good turns out to be activity of soul in accordance with virtue, and if there are more than one virtue, in accordance with the best and most complete.[20]

The force of Aristotle's demonstration lies in the considerations concerning theoretic and practical science to which we have already given some attention. It should be observed that Aristotle is here saying that if in respect of the various arts, we find spe-

[20] *Ethics* I.1097b.23–1098a.17.

cialized functions coming to fruition in man—in man as sculptor, man as physician, etc.—it is more to be expected that man himself, as a work of the divine art, should have an activity proper to him. The subject matter of what we designate *theoretic* from the point of view of our own intellect (the whole order of nature), is "operable" by the divine intellect, and hence is the work of God's practical knowledge. The following diagram illustrates the relationship:

Divine Nature—Divine Art—Nature—Theoretic Science—Human Art

The knowledge of God is to all things other than Himself what the knowledge of an artist is to the things made by his art. Natural things stand midway between the knowledge of God and our human knowledge in the way, for example, that a house that has been built stands midway between the knowledge of the builder who made it and the knowledge of the one who sees it already built. We must, then, approach, as it were, the art of God and see how man has been made and what his activity is. For we see, as Aristotle remarks, an order of natural inclinations in man. There is first an inclination that he has in common even with plants—life itself; and above this vegetative and nutritive activity we find sensitive knowledge, which man has in common with all other animals. Finally there is a principle that is proper to man alone among corporeal things, namely, rational activity. Hence happiness turns out to be activity of soul in accordance with reason, and since "the well and the good" reside in the function, the good performance of reason, which is virtue, is added to the definition: Happiness is activity of soul according to virtue in a complete life, and if there be more than one virtue, then it is in accordance with the highest virtue.

Of the element that has a rational principle we have just seen Aristotle say, "one part has such a principle in the sense of being obedient to one, the other in the sense of possessing one and exercising thought." We see in man, then, a capacity for self-government. The sensitive part of the irrational element (unlike the vegetative part) participates in the rational; for we praise the rational principle in the continent and incontinent man since it urges them aright and toward the best objects: The continent man *has* disordered concupiscences but does not act according to them; and the temperate man even more perfectly overcomes them, for he controls even the interior movements. If indeed Plato was right in seeking to establish the proper good of man by analogy with the arts and with the distinct natures found in the universe, and in finding this good to consist in the harmony of man's "inward faculties," he failed to perceive what man's precise dignity is: that it consists in *freely* ordering himself to his proper end. For Plato, the appetitive and spirited "souls" were not rational by participation and hence were conceived as subject in a despotic way to the rule of an extraneous "reason." But the principle of self-government belongs to man's nature and constitutes his precise dignity. To see this more fully we must advert once more to the second book of Aristotle's *Physics*. In the course of this book Aristotle demonstrates in many ways that all of nature acts for an end. But although natural things act for an end, they do so without knowledge of the end, the sign of which is that nature acts always, or for the most part, in the same way: That ants and spiders and bees act for an end, but not in virtue of an intrinsic intellectual principle, not independently, is evident, Aristotle points out, from the fact that they operate always, or for the most part, in the same way. For if action of this sort indicates some purpose and intelligence (for it is events outside the intention of an agent that happen infrequently and are called chance events) by the same token this very regularity is a sign of stupidity—or as St. Thomas views it, "substitute intelligence." Swallows would not build their nests over and over again in the same way if they acted by intelligence and art. Architects do not all build the same kind of house because an architect can make judgment about the form artifacts and can vary them.[21] But that which is necessarily

---

[21] That this kind of argument is not outmoded is shown by the fact that two distinguished representatives of two contemporary and opposed social philosophies rely in their own fashion upon these notions. Karl Marx writes: "A spider accomplishes operations which resemble those of a weaver; a bee, by the construction of its cells of wax, resembles more an architect. But that

determined by its nature to one course of action does not permit any principle of government within itself. The very condition of the rational creature, namely, that he has mastery over his actions, that he governs himself, means that alone among corporeal creatures he is said to be free, for "he is free who exists for his own sake and not for another's. . . ." [22]

---

which . . . distinguishes the worst architect from the most skilled bee is that the former has constructed his cell in his head before he has put it in wax." (Marx, *Capital*, pt. III, chap. 7; English translation, Vintage Books, Random House, Inc., New York, pp. 197–198.) And a distinguished American jurist, Judge Learned Hand, exhibiting a less clear grasp of these matters, sees in the "willingness" of the ants and the bees a sign of liberty in these creatures but, of course, a liberty unworthy of human beings. While Marx thinks that man is a "generic being" containing in himself the common good of the universe, Judge Hand thinks that the specific difference between man and other natures lies in the absence in human affairs of any "indefectible" first principles and ends; and this is why, in Judge Hand's view, man is not like an ant or a bee. ("The Quest for Liberty," Edwin Newman (ed.), *The Freedom Reader*, Oceana Publications, New York, 1955, pp. 22–26.) See Chaps. VIII and X.

[22] *Metaph.* I.982b.26. This doctrine of Aristotle is explained at length in the following discussion by St. Thomas on the nature of intellectual substances: "The principle of every operation is the form by which a thing is in act. So, the mode of operation consequent upon a form must be in accordance with the mode of that form. Hence, a form not proceeding from the agent that acts by it causes an operation of which that agent is not the master. But if there be a form which proceeds from the agent acting by it, then the consequent operation also will be in the power of that agent. Now, natural forms, from which natural motions and operations derive, do not proceed from the things whose forms they are, but wholly from extrinsic agents. For by a natural form each thing has being in its own nature, and nothing can be the cause of its own act of being. So it is that things which are moved naturally do not move themselves . . . in brute animals the forms sensed or imagined, which move them, are not discovered by them, but are received by them from extrinsic sensible things which act upon their senses and are judged of by their natural estimative faculty. Hence, though brutes are in a sense said to move themselves, in as much as one part of them moves and another is moved, yet they are not themselves the source of the actual moving, which, rather, derives partly from external things sensed and partly from nature. For, so far as their appetite moves their members, they are said to move themselves, and in this way surpass inani-

Aristotle discerns two types of rule within man himself: a rule of the soul over the body, which he calls "despotic" because in a healthy constitution the limbs obey the rule of the soul immediately and without any power of opposition. But there is a second kind of rule—the rational principle over the sensitive part which Aristotle calls "political and royal." [23] The meaning of the word "political" in this phrase may be understood by considering the fact that the sensitive appetite stands in relation to the reason in a position of some independence: This is evident in the fact that, unlike the limbs of the body, the sensitive appetite can initiate a movement of its own, independently of the command of reason. We become hungry and thirsty without telling ourselves to become hungry and thirsty. Now it is this very independence that establishes the sensitive part as "other" and therefore gives it "rights"; there is a relation of "justice" between it and the rational principle. [24] Since, on the contrary, the body cannot move without the

---

mate things and plants; but so far as appetition in them follows necessarily upon the reception of forms through their senses and from the judgment of their natural estimative power, they are not the cause of their own movement; and so they are not master of their own action. On the other hand, the form understood, through which the intellectual substance acts, proceeds from the intellect itself as a thing conceived, and in a way contrived by it; as we see in the case of the artistic form, which the artificer conceives and contrives, and through which he performs his works. Intellectual substances, then, move themselves to act, as having mastery of their own actions." (*Contra Gentiles* II.chap.47. Cf. *Summa Theol.* I.Q.18 a.3.)

[23] *Politics* I.1254b.5.

[24] We must observe, of course, that man's dealings with himself, though rectified by the reason, are not, properly speaking, relations of justice and right. For as St. Thomas explains, ". . . since justice by its name implies equality, it denotes essentially relation to another, for a thing is equal, not to itself, but to another. And forasmuch as it belongs to justice to rectify human acts, as stated above (Q.57 a.1; I–II.Q.113 a.1), this otherness which justice demands must be between beings capable of action. Now actions belong to *supposita* (I.Q.29 a.2) and wholes and, properly speaking, not to parts and forms or powers, for we do not say properly that the hand strikes, but a man with his hand, nor that heat makes a thing hot, but fire by heat, although such expressions may be employed metaphorically. Hence, justice properly speaking demands a distinction of *supposita*, and consequently is

soul, it is impossible to speak of it as having "rights" in relation to the soul; but it is precisely the independent power of the sense appetite that establishes it as "other" and gives it a kind of "equality" in relation to the ruling principle of the reason, and in this way we may speak of "justice" between them. Hence, the term "political" applies to rule that is over subjects that are free, and because they are free, they have a certain equality in relation to the ruler, and because there is this equality, there is justice between them by which their respective rights (that of ruler and that of subject) are established.

The term "royal" signifies the perfection of the governing principle over subjects that are free. It is a rule that realizes the proper good of the subjects and does so in accordance with their freedom. The virtuous man does easily and with pleasure *what* he *ought* to do and *how* he ought to do it. For ". . . if the acts that are in accordance with the virtues have themselves a certain character, it does not follow that they are done justly or temperately; it is not the man who does these that is just and temperate, but the man who . . . does these as just and temperate men do them." [25] In the just man and the temperate man there is government over the appetites in accordance with their proper freedom which, in these men, presents no hindrance to the rule over them. Both freedom and government are present and there is no element of violence.

Contrary to the virtuous man, the vicious man does easily and with pleasure the things he ought not to do; and because he perverts the essential freedom of his nature, he establishes a despotic rule within himself. He becomes the "slave" of his passions which

---

only in one man toward another. Nevertheless in one and the same man we may speak metaphorically of his various principles of action such as the reason, the irascible, and the concupiscible, as though they were so many agents: so that metaphorically in one and the same man there is said to be justice in so far as the reason commands the irascible and concupiscible, and these obey reason; and in general in so far as to each part of man is ascribed what is becoming to it. Hence the philosopher calls this *metaphorical justice*. (*Ethics* V.II)." (*Summa Theol.* II.II.Q.58 a.2.)

[25] *Ethics* II.1105a.30–1105b.7.

exploit their proper freedom and seduce the governing principle. The merely "continent" man (he who *"has* disordered concupiscences but does not act according to them") performs the acts of the virtuous man but with reluctance and difficulty. He is said to establish a simple "political" rule over himself because the equality of reason and sense appetite in this kind of man is such that these powers take turns, as it were, in ruling.

Finally, the incontinent man performs the acts of the vicious man but with some protest and remorse. In both the continent and incontinent man the governing principle is imperfect and their internal freedom is in jeopardy. There is in each man an element of violence, although—we may note—in the vicious man there is a kind of natural (from the "second nature" of habit) despotism which, precisely because it belongs to his "second nature," largely conceals the state of violence. Aristotle will analogize this condition of soul to political tyranny, as we today may indeed analogize it to the "peace" and "freedom" of totalitarian rule.

The political life and the contemplative life

The activity of soul that we have been considering is of course the activity that is, metaphorically, the "political life" of man. It is metaphorically such because, as we have seen, man's dealings with himself, though ruled by the reason, are not properly speaking relations of justice and right; these require a relation between independent agents.[26] Aristotle had not rejected the political life as he had rejected the claims of the life of pleasure and the life of money. What then is the ground of its claim, if it is not honor nor even virtue itself? For answer we must look beyond the directly pertinent considerations, already made, of man's proper activity. This activity, as we have noticed, is twofold: "Of the element that has a rational principle one part has such a principle in the sense of being obedient to one, the other in the sense of

[26] Above, n. 24.

possessing and exercising thought." [27] This latter is more principally the rational part, for the sensitive part is rational only by being regulated by the reason. And because happiness is the most principal good of man, and man is distinguished in species by his rationality, his happiness consists in that which is essentially rational rather than in that which is rational by participation. This happiness is the happiness of the "contemplative life," the life of the speculative virtues of science, wisdom, and understanding. Since Aristotle considers this life to be, absolutely speaking, better than the political, his reasons for considering the political life a good one will derive from his absolute preference for the contemplative life.

Now then we should observe first that the integrity of the political life depends on the primacy of the contemplative: The rule of the appetite by the rational principle (which produces the political virtues) presupposes theoretic rectitude concerning man's nature and end. Granted, as we have seen, that there is a certain "freedom" and "equality" of the sense appetites in relation to the ruling principle of the reason, the very contrariety of sense and reason in man can jeopardize his capacity for freedom by fostering a revolt against the constitutional exigencies of his very nature—against the human condition. Such a revolt would take the form of man denying what Aristotle called (as we have seen) the "axiomatic" first principles of human nature. Without the primacy of speculative truth, all practical regulation dissolves: Man, human good, and society become simply and wholly what we want them to be. Political rule is transformed into universal despotism and the reign of whim and hazard. Indeed, a good part of political thought and practice as we find it in the history of Western Europe has been engaged in this revolt against the human condition put forward in terms of "freedom" and the emancipation of man. We have noted Aristotle's observation that human nature, compared to perfect intellectual natures—the "separate substances"—may be said to be in a condition of bondage. This bondage produces in man a tendency to revolt and

[27] *Ethics* I.1098a.3.

escape from his condition. But this type of emancipation—from the human condition itself—can lead only to the supremacy of force. Hence true freedom, the "political" freedom of man's very nature, is protected by an insistence on the primacy of theoretic (speculative) truth concerning man's nature and end.

We must now see that the ultimate reason why the political life is at all good derives from the reason why the contemplative life is, absolutely speaking, best. If man were the best thing in the universe, then, Aristotle tells us, "political science and prudence would be the most perfect knowledge; but the most perfect knowledge is rather of the highest objects—of the highest objects, we say; for it would be strange to think that the art of politics, or practical wisdom, is the best knowledge, since man is not the best thing in the world." [28] Now in asking in what way the universe contains the good and the highest good—whether in the order of its parts or in something separate—Aristotle answers as follows:

. . . probably in both ways, as an army does; for its good is found both in its order and in its leader, and more in the latter; for he does not depend on the order, but it depends on him.[29]

And of the life of this "leader" upon whom "depend the heavens and the world of nature," Aristotle observes further:

And it is a life such as the best which we enjoy, and enjoy but for a short time (for it is ever in this state which we cannot be). . . . And thinking in itself deals with that which is best in itself, and that which is thinking in the fullest sense with that which is best in the fullest sense. And thought thinks on itself because it shares the nature of the object of thought; . . . For that which is *capable* of receiving the object of thought, i.e., the essence, is thought. But it is *active* when it *possesses* this object. Therefore the possession rather than the receptivity is the divine element which thought seems to contain, and *the act of contemplation is what is most pleasant and best*. If, then, God is always in that good state in which we sometimes are, this compels

[28] *Ethics* VI.1141a.20.
[29] *Metaph.* XII.1075a.12.

our wonder; and if in a better this compels it yet more. And God *is* in a better state. And life also belongs to God; for the actuality of thought is life, and God is that actuality; and God's self-dependent actuality is life most good and eternal. We say therefore that God is a living being, eternal, most good, so that life and duration continuous and eternal belong to God; for this *is* God.[30]

The argument, then, is this: Since "thought thinks on itself because it shares the nature of the object of thought [and] it is *active* when it possesses this object," it follows that man's chief good and highest activity consist in the possession of the "highest object" of thought, viz. God: "the self dependent activity of thought which is life most good and eternal." And again, it is this contemplative activity in man that is most akin to God, whose activity "surpasses all others in blessedness" and is contemplative. This life, then, Aristotle calls "divine" rather than human, for, as St. Thomas makes clear, "the likeness of the speculative intellect to God is one of union and informing." [31] Although "such a life would be too high for man—for it is not insofar as he is man that he will live so, but insofar as something divine is in him"—nonetheless Aristotle warns that "we must not follow those who advise us, being men, to think of human things, and being mortal, of mortal things, but must so far as we can . . . strain every nerve to live in accordance with the best thing in us; for even if it be small in bulk much more does it in power and worth surpass everything." [32]

---

[30] *Ibid.* 1072b.14ff.

[31] *Summa Theol.* I.II.Q.3 a.5 ad 1.

[32] *Ethics* VI.1141a.20. "The classical political philosopher," Prof. Leo Strauss has said, "is ultimately compelled to transcend not merely the dimension of common opinion, of political opinion, but the dimension of political life as such; for he is led to realize that the ultimate aim of political life cannot be reached by political life, but only by a life devoted to contemplation, to philosophy. This finding is of crucial importance for political philosophy, since it determines the limits set to political life, to all political action and all political planning. Moreover, it implies that the highest subject of political philosophy is the philosophic life: philosophy—not as a teaching or as a body of knowledge, but as a way of life—offers, as it were,

Now the contemplative life "surpasses everything" because its object is that life upon which "depend the heavens and the world of nature." And this order of the heavens and the world of nature —the intrinsic common good of the universe—is "more divine" than a proper good of the same order because it is a better imitation of the ultimate final cause which draws all things to itself.[33] Similarly, then, the common good of men is "more divine" than a private good of the same order because it is a more perfect imitation of the ultimate essential goodness which draws all things to itself. This is Aristotle's first reason for characterizing the good of the political life of the individual as "more divine" than the private good of the same individual. The good, he says, has the nature of a final cause and is thus diffusive of itself: that is, "everything else is desired for the sake of [the end of the things we do]," and "if the end is the same for a single man and for a state, that of the state seems . . . more godlike." [34] It is more diffusive of goodness because of its communicability to many; and it is communicable, or common, not because all the citizens find their private good therein, but because for each of the citizens this good is also the good of the others. The second reason for calling the good of the political life of the individual more divine than the private good of the same individual is that the likeness to God of the practical life is one of "proportion," that is, by reason of standing in relation to what it knows as God does to what He knows: Men are the more like God in this way as by their actions or practical knowledge they cause goodness not only in themselves but also in others. Indeed, both the activity of the speculative and practical reason is nothing but a participation of man's intellect, which is "separable indeed but [does] not exist apart from mat-

---

the solution to the problem that keeps political life in motion. Ultimately, political philosophy transforms itself into a discipline that is no longer concerned with political things in the ordinary sense of the term. . . ." Leo Strauss, *What Is Political Philosophy?* The Free Press of Glencoe, New York, 1959, p. 91.

[33] *Metaph.* XII.chap.7.

[34] *Ethics* I.1094a.18, 1094b.7–10.

ter" [35] in the life of the Prime Intellect, upon whose perfect freedom "depend the heavens and the world of nature." This profoundly spiritual root of the concept of political common good has been lost in the West in modern times. It is, however, restored in profoundly perverted form in Marx's view of the individual as a "universal being" which "relates itself to the species as to his own proper being, or which relates itself to itself as a universal being." [36]

The primacy of the common good

There are three aspects of the doctrine of the primacy of the common good to which we must give special attention. We must, first of all, take careful note of the fact that this common good, which Aristotle calls more "godlike" than the good procured for a single man, is not taken in opposition to the good of a single man. The unity of this common good is not the unity of the logical whole which absorbs the real parts in a collective, indeterminate "genus"; this was the common good that Plato, confusing the logical and real orders, sought to achieve by the simplest possible unity in his ideal State. Rather, in Aristotle's doctrine the common good extends to many not by reason of any indetermination of individuals (in the way, for example, that "man" applies indeterminately to Peter and John), but it extends to them in their very *diversity* and by reason of this diversity. As Aristotle observes, in speaking of the order of the universe, "all things are ordered together somehow, but *not all alike.* . . ." [37] But this very diversity

---

[35] *Physics* II.194b.10–15; *Metaph.* XI.I.1072b.13.

[36] Marx, *Oekonomische-philosphische Manuscript*, in D. Rjazanou and V. Adoratski (eds.), *Gesamtausgabe*, Marx-Engels-Verlag, Berlin, 1932. An English translation of the philosophical portions of the *Economic and Philosophical Manuscripts* (pt. 1, vol. III in the *Gesamtausgabe*) has recently been made by T. B. Bottomore and reproduced in Erich Fromm, *Marx's Concept of Man*, Frederik Ungar Publishing Co., New York, 1961, pp. 87–196.

[37] *Metaph.* XII.1075a.17.

comes from the order of the parts in any whole; and thus the common good is the good of individuals as parts and members of society, and is sought by them precisely as *members of society and as being not all alike.* The common good thus extends to individuals by reason of its very elevated determination, reaching to that in them which is most determinate and most actual: "It extends to Peter not primarily insofar as Peter is an animal, nor even insofar as he is a rational animal, but insofar as he is *this* rational animal: it is the good of Peter envisaged in his most proper person." [38]

The common good is common, then, *as a universal cause* whose power extends to many different kinds of effects. And therefore we must understand a second point about the common good: If indeed it extends to that which is most determinate and actual in individuals, it is not for that reason to be identified with the singular, private good of these individuals; rather, it is common by reason of its *communicability* to these many different individuals, and not because it includes the singular good of all of them. This may be made clear by the following considerations: The singular good of the eye is vision and that of the ear is hearing, but the common good of these different organs is not common as including the different singular goods of each of them. Rather, it is a good of the man who hears and sees—that is common to each organ and in which each shares. In like manner, "the good of the family is better than the singular good of its members not because all the members of the family find their singular good there-in; the good of the family is better because for each of its members this good is also the good of the others." [39]

Having said that the common good is a good that extends to that which is most actual and determinate in things, and secondly that it is nonetheless a truly common good in the sense that none of these diverse and singular things is the absolute measure of the good that is theirs, we must finally distinguish the common good

[38] Charles DeKoninck, *De la Primauté du bien commun,* Éditions Fides, Montreal, Canada, 1943, p. 55.

[39] *Ibid.,* pp. 8–9.

of the whole which is a civil multitude, a family, or any association of human beings, from the common good of an organic whole
and that of a collectivity.[40] The unity of these latter is a *simple
unity:* In an organic whole, in a collectivity (and in a continuum)
there is no action of the parts which is not either simply or principally the same as the action of the whole: In a continuum the
movement of the whole is the same as that of the part, and in a
composite the movement of the part is principally of the whole
(we do not say that the eye of the man sees, but that man sees
with his eye); and in a collectivity (such as a society of bees or
ants) the action of the parts is principally of the whole because
the parts have no principle of self-government within them and
are not themselves the source of their actual moving.[41] A society
of human beings, on the other hand, is one whose parts have an
action independent of the whole, for here the part governs itself.
Such a whole has merely *unity of order;* for this union is brought
about by the collaboration of parts that are self-governing. Therefore, if these parts are ordered to the common good as to their
chief good, this direction is not accomplished except by self-government. In Aristotle's doctrine the action of the ruling element in
the political community is in no sense divorced from the participation of the citizenry. Contrary to a rather commonly held opinion, the political science of Aristotle can in no sense be called
"totalitarian"; those who call it so do an injustice to his teaching.

Economics and politics

The first order of common good to which the individual directs
his action is of that association without which man cannot exist at
all: the family or the household. The first relation of the persons
is that between man and woman, for

. . . there must necessarily be a union or pairing of those who cannot
exist without one another. Male and female must be united for the

[40] See *In I Ethics* lect.I.
[41] See above, p. 43, n.22.

reproduction of the species—not from deliberate intention, but from the natural impulse, which exists in animals generally as it also exists in plants. . . . Next there must necessarily be a union of the naturally ruling element with the element which is naturally ruled, for the preservation of both. The element which is able, by virtue of its intelligence, to exercise forethought is naturally a ruling and master element; the element which is able, by virtue of its bodily power, to do what the other element plans is a ruled element, which is naturally in a state of slavery; . . .

The first result of these two elementary associations (of male and female, and of master and slave) is the household or family. . . . The factors to be examined therefore are three—first, the association of master and slave; next, what may be called the marital association; and lastly, what may be called the parental association. But besides the three factors which thus present themselves for examination there is also a fourth, which some regard as identical with the whole of household management, and others as its principal part. This is the element called "the art of acquisition"; and we shall have to consider its nature.[42]

Although our chief interest must be in that association—the political—which lies beyond the "economic" or wealth-getting association of the family (and that economic association of families that Aristotle calls the village), our appreciation of the political community will depend upon our giving some attention to the matters contained in the above selection—however curious some of these may sound to modern ears. First of all we must notice that the household is said to be natural to man in a much more primordial way than is political society: The family and its management (the "art of acquisition") are designed primarily to safeguard the very *living* of men; and property is an instrument of mere life, which pertains to economic associations.[43] The natural-

---

[42] *Politics* I.1252a., 1253b.

[43] We have already seen that Aristotle does not consider wealth to be the final end and the chief good of human life, but merely a useful good. And on this point St. Thomas observes that if wealth were the end of human life, then "financiers and not kings would be the heads of states." We shall have occasion later to see that a political community whose government is con-

ness of the relation between male and female is found in the intention of nature to generate the species, thus making this relationship of persons primary in the sense precisely that it is found also among other animals and in plants.[44] After the natural difference between male and female, Aristotle speaks ("Next there must necessarily be a union of the naturally ruling element . . .") of a natural difference founded on the nature which is proper to man, namely, the rational. And here the primary distinction is in terms of the minimum of the reason's ability with respect to the ordering of human acts to the whole end of human life: that is, the distinction is in terms of self-government, of practical reason or prudence. This last difference establishes the relation between the so-called natural slave and natural master.[45]

---

trolled by men who are chiefly interested in wealth is, in Aristotle's classification of governments, a perverted form known as "oligarchy."

[44] Since, however, man's nature is *rational animal,* those things that are natural to him in virtue of that nature which he has in common with other animals are not fully accomplished without some participation, more or less, of the reason. In the generation of the species, reason plays only an extrinsic role; but in the conservation of the individual, nature, whose intention it is (for nature intends the individual for the sake of the species), does not carry out this intention without the aid of reason. The primary foundation of marriage is here; a permanent union of the sexes is necessary for the protection, nourishment, education of the offspring. See de Monléon. "Petites notes autour de la famille et de la cité," pp. 267–268. See the treatment of natural law, Chap. III.

[45] It will be sufficient to summarize very briefly here Aristotle's doctrine of natural slavery and its essential political import. "Natural slavery" is to be clearly distinguished from "legal" or "institutional slavery." The latter, imposed in ancient times under the law of war, was considered by Aristotle to have some justification, but he pronounced it to be "simply speaking" not just: It was considered by him not to be just "simply speaking" because under the law of war it could happen that men who were by nature free could be enslaved. The man who "by nature" is a slave is any man who, on the part of his reason, is so defective in prudence that he requires direction before he can effectively govern himself in everyday affairs, and on the part of his body, is of such physique to be fitted for servile or heavy labor. Such a man, Aristotle says, "naturally belongs to another," and he is compared to the other as the "species" *brute animal* is compared to the species "man." He is said to be "part of the master," and therefore does not actively par-

Our concern is to notice that the relations in the household—
of husband and wife, parent and child, master and slave—are
not "political" in the proper sense of the word, although Aristotle

---

ticipate in the political community of freemen. We must note that Aristotle's
definition of the natural slave as "a man who belongs to another as an active,
living, separate instrument" includes "man" as one of the five differentiae
(the genus of the definition is "instrument"). This means that the slave is,
of course, not a brute animal and has human rights if not political rights. As
St. Thomas points out in his treatment of Aristotle's doctrine, the natural
slave, considered as a man, is something having separate existence from the
master, and hence there is justice toward him in a way; and "for this
reason . . . there are certain laws regulating the relation of a master to
his slave." (*Summa Theol.* II–II.Q.57 a.4 ad 2.) But Aristotle's slave would
be excluded from participation in the political life much as contemporary
constitutions exclude those failing to pass literacy tests.

There are both harsh and benign aspects to Aristotle's doctrine. He writes,
"The abuse of this authority [of the master] is injurious to both; for the
interest of part and whole . . . are the same. . . . Hence where the relation
of master and slave between them is natural, they are friends and have a
common interest, but where it rests merely on force the reverse is true."
(*Politics* I.1255b.10–15.) Legal or institutional slavery rests, of course, on
force. There is a very subtle and sympathetic understanding of this natural
relation in Joseph Conrad's novel *Heart of Darkness.* Marlow, the narrator of
the tale, is speaking of the cannibal who had been indispensable to him in
negotiating a difficult river in the heart of Africa and who had been killed
in the course of the voyage: "I missed my late helmsman awfully—I missed
him even while his body was still lying in the pilothouse. Perhaps you will
think it passing strange, this regret for a savage who was no more account
than a grain of sand in a black Sahara. Well, don't you see, he had done
something, he had steered; for months I had him at my back—a help—an
instrument. It was a kind of partnership. He steered for me—I had to look
after him, I worried about his deficiencies, and thus a subtle bond had been
created, of which I only became aware when it was suddenly broken. And
the intimate profundity of that look he gave me when he received his hurt
remains to this day in my memory—like a claim of distant kinship affirmed
in a supreme moment." (In *Three Great Tales,* Random House, Inc., New
York, 1958, p. 128. By permission of the Joseph Conrad Estate and J. M.
Dent & Sons, Ltd., Publishers, London. U.S. edition published by Doubleday
& Company, Inc., Garden City, New York.) There you have an appreciation
by a very noble mind of what Aristotle meant by the relation of the natural
master and the natural slave.

finds analogies of civil rule in these relationships. The father's rule over his children is like "royal" rule in civil society because the father rules over them by love and for their own good; but it is not properly royal rule, for the children are not "freemen" and do not choose their father. A king, on the other hand, should not rule over his subjects as though they were children. His rule is over free men who choose their ruler by knowledge and will: A king's rule is "royal and political." Aristotle calls the rule of the husband over his wife "political" (in a sense narrower than that which embraces "royal") by analogy with the rule of equals over equals in civil society; but although there is greater equality between husband and wife than between father and children, this relationship is not properly political because the difference between man and woman is brought in by nature: There is then, no genuine "rotation in office"; but in a genuine democracy the freemen and equals are all entitled to rule. The wife, then, is naturally subject to her husband.[46] Finally, the "despotic" rule of the "natural master" over the "natural slave" clearly lies outside the whole concept of political rule, which is over freemen and equals. It is in this way that Aristotle shows that household government differs in kind from that of the State; contrary to Plato's view, the nature of the household, however large, is not the same as that of the state, however small, "but they differ in regard to government."

[46] *Politics* I.1259b, 1260a.14. Aristotle says that woman has the deliberative faculty, but it is without authority in her. "Although there may be exceptions to the order of nature, the male is by nature fitter for command than the female." With the disinterestedness that is compatible with making it, I should like to make the suggestion that Joseph Conrad wonderfully expresses Aristotle's view in the following passage: "It's queer how out of touch with truth women are. They live in a world of their own, and there has never been anything like it, and never can be. It is too beautiful altogether, and if they were to set it up it would go to pieces before the first sunset. Some confounded fact we men have been living contentedly with ever since the day of creation would start up and knock the whole thing over." *Op. cit.,* p. 228. (By permission of the Joseph Conrad Estate and J. M. Dent & Sons, Ltd., Publishers, London. U.S. edition published by Doubleday & Company, Inc., Garden City, New York.)

Political science: architectonic and principal science

If the task of the household is that of procuring the indispensable daily needs of life, and that of the village goes beyond these daily requirements, the diversity of trades and activities made possible by the union of villages marks the beginning of the political community. And with this beginning in a sufficiency of material goods, the State continues in existence for the sake of the perfection of life in the virtues and the arts. There now open up for man possibilities of a common good of the highest sort. For the state is a community—a communication—of men not merely for activity of life but for activity of life according to the highest virtues. The political community is organized for the procurement of this common good of its members: the good of the virtues, both speculative and moral, and of the arts; and for this reason the "art" of government is declared by Aristotle to be "the most authoritative art":

for it is this which ordains which of the sciences should be studied in a state, and which each class of citizens should learn and up to what point they should learn them; and we see even the most highly esteemed of capacities to fall under this, e.g., strategy, economics, rhetoric; now, since politics uses the rest of the sciences, and since, again, it legislates as to what we are to do and what we are to abstain from, the end of this science must include those of the others, so that this end must be the good for man.[47]

We have already observed that the common good of the political community extends to the many who make up that community in their very diversity and for this reason the unity of the common good is a unity of order. The "authoritative" character of politics, then, is to be understood as being that of a "master art" with respect to autonomous, if subordinate, arts: ". . . as there are many actions, arts, and sciences, their ends also are many; the end of the medical art is health, that of shipbuilding a vessel,

[47] *Ethics* I.1094a.28–1094b.8.

that of strategy victory, that of economics wealth"; but the art that directs all of these autonomous activities to the human common good—that art is "the most authoritative."

In the above cited paragraph we may discern two properties of an authoritative art: It prescribes what the sciences under it ought to do (as the equestrian prescribes for the art of bridle-making), and it uses the subordinate sciences for its own end (the equestrian uses the bridle for riding horses). Now we must be careful to observe, as St. Thomas points out in his Commentary, that political science, itself being a practical science, is authoritative with respect to all other sciences only insofar as these deal with things that are operable by man; and, therefore, we may observe in the text of Aristotle cited above that politics is authoritative with a difference in regard to speculative and practical sciences. With respect to the theoretic sciences, the first of the above-mentioned properties of an authoritative science belongs to politics only to the extent that the State prescribes that they be pursued; the State may issue orders for the sake of truth, but not to it: It ordains, for example, that some should teach geometry and lays down qualifications for teachers, but it does not prescribe for geometry what should be the conclusion concerning the triangle; for this is a matter that does not lie under the will of man (the sphere of practical science) but depends on the very nature of things (the sphere of theoretic science).[48] Aristotle was very clear about the

[48] This holds for art too, in its essential nature, for we have noticed that art resembles the habits of the theoretic intellect in that both are concerned with the disposition of the things considered by them and not with the disposition of the will toward these objects. What makes the excellence of art is not touched by the "authoritative" rule of politics; and art—in the point in which it is unlike theoretic science, namely, its consideration of the disposition of things being for the sake of beauty in imitation of nature —lends itself less than the theoretic sciences to violation by political authority. Willa Cather as a great artist understood this matter perfectly: "The condition every art requires is, not so much freedom from restriction, as freedom from adulteration and from the intrusion of foreign matter. . . . The great body of Russian literature was produced when the censorship was at its strictest. The art of Italy flowered when the painters were confined almost entirely to religious subjects. In the great age of Gothic architecture

stupidity of such things as our own times have known in Nazi biology or Marxist genetics; but this safeguard to liberty cannot be had—it may be noted with profit—except man recognize the existence of truths not dependent on his own will (something that contemporary democratic philosophy is as hesitant in accepting as totalitarianism is unhesitant in denying). With regard to practical sciences, Aristotle holds that politics may prescribe for them not only with respect to putting and not putting them to use, but even with respect to the determination of their work: what kind of roads to build, where to build houses, where not to build them.

The second attribute of an authoritative science—that it use the subordinate science for its own end—pertains to political science only with respect to the practical sciences; whence it is, Aristotle says, we see that the most esteemed capacities fall under the direction of the State, viz., military science, economics, and rhetoric. The theoretic sciences, however, may not be used by the State for its own end. This is because the end of the theoretic sciences is a good which lies outside the sphere of the human will: the truth of the theoretic (speculative) intellect. The contemplative life, most perfectly ordained to this intelligible good, is the life to which the political virtues and the arts themselves are ordered. This is the life which we have seen Aristotle call "too high for man"; but it is the life which he nonetheless bids us "strain every nerve" to live, for "even if it be small in bulk, much more does it in power and worth surpass everything." The dictum

---

sculptors and stone-cutters told the same stories (with infinite variety and fresh invention) over and over, on the faces of all the cathedrals and churches in Europe. How many clumsy experiments in government, futile revolutions and reforms, those buildings have looked down upon without losing a shadow of their dignity and power—of their importance!" (*Willa Cather, On Writing*, Alfred A. Knopf, Inc., New York, 1949, pp. 26–27.) It is precisely those artists who, as Willa Cather puts it, are mainly interested in "the Preservation of the Indian, or Sex, or Tuberculosis" and ought to "be working in a laboratory or bureau" (where they could do their work honestly) who complain most about censorship; and this because they attempt to be administrators themselves in morals and politics, transforming their art into sociology or psychology. (*Ibid.*, p. 125.)

commonly made concerning Aristotle's alleged straitening of man in the confines of the polis rests on a simple misunderstanding of Aristotle's doctrine. On the contrary, Aristotle's teaching is calculated to show man the way of freedom by approaching that Life upon which "depend the heavens and the world of nature." Indeed, the reason why politics is the "most principal" as well as "the most authoritative science" is that this science provides the way for man to approach the perfect freedom of God— by way of proportion in the virtues and the arts and by way of "informing" in the theoretic sciences, and especially in Wisdom. This is why Aristotle calls the political life "godlike."

The political community—forms of government

The political community is indeed, then, a community for freemen. It is defined, in contradistinction to the household, precisely in that way: It is a community of freemen and equals.[49] But if the household is a kind of natural monarchy, as Aristotle says, it does not follow that the political community is a kind of natural democracy. For there are elements other than freedom and equality that go to make up the political community. Indeed a man is said to be free as being "cause of himself"—of that *second* self of the political virtues—and so, in Aristotle's view, virtue has a better title to political rule than do freedom and equality. The members of a political community are free because of their *capacity* for self-government, and they are equal in *having* this capacity. It does not follow that they have this capacity equally, nor, where they may have it equally, that they use it equally, nor that all are equal in the ability to govern others. Consideration must also be given to the claims of wealth to political rule, for the political community is in the first instance distinguished from the household and village by reason of the sufficiency of material goods that it makes possible. The forms of government for the political community are therefore distinguished most basically in terms of

[49] *Politics* I.1255b.19–20, III.127a.21.

the character of the ruling class and secondarily in terms of the number of the ruling class. Aristotle recognizes three main forms of good government—good because they respect the nature of a freeman and work for the common good: monarchy and aristocracy, in which, respectively, the one most virtuous man and a few most virtuous men exercise power; and moderate democracy, in which the many, on the principle of equality, rule for the common good. The first two forms rightly consider that freedom, equality, and wealth are merely the material and not the final cause of political life; they take virtue to be this final cause. Royal and aristocratic rule, Aristotle suggests, are suitable forms for a people neither too rich nor too poor, secure from attack, with no desire for great wealth, homogeneous in culture, unambitious, virtuous, self-sufficient but not aggressive, "great" but not large. Where rule is in the hands of the many "who neither are rich nor have any merit of virtue," the government is a moderate democracy or simply called "polity" as signifying the "political" rule of equals over equals in contradistinction to the "royal and political" rule of the most virtuous. Insofar as freedom and equality are just claims to rule, moderate democracy is a good form of government. Insofar as freedom and equality are taken to be the final cause of political life (to the point of ostracizing those who are eminent in virtue), it is not, simply speaking, just and tends to its natural perversion, extreme democracy. This perverted form of democracy, like the perversions of monarchy (tyranny) and of aristocracy (oligarchy), is improperly "political," for they all imply a violation of man's freedom and its purpose of virtuous living. The tyrant seeks power for his own sake and not to perfect the freedom of the members of the political community; oligarchical rule places wealth as the end of the human life and exploits the poor for the benefit of the rich; extreme democracy exploits both the rich and the virtuous in behalf of absolute equality in everything.

We must notice, in the listing of the forms of government, a fourfold signification of the term "political." Its first and most generic meaning is intended simply to distinguish the members of the polis, as persons *capable* of governing themselves, from the members of the household, who for one reason or another are not fully capable of self-government—the child because of its immaturity, the woman because of the alleged instability of her prudence, and the "natural slave" because of his inability to initiate self-direction. The term political in this most generic sense applies to all forms of state, good and bad; it simply distinguishes the polis as a community of men who are free by nature from the "natural monarchy" of the household. Beyond this basic freedom and equality that distinguishes the state as such from the household, lies the distinction, founded in nature, between ruler and subject even among free men, and this distinction leads to a second meaning of "political." [50] Here the term signifies the different good forms of government—forms that do in fact (and not merely in name) take into account, however differently, man's basic freedom and equality. This second meaning of "political" poses the good forms of government against the bad. Thirdly, the term "political"

[50] This second meaning is brought out by Aristotle in the following text: ". . . there are many kinds both of rulers and subjects (and that rule is the better which is exercised over better subjects—for example, to rule over men is better than to rule over wild beasts; for the work is better which is executed by better workmen, and where one man rules and another is ruled, they may be said to have a work); for in all things which form a composite whole and which are made up of parts, whether continuous or discrete, a distinction between the ruling and subject element comes to light. Such a duality exists in living creatures, but not in them only; it originates in the constitution of the universe. . . . We will . . . restrict ourselves to the living creature, which, in the first place, consists of soul and body: and of these two, the one is by nature the ruler, and the other the subject. But then we must look for the intentions of nature in things which retain their nature, and not in things which are corrupted. And therefore we must study the man who is in the most perfect state both of body and soul, for in him we shall see the true relation of the two; although in bad or corrupted natures the body will often appear to rule over the soul, because they are in an evil and unnatural condition. At all events we may . . . observe in living creatures . . . a constitutional rule; for . . . the intellect rules the appetites with a constitutional and royal rule. And it is clear that the rule of the mind and the rational element over the passionate, is natural and expedient; whereas the equality of the two or the rule of the inferior is always hurtful . . . this principle of necessity extends to all mankind." (*Politics* I.1254a.24–1254b.15.)

is used in a still more restricted sense to signify that particular form of good government known as moderate democracy: This form deserves especially to be called "political" because it puts forth freedom and equality as titles to political authority. Here then the term "political" is opposed to "royal" and "aristocratic," though these latter are political in the second sense—and indeed, in Aristotle's view, in the sense of what is best absolutely speaking: for the term "royal," we must remember, essentially signifies the perfection of the governing principle over subjects who are free, whereas the simple "political" form is defective in political wisdom. There is, finally, a fourth usage of this term. Aristotle calls "polity" that form of government which he considers best not absolutely but best in the sense of what is most generally attainable and practicable. This polity—of which we shall presently speak—seems most especially to deserve the appellation "political" because by avoiding the evils of oligarchy and of extreme democracy, it at once insures political wisdom (by, essentially, the economic stability that is the product of wide property distribution) and the greatest possible share in government by the whole people. To this form, also, is given by a special appropriation, as it were, the designation of "rule according to law." And every good government, Aristotle says, must observe the principle of rule according to law. An examination of this principle will throw further light on Aristotle's scheme of governments.

Rule according to law and the forms of government

The reading of Book III of the *Politics,* in which Aristotle treats of the forms of government in general, is a very bewildering experience. The riddle of this book arises from four propositions that Aristotle makes in the course of his examination of the question of the best form of government. He says first that all good government is government according to law; he then rather surprisingly raises the question whether it is better to be ruled by law or by one best man; thirdly, he goes on to say that the rule of many is itself rule according to law; and finally, he concludes the whole discussion by saying, quite unexpectedly, that rule by one best man is best. If Aristotle means what he says, then we must conclude that rule by one best man is also rule according to law (for Aristotle prefers rule by one best man and also says that every good government exemplifies the principle of rule according to law). We are forced to conclude also, then, that where the rule of law is *contrasted* with rule by one best man, it signifies a special kind of rule of law. The solution to this riddle[51] seems to lie in recognizing four distinct ways in which law may be said to rule. These four ways correspond to the four meanings which we have said are attached to the term "political."

The question at issue is not whether there should be law, but whether law should rule: Law, indeed, there must be, for law is nothing but an ordinance of reason for the *common good* (and not for any particular interest). Hence general rules (laws) must of necessity precede particular determinations and decrees in the political community, for the measure of a thing must suit the thing measured, and the common good is measured by common or general enactments. When it is said, then, that law should *rule*, the question is not whether there should be law (for law there

---

[51] Book III is generally considered a quite insoluble riddle. Professor Ernest Barker, a renowned Aristotelian scholar, explains the argument of Chapter XVI of Book III as follows: "Aristotle had started the previous chapter by an examination of the antithesis, *aut rex aut lex* (either king or law). But by the end of that chapter he had abandoned the antithesis: he had assumed the general principle of the sovereignty of *lex*. . . . Now, however, at the beginning of Chapter XVI, he returns to the antithesis, *aut rex aut lex*. In spite of the general assumption in favor of the sovereignty of law, there *may* (he feels) be a case, or cases, in which one man is so eminent and so good, that his free discretion may be a better mode of sovereignty than the rule of law." (*The Politics of Aristotle*, trans., with notes by Sir Ernest Barker, Oxford University Press, Fairlawn, N.J., 1948, p. 170, n. 1.) And Prof. George H. Sabine, having written quite absolutely that "Aristotle accepted the point of view . . . that in any good state the law must be the ultimate sovereign and not any person whatsoever," goes on to say that "Aristotle recognizes that . . . this (the supremacy of the law) cannot be asserted quite absolutely" and that in fact Aristotle apparently "believed that monarchy and aristocracy alone have any claim to be regarded as ideal states." (Sabine, *A History of Political Theory*, pp. 93, 103.)

must be); the question rather is whether law, in some sense, measures and rules every form of government, even that of the best man. It is this consideration that leads us to see four distinct meanings of "rule of law" in Aristotle. First and most generically, rule of law marks the kind of rule that distinguishes the political community from the household. To understand this we must note that law is an ordinance of *reason:* As Aristotle teaches, the practical reason makes use of a syllogism in respect of actions to be done;[52] hence universal propositions of the practical intellect that are directed to actions have the nature of law. Law, then, is something that belongs, properly speaking, to rational natures; it applies to nonrational creatures only by way of similitude. Now the household association, insofar as it is distinguished from the political community, is governed rather by instinct than by rational activity as intrinsically constituting it.[53] It is rooted in a much more primordial nature than is the political community. The latter, though natural in the sense of constituting the integration and purpose of other communities, is not brought in by nature but needs to be instituted by man: Law is an ordinance of reason. The founding of the State, as a work of reason, is effected by a rule of law—the law of the constitution; thus the State, by its very nature, ought to originate in law and needs some kind of consensus on the part of the free community.[54] All the forms of

---

[52] *Ethics* VII. 1145b.22ff.

[53] But see p. 55, n. 4. In the *Physics* Aristotle's demonstration of nature's action for an end leads St. Thomas in his Commentary to define nature as a *ratio indita rebus qua ipsae res moventur ad finem determinatum"* (a reason put into things by which they are moved to a determined end). (*In II Physics* lect.14.) Hence, the "actions" of nature are directed to an end, as Aristotle shows, not by an intelligence intrinsic to the nature. Thus, although we may indeed speak of "natural law" in referring to the regularity of natural operations, the term is applied, as St. Thomas says, by way of similitude only. (*Summa Theol.* I.II.Q.91 a.2 ad 3.)

[54] Aristotle does not treat the question of the origin of the State except to say that the State is natural and at the same time needs to be instituted by man: ". . . if the earlier forms of society are natural, so is the state, for it is the end of them, and the nature of a thing is its end. For what each thing is when fully developed, we call its nature, whether we are speaking of a

government, including that of the best man, are or ought to be, then, under a constitutional law.

There is next a more restricted meaning of rule of law which distinguishes the rule of good forms of government from its perversion in the bad. If the State is a work of reason, it is the reason of prudence and not of art that establishes the law of its constitution. The virtue of a prince, Aristotle says, is the practical reason making use of a syllogism in respect to *actions to be done,* not in respect to *things to be made.* Law is a work of political prudence. The second signification of "rule of law" opposes rule of law to rule of art and distinguishes the good constitutions from the bad. We have already adverted to the constitutional implications of the difference between art and prudence.[55] Precisely because prudence does not—unlike art—determine the end to be achieved (the proper human common good), the virtue of government is bounded by jurisdiction, namely, the order of rights that follow from the nature of man and the true end of human life. These rights may conveniently be summed up by the terms "substantive" and "procedural." By the first is meant all that is implied in living and living well (the burden of the first book of Aristotle's *Ethics*); by the second is implied the various acts that are indispensable to the making of choice by free men: deliberation, counsel, judgment. The rule of art in politics perverts these rights: Tyranny seeks political power for its own sake; oligarchy seeks wealth as the end of human life; extreme democracy seeks equality in everything.

This second meaning of the "rule of law" is best fulfilled, in Aristotle's opinion, by the rule of the man who is most wise in practical matters. This is Aristotle's "absolute kingship" which he maintains—at least in the abstract, in theory—is the best form

---

man, a horse, or a family. Besides, the final cause and the end of a thing is the best, and to be self-sufficing is the end and the best. Hence it is evident that the state is a creation of nature, and that man is by nature a political animal. . . . A social instinct is implanted in all men by nature, and yet he who first founded the state was the greatest of benefactors." (*Politics* I.1252b.30–1253a.30.) See Chap. V, pp. 134–138.

[55] *Above,* pp. 31–35.

of government. Such a government is under a constitution—that is to say, it exists by consent—but enjoys a plenitude of power in the making of laws under the constitution. The virtue of Aristotle's royal ruler must exceed that of the whole community together, not merely in quantity but in quality. And this means, as St. Thomas points out in his Commentary, that absolute kingship requires in the ruler "divine" or "heroic" virtue—virtue altogether surpassing the human mode.[56]

But if Aristotle's absolute kingship fulfills perfectly the second meaning of rule of law by ruling with the greatest practical wisdom, the fact that none of the subjects ever has a turn at ruling leads Aristotle to speak of absolute kingship as "rule by one best man" in contrast to what is now a third meaning of "rule of law." For ". . . it is thought to be just that among equals every one be ruled as well as rule, and therefore that all should have their turn. We thus arrive at law; for an order of succession implies law." [57] Absolute kingship is not simply "political rule" because the king's authority is not divided with the citizens; to be simply speaking "political," the rule itself must be subject to laws laid down by the citizens.[58] Absolute kingship is modeled on the virtuous man's government of himself and represents the perfection of the governing principle. But if "we must study the man who

[56] ". . . such a person, exceeding all the others in virtue, appears as it were 'god-like.' Concerning this, it should be understood that anyone can attain perfect virtue and its acts in a two-fold manner: in one way according to the common human state; in another way, beyond the common human mode: but this is done through heroic virtue . . . but this is something divine, accomplished through something divine in man, viz., his intellect: it is in this way that Aristotle speaks here: for such a man, exceeding all others in virtue is, he says, like God." (*In III Politics* lect.XII.) This leads St. Thomas to observe that Aristotle's absolute kingship, as a pure form, is "supra-political." See Chap. V, pp. 142–143.

[57] *Politics* III.1287a.17.

[58] Cf. *In I Politics* lect.1. "But the state can be ruled by a two-fold government: namely, political and royal. The regime is royal indeed when he who is head of the state has a plenitude of power. But the government is political when he who is the ruler has power which is constricted by certain laws of the state. . . ."

is in the most perfect state of both body and soul" in order to find
the true relation of ruling and subject principles (which "of
necessity extends to all mankind"), it is nonetheless also the case
that perfect virtue is very rarely found in men. And so political
communities tend, by and large, to organize on less desirable lines.
Now we notice that in the individual man who is merely continent
(as distinct from the man who is virtuous) there is found an
imitation of the perfect rule of law by which the virtuous man
governs himself. And it is on this basis that Aristotle introduces the
third meaning of "rule of law," which applies to the rule of many
in a democracy. This third signification is derivative, and the rule
of law here is imitative and less good in precisely the same way
that the condition of mere continence is less good than true virtue.
At the same time, we must take care to notice that the concept
"rule of law" applies more appropriately to the continent man
(and thus to democracy) than it does to the perfectly virtuous
man (and to royal rule)—a fact that explains Aristotle's contrast-
ing rule of law (taken as being the same as the rule of many) with
rule by one best man. For in the merely continent man there is no
clearly recognizable governing principle: The rational principle
is too affected by desire, and the desire is too little under the rational principle, yet not so little as to destroy the proper order. The
sense appetites in such a man are fairly equal with the rational
principle in the position of authority, and it is only *the fact of this
equality* (in itself not be wished for) that allows him to perform
acts of virtue without having the virtue itself. The law is in such
a man as in *that which is measured* rather than in him *as the ruler
and measurer*. This third sense of rule of law is clearly, then, a
substitutional sense: For law, being an ordinance of reason, is
imperfectly in the continent man; it is there only by the fact of
order which "implies law" and which is not destroyed in the continent man as it is in the vicious man. This law substitutes for the
perfection of government through the rational principle. In a
similar way, rotation in office in a community of equals substitutes
for the perfection of the governing principle in the one best man
and itself constitutes the "rule of law." Aristotle indicates the substitutional character of rule by equals by observing that "we

endeavor (in such a case) to create a difference of outward forms and names and titles of respect, which may be illustrated by the saying of Amasis about his foot-pan." [59] In both cases—that of the continent man and that of democracy—we find relative weakness of rule due partly to less clearly fixed responsibility and partly to the tendency to eliminate the better element. And just as the continent man, unless he devises a special rule of life, tends to a worse condition, so simple democracy, unless it devises a rule to safeguard the good it has, tends to demand equality in everything. It is the need for this special device that leads to the fourth sense of "rule of law"; it is exemplified in that mixed constitution, the Polity, that Aristotle proposed as the best in the sense of what is most practicable and attainable.

The mixed forms of government and the Polity

Royal rule, aristocracy, and democracy are the three "pure" forms of government and they are distinguished not only in terms of the number of the ruling element but more basically in terms of the values prized by the community: Democracy prizes freedom and equality above all other things, while the other two forms assert the political primacy of practical wisdom. Aristotle notes a certain disadvantage in each of these forms. Although he believes that absolute kingship is without defect in principle and is, absolutely speaking, the best, this very superiority renders it difficult of attainment; and further, he seems to think that the citizens of such a state would feel dishonored in being excluded from the highest office. Democracy, on the other hand, is defective in principle, for it leads to the ostracizing of the wiser men. For just as the equality and freedom of the sense appetites and the

[59] *Politics* I.1259b.7. Amasis, having been a subject, became a ruler and made a golden foot-pan which the Egyptians reverenced. Amasis likened himself to this foot-pan, explaining that he too had been formerly a mere utensil and then had become, like his foot-pan, an object of veneration.

rational principle in the continent man cannot serve as a measure and rule for him, so democracy, if taken absolutely, leads to an evil condition. These considerations lead Aristotle to suggest a criterion of the "best" that is based not on the formal considera- tion of virtue (not on what is, absolutely speaking, best) but simply on the consideration of avoiding the worst. The most prac- ticable scheme for this, he suggests, lies in some constitutional de- vice for avoiding the extremes of democracy and oligarchy; this intermediate constitution calls for a special "construct." As the continent man, who by nature is inclined to the extreme of over- indulgence, avoids a worse state by imitating the intermediate (virtue) by moving in the direction of the opposite extreme (from overindulgence he moves toward total abstinence, thus imitating the intermediate condition of temperance by a precarious com- bination of both extremes), so the political community can avoid the extremes of oligarchy and democracy by combining the ex- tremes of the wealthy few and the many poor in a large middle class. This avoidance of the extremes of oligarchy and democracy is accomplished by having the middle class possess the preponder- ance of power in the State. Any number of mixed constitutions is possible by different combinations of political factors (voting and office-holding qualifications) joined to economic factors (the dis- tribution of wealth) and by the way in which both sets of factors are combined with each other. If wealth, for example, is widely distributed the community is disposed toward democracy; if high property qualifications for voting and office-holding are enforced, the community tends toward oligarchy. The chief objective in the modeling of the "best" constitution in these terms is to avoid the extremes of oligarchy and democracy by balancing birth, wealth, education, and position with sheer number. The Polity places supremacy in the hands of the class that lies between the extremes of the very rich and the very poor and its success is made to de- pend largely on the numbers and political strength of this inter- mediate class. If possible, the middle class should be stronger than the very rich and the very poor taken together, or at least stronger than either of them.

Aristotle's analysis of the most generally practicable State thus

III

The political philosophy of Later Greece and Rome

The two features that characterize the political world after the death of Aristotle (322 B.C.) are the disappearance of the city-state as a vital force and the development, within the milieu of empire, of the sense of the individual and his self-sufficiency expressed by the new "philosophies of conduct." The city-state was on its way out even in Aristotle's time, giving way first to the Macedonian Empire of Alexander the Great (Aristotle's own student) and finally coming under the domination of the Roman Empire. The Greek federations and alliances had failed to make stable States; their fate indeed had depended less on themselves than on Carthage, Asia, and Italy.

In presenting these developments it has been customary to charge Aristotle with short-sightedness in his notion of the self-sufficient polis, and to find him curiously obtuse to the vision of world empire and universal humanity. Professor Sabine says, for example, that neither Plato nor Aristotle "was as keenly aware as he should have been of the part which foreign affairs played even in the internal economy of the city-state." His stricture is more severe against Aristotle than it is against Plato: "If Plato had been as closely associated with Macedonia as Aristotle, he would hardly have failed to perceive the epoch-making importance of the career of Alexander. It is interesting to conjecture what might have happened if it had occurred to Aristotle to consider the hypothesis that the city-state needed to be absorbed into some still more self-sufficing political unit, as it had itself absorbed the family and the village. But this was beyond the power of his imagination." [1] Agreeing with this observation, Professor Catlin remarks that "This lack of interest [on Aristotle's part] was . . . a strange distortion of perspective due to ethical disregard of quantity in the name of quality." [2]

There are certain considerations, however, which this kind of criticism entirely neglects, and they are considerations that bear upon the deepest import of Aristotle's conception of politics. The simple fact of relevance here is that in Aristotle's view military alliances and economic agreements and administrative arrangements are conditions without which a State cannot exist, but all of them together do not constitute a State. To be preoccupied with military and economic security is indeed to be in a prepolitical, a precivilized condition, in a condition just this side of barbarism. Aristotle fully recognized the need for military and economic alliances. Speaking of the laws devised by Phaleas of Chalcedon, he says: "There is another objection to them. They are chiefly designed to promote the internal welfare of the State. But the legislator should consider also its relation to neighboring nations, and to all who are outside of it." [3] Aristotle's notion of self-sufficiency did not, then, exclude need for international agreements; but such agreements he considered to be a mere preamble and auxiliary to the communication of men in the highest goods:

Nor does a state exist for the sake of alliance and security from injustice, nor yet for the sake of exchange and mutual intercourse. . . . It is clear . . . that the state is not a mere society, having a common

[1] Sabine, *A History of Political Theory,* p. 126.
[2] George Catlin, *The Story of the Political Philosophers,* McGraw-Hill Book Company, Inc., New York, 1939, p. 105.
[3] *Politics* II.1267a.20.

place, established for the prevention of mutual crime and for the sake of exchange. These are the conditions without which a state cannot exist; but all of them together do not constitute a state, which is a community . . . for the sake of a perfect and self-suffing life. . . . The end of the state is the good life, and these are the means towards it.[4]

Nor then, we may notice, is distance a decisive point. Indeed, considering the possibility of men "dwelling at a distance from one another but not so far off as to be unable to associate, Aristotle makes it clear that distance would not itself prevent the forming of a State: Whatever the distance, if it permits the will to live together—which is friendship—it permits the forming of a State.[5] For we must consider that, as he points out, although "all things are ordered together somehow" they are not ordered "all alike." Indeed, it is in extending his vision from the polis to not the empire but the entire universe that Aristotle makes this point:

We must consider also in which of two ways the nature of the universe contains the good and the highest good, whether as something separate and by itself, or as the order of the parts. Probably in both ways, as an army does; for its good is found both in its order and in its leader, and more in the latter; for he does not depend on the order, but it depends on him. And all things are ordered together somehow, but not all alike—both fishes and fowls and plants; and the world is not such that one thing has nothing to do with another, but they are connected. For all are ordered together to one end . . .[6]

These remarks should suggest to us that the reason why Aristotle did not consider a larger unit than the city-state as politically viable lies in the fact that any larger unit in the fifth century Mediterranean world would not have met the exigencies of a truly "political" life but rather would have favored a kind of random freedom befitting not men but animals and slaves. In that very same passage in which he says that the world is not such that one

[4] *Politics* III.1280b.35ff.
[5] *Ibid.*
[6] *Metaph.* XII.1075a.12–20.

thing has nothing to do with another, but all are ordered together somehow, he observes that this ordering together of all things in the universe

is as in a house, where the freemen are least at liberty to act at random, but all things, or most things are already ordained for them, while the slaves and the animals do little for the common good, and for the most part live at random.[7]

We must notice that in this analogy the "separate substances"— the separate intelligences—are to the universe what freemen are to the house, and man is compared to the separate substances as the slave in the house is to the freeman. If, as Aristotle says in Book I of the *Politics,* there are some men who are "natural slaves," all men, by reason of the whole of human nature, are in a condition of bondage compared to perfect intellectual creatures —the separate substances. Indeed, at the very beginning of the *Metaphysics* Aristotle remarks: "the possession of wisdom might be justly regarded as beyond human power; for in many ways human nature is enslaved."[8] Now the slave lived principally on the margin of society. He lived, as Aristotle remarks, for the most part at random. Was it not Aristotle's opinion that in the milieu of empire men would live at random on the margin of society, contributing little or nothing to the common good, all readily victimized by the common slavery to which the whole of human nature is subject? It is in any case a most remarkable fact that this random freedom became the most characteristic expression of the philosophies of conduct that succeeded Aristotle. Far from introducing a loftier conception of common good, the new concepts of world empire and world humanity were accompanied by philosophies that emphasized opposition between the common good and individual good. The great empire spelled the end of active intimate participation in the life of the State that had defined man as a "political animal." "The ideal of free citizenship was transformed to meet a situation in which the holding of public office

[7] *Ibid.*
[8] *Ibid.* I.982b.20.

and the performance of political function played a negligible role, and yet the ideal . . . persisted as the conception of a legal status and a body of rights in which the individual could claim the protection of the State." [9]

The philosophies of conduct

The task of adjusting men's ideas and ideals to the new world of empire was carried out by the so-called "philosophies of conduct" —Stoicism, Cynicism, and Epicureanism. Whatever their differences, these philosophies were at one in their preoccupation with the fate of the individual in the great new world. The new sense of the individual introduced by these philosophies is thought by most scholars to have ushered in a conception hitherto alien to the Greek mind—the conception of individual human rights. Aristotle's concern for the city-state—so runs the common opinion— was an obstacle to an appreciation of the rights of man. Professor Tarn observes:

Man as a political animal, a fraction of the *polis* or self-governing city-state, had ended with Aristotle; with Alexander begins man as an individual. This individual needed to consider both the regulation of his own life, and also his relations with other individuals who with him composed the "inhabited world"; to meet the former need there arose the philosophies of conduct, to meet the latter certain new ideas of human brotherhood.[10]

How Professor Tarn regards Aristotle's division of moral philosophy into ethics, economics, and politics—the first of which is concerned with the individual's regulation of his own life—is not entirely easy to understand. But in common with many others, Professor Tarn evidently looks upon the new interest in the individual man as introducing to Western civilization the idea of a

[9] Sabine, *op. cit.*, pp. 144–145.
[10] W. W. Tarn, *Hellenistic Civilization*, St. Martin's Press, Inc., New York, 1927, p. 79.

"higher law" which bears fruit centuries later in the doctrine of the rights of man. This is also the view of Carlyle, who has possibly been most responsible for its propagation among later students of political thought. Professor Carlyle's statement is that "There is no change in political theory so startling in its completeness as the change from the theory of Aristotle to the later philosophical view represented by Cicero and Seneca"; for it is here that "we are indeed at the beginnings of a theory of human nature and society of which the 'Liberty, Equality and Fraternity' of the French Revolution is only the present-day expression." [11]

But if scholars agree that a turning point in the history of political thought occurs here, and that it involves a new conception of the rights of man, there has been no adequate effort to understand in what this turning point precisely consisted. There are to be found, certainly, many dicta: that a new doctrine of the equality of men is for the first time introduced; that for the first time men understand the State in terms of law and do not, like the classical Greeks, understand law in terms simply of the State; that there is a new sense of human brotherhood and benevolence in the philosophies after Aristotle. But there is ambiguity in all these dicta. In regard to the first, we may recall that Aristotle puts "man" as one of the five differentiae in his definition of the "natural slave"; with regard to the second, Aristotle's division of States into good and bad is in terms of their conformity or lack of conformity with the general principles of natural law; and with regard to the third of these dicta, we observe Aristotle remarking that friendship, which seems to exist even among birds and most animals, ". . . is felt . . . especially by men, whence we praise lovers of their fellowmen. We may see even in our travels how near and dear every man is to every other." [12]

One would be tempted to assign as a reason for the obscurity in the presentation of this portion of the history of political philosophy the fact that later Stoicism, as represented by Panaetius and

[11] R. W. Carlyle and A. J. Carlyle, *A History of Mediaeval Political Theory in the West,* William Blackwood and Sons, Ltd., Edinburgh, 1930, vol. I, p. 9.

[12] *Ethics* VIII.1155a.20.

Cicero, was modified in a superficial way by the inclusion of ideas drawn from Plato and Aristotle.[13] One would be tempted to assign this reason were it not for the fact that what is insisted upon in the presentation of the development of political ideas in this period is precisely the complete break with the past. And clearly, if a new theory of human rights arises between the death of Aristotle and the writings of Cicero, its novelty is not to be looked for in its revision through a return to ideas drawn from Plato and Aristotle. The task remains of isolating, if possible, the distinctive features of the new natural rights doctrine from the ambiguity of late Stoicism. This will not only enable us to see with greater precision the foundations of the modern theory of politics to which Carlyle refers; it will also permit us to discover what in the new concepts represents an authentic extension and clarification of genuine Aristotelian positions.

We will be helped toward the resolution of the ambiguities to which we have alluded if we notice that the kind of value placed on the individual by the new philosophies of conduct was indeed very different from that with which Aristotle and Plato had been concerned. As we have seen at some length, Aristotle had himself insisted on values for the individual higher than those represented by the political life: The pursuit of truth for its own sake is the best life, for by this activity we approach most closely to the source of the common good of the whole universe; this is the life that, as both Plato and Aristotle said, is "better than the political," for it attains to things that are better than man. For the post-Aristotelian philosophies of conduct, there is, on the contrary, nothing better in the universe than man himself, and so the "higher values" prized by these philosophies are in an order that is the reverse of Aristotle's. If for Aristotle the contemplative life is better than the political, and the political life better than the life that perfects

[13] Professor Carlyle admits this difficulty but then "ventures to think" that it is not one: "There can be little doubt that . . . we find Cicero . . . speaking under the influence partly at least of the Aristotelian principle of the fundamental distinction in human nature. . . . But we venture to think that such passages do not . . . weaken the effect of those which we have already discussed." (Carlyle, *op. cit.*, vol. I, p. 12.)

one in the line of his private satisfaction, the philosophies of conduct taught that the life of personal, private satisfaction, of individual self-sufficiency, is better than any other. These philosophies are aptly called philosophies of "withdrawal" and "protest" —withdrawal from the political life as well as from the contemplative. They protest against the order to the common good which is implied by both kinds of life.

Stoicism, founded by Zeno of Citium at the end of the fourth century, sought happiness in "apathia," a kind of victory over fate and nature achieved through a studied insensibility to every kind of pleasure. Epicureanism, founded at Athens in 306 B.C. by Epicurus had as its fundamental doctrine individual self-sufficiency attained by a negative sort of pleasure consisting in confining oneself to the company of chosen friends and in avoiding the painful sense of obligation with its attendant anxiety and fear. Epicurus considered the anxieties of the moral and religious conscience to be the chief obstacles to human happiness. Cynicism, founded by Antisthenes of Thrace (445–365 B.C.) was also a philosophy of revolt and escape to a curious self-sufficiency amounting to self-annihilation. Everything but "moral character" indeed was regarded as a matter of indifference, but the things which the Cynics included as indifferent—marriage, the family, property, citizenship—were precisely the things that traditionally had been thought to test moral character. The equality asserted by the Cynics, as Professor Sabine says, was "an equality of nihilism."

The character of all the post-Aristotelian philosophies of conduct is suitably suggested in Professor Catlin's description of early Stoicism:

Stoicism . . . asserted as central in its philosophy that Man, autonomous in his Will, was master of his soul and hence captain of his fate. The right to suicide—in the final need, the right to turn the keys of the portals of death—was at once a theoretical concession and a practical corollary . . . the resolve to do nothing save on one's own moral choice and at one's own will, was the core of the philosophy.[14]

[14] Catlin, *op. cit.*, p. 114.

The Stoic principle of the autonomy and self-dependence of the human reason was curiously unlike everything that Aristotle had had to say about man, whom he regarded as the most dependent and uncertain of intellectual creatures. Do not the "rights" asserted for man in the philosophies of conduct strangely free the *form* of human life from all determinations? For Aristotle the form of human life is made determinate and complete through (good) acts, habits, laws, and institutions—all manifestations of self-government. The early Stoic concept of self-sufficiency demanded a "natural right" and a "higher law" that were the expression of a nature that is universal in the sense of being tied to no determinate form: The "higher law" binds only in ensuring the free act of man which creates a world of his own total making. In what else, indeed, is the Stoic conception of the equality of all men grounded? Stoicism did not deny the reality of physical, moral, and intellectual differences; and on the other hand, Aristotle's definition of the natural slave has "man" as one of its five differentiae. Thus the Stoic doctrine of equality of men consists precisely in a self-dependent reason which makes one's moral worth dependent exclusively on one's own judgment in merging moral, domestic, and political distinctions "in a far-off dream of the fellowship of cosmopolitan philosophers."

Neither Plato nor Aristotle was unaware of the ethics of withdrawal. Indeed, beyond the explicitness of its formulation there was little in it that was not present in the discussions of the early sophists. Cynicism was founded during Plato's lifetime. Its abandonment of the amenities of life is derisively pictured by Plato in the "pig-state." [15] Aristotle had declared man to be by nature a political animal and had observed that he who was not must be either a god or a beast: The god-like life was the life of the contemplative virtues, the life of the "divine element" in man, to live in accord with which Aristotle advised, indeed, that we "strain every nerve." It is precisely the extreme difficulty of the truly god-like life—human nature being in a "condition of bondage"—that produces the tendency to revolt and escape: We will be as

[15] *Republic* p. 372.

gods ourselves, declare our independence and self-sufficiency by appealing to a "higher law" by which we are a law unto ourselves. We will protest and withdraw. Now in Aristotle's view, to withdraw from the practical life for unworthy reasons placed one with the beasts: If the "natural slave" is compared to the brute animal because both live on the margin of society and at random, contributing little or nothing to the common good, the freeman who seeks his private satisfaction over the common good is more beastly than the brute because he employs his reason to serve brutish ends. The "god-like" life pursued by men of the Cynic and Epicurean and early Stoic stamp was a "godliness" that was inhuman on the side of beastliness.

In late Stoicism, as refounded by Chrysippus and revised by Panaetius and Cicero, the primacy of the individual gives way to the primacy of the political virtues. Since, however, these latter enjoy, among the late Stoics, a primacy over the speculative virtues, the sense in which Stoicism is revised back in the direction of Plato and Aristotle is a very limited one. Later Stoicism perpetuates the radical difference between the ethical doctrine of Aristotle and all the post-Aristotelian philosophies of conduct. Evidence of this very real difference is found in the appearance among the Romans of a quite new virtue—the virtue of *humanitas*. Professor Cassirer has described this new virtue as follows:

If we study the classical works of Greek ethics, for instance Aristotle's *Nicomachean Ethics,* we find there a clear and systematic analysis of the different virtues, of magnanimity, temperance, justice, courage, and liberality, we do *not* find the general virtue called "humanity" (*humanitas*). Even the term seems to be missing from the Greek language and literature. The ideal of humanitas was first formed in Rome; and it was especially the aristocratic circle of the younger Scipio that gave it its firm place in Roman culture. Humanitas was no vague concept. It had a definite meaning, and it became a formative power in private and public life in Rome. It meant not only a moral but also an aesthetic ideal; it was the demand for a certain type of life that had to prove its influence in the whole of man's life, in his moral conduct as well as in his language, his literary style, and his taste.[16]

[16] Cassirer, *The Myth of the State,* pp. 101–102.

What exactly was this virtue of *humanitas* which Professor Cassirer says was "no vague concept?" We may best understand its meaning if we inquire why, as Professor Cassirer observes, the term was missing not only from Aristotle but from the whole of Greek language and literature. Aristotle says in the *Ethics* that if man were the best thing in the universe, then political science and prudence, not philosophic wisdom, would be the most perfect knowledge. But the most perfect knowledge is rather of the highest objects—"of the highest objects, we say; for it would be strange to think that the art of politics, or practical wisdom, is the best knowledge, since man is not the best thing in the world." [17] We have already adverted to Aristotle's saying that the possession of wisdom is in a way beyond human power, for the nature of man is in many ways enslaved. The speculative life is not as proportionate to human nature as the practical life. The important thing to notice is that in Aristotle's opinion the better part of man is his weakest part, and his "humanity"—the things most proportionate to his human nature—is at once the strongest thing in him and the less good part. Now the Roman virtue of *humanitas* could be cultivated only where man was indeed considered the best thing in the world. The new sense of "brotherhood" of which scholars speak in presenting the development of political thought in this period was new because it was based on a love of man for himself as a being than which there is none better in the universe.[18] And because practical knowledge, as the knowledge that

---

[17] *Ethics* VI.1141a.20.

[18] In the book *To Himself* the Stoic Emperor Marcus Aurelius remarks: "Call none of those things a man's that do not fall to him as a man. They cannot be claimed of a man; the man's nature does not guarantee them; they are no consummations of that nature. Consequently, neither is the end for which man lives placed in these things, nor yet that which is perfective of the end, namely the Good. Moreover, if any of these things did fall to a man, it would not fall to him to condemn them, . . . but as it is, the more a man can cut himself free, . . . from these and other such things . . . by so much the more is he good." (C. R. Haines, *The Communings with Himself of Marcus Aurelius Antonius*, Loeb Classical Library, Harvard University Press, Cambridge, Mass., 1916, bk. V, par. 15.) As Cassirer astutely observes, the Socratic injunction "know thyself," from being merely a moral injunction

is most proportionate to human nature, has to do with the things that are operable by man, the virtue of *humanitas* included, as Professor Cassirer remarks, not only a moral but an aesthetic ideal. When Professor Cassirer says that *humanitas* was a demand for a certain type of life that had to prove itself in the whole of man's life, in his moral conduct as well as in his language, his literary style, and his taste, he very rightly and significantly omits any reference to the life that is "too high for man." We can hardly fail to be startled by the oversights in the histories of political thought when we consider that it was Aristotle who, reputed to have absorbed the individual in the polis, insisted on a wisdom for man higher than that of the State; and that among the Romans, reputed to have engendered a doctrine of individual right against the State, "political science" and "prudence" came to hold the highest place.

I have put quotation marks around political science and prudence to indicate that when these forms of knowledge are accorded the highest place, they are neither, respectively, scientific nor prudential: For in the Aristotelian ethic political science and prudence depend on speculative rectitude—the critical point which in the restoration of the political virtues under the aegis of

---

becomes a metaphysical inquiry. (Cassirer, *Essay on Man*, p. 22.) An interesting present-day expression of the same philosophy is to be found in Erich Fromm: "In all theistic systems . . . there is the assumption of the reality of the spiritual realm, as one transcending man, giving meaning and validity to man's spiritual powers. . . . In a non-theistic system, there exists no spiritual realm outside of man or transcending him. The realm of love, reason, and justice exists as a reality only because . . . man has been able to develop these powers in himself. . . . In this view there is no meaning to life, except the meaning man himself gives to it; man is utterly alone except inasmuch as he helps another . . . the concept of God is only a historically conditioned one, in which man has expressed his experience of his higher powers . . . at a given historical period." (Erich Fromm, *The Art of Loving*, Harper & Row, Publishers, Incorporated, New York, 1956, p. 72.) The notion here expressed by Fromm was formulated by the celebrated nineteenth-century German philosopher, Ludwig Feuerbach, and was taken over by Karl Marx in his doctrine of the "generic being" of man. See Chaps. IX and X.

"humanitas" is ignored. As we have had occasion to observe, one of the reasons why the speculative virtues are considered by Aristotle to be better than the practical virtues is simply that they guarantee the integrity of the practical life by appointing the ends of human life: The rule of the appetite by the rational principle (which produces the political virtues) presupposes speculative knowledge of man's nature and end. Granted, as we have seen, that there is a certain "freedom" and "equality" of the sense appetites in relation to the ruling principle of the reason, the very contrariety of sense and reason in man can jeopardize his capacity for freedom by fostering a revolt against the constitutional exigencies of his very nature—against the human condition. Such a revolt takes the form of denying what Aristotle called the "axiomatic" first principles of human nature; the consequence is that the "operables" of practical science become limitless, and human reason, by its own free constructions, becomes the source of every law. The ambiguity created by later Stoicism's simple reassertion of the moral and political life veils the precision of its basic identity with the earlier philosophies of conduct: which is its avowal, in common with them, of the primacy of practical knowledge.[19] It is precisely this that constitutes the inarticulated begin-

---

[19] The quite crude identification of Stoic principles with Christian doctrine is part of the impossible ambiguity in which this period in political philosophy is shrouded. It should be clear that if we isolate from the incoherence of later Stoicism the formality of its point of view, by which it distinguishes itself from Aristotle, then the substance of the Stoic doctrine is the self-dependence of the reason of the universal Man, whose dignity consists in the very affirmation of his complete self-dependence. And this, of course, is clearly against the whole burden of the Christian message. It is true that St. Augustine and the other Church Fathers were greatly affected by their reading of the Stoics, and particularly of Cicero, but it must be remembered that Cicero's literary exposition of Stoic ethical teaching already reflects the revision of Stoicism back in the direction of Plato and Aristotle. When St. Thomas Aquinas, in the thirteenth century, comes to write his treatise on the moral virtues he does two significant things: First, he cites St. Augustine's opinion that the Stoics and Peripatetics differ more in word than in opinion, and then he goes on to show that the verbal difference is nonetheless rooted in a real inadequacy of analysis. (*Summa Theol.* I.II.Q.59 a.2.) The Stoic position on the role of passion in virtue can be best understood correctly by making

nings—of which Carlyle speaks—of the "theory of human nature and society of which the 'Liberty, Equality and Fraternity' of the French Revolution is only the present-day expression." For in the political theories of the eighteenth century the State, far from having its origin even remotely in the "givenness" of man's nature, is, on the contrary, something wholly produced by man who is conceived as being originally quite independent and "withdrawn." Thus the ethics of withdrawal and protest assume in this late revival a specifically *political* character in the notion of the State arising out of an original "equality of nihilism" and coming into existence simply by a voluntary contractual submission of the governed. These then are the decidedly novel meanings of "equality" and "the state conceived in terms of law" that make the post-Aristotelian period rightly thought of as a turning point in the history of political thought.

These new conceptions—we may observe here—have been no more astutely evaluated and turned to advantage than by Karl Marx. In Marx's view the philosophies of conduct were a natural outcome of the Aristotelian system which "closes itself into a completed, total world" and forces its heirs to turn against their age. Withdrawal and protest were important steps in the liberation of man from such a world, but they resulted in antiquity in "an intolerable attitude of half-contemplation and half-action." [20] The seventeenth- and eighteenth-century political

---

use of Aristotle's *Ethics*. Similarly, the Stoic doctrine of the fundamental equality of men is verbally good, but Aristotle's doctrine of the fundamental equality of men has the advantage of being intelligible. And it is instructive to observe that when St. Thomas treats the virtues which relate to justice, he interprets the Roman virtue of *humanitas*—which is perhaps the most finished expression of the new natural law doctrine—not in its characteristically Stoic meaning, but in the sense of Aristotle's *friendship*. (*Ibid.* II.II.Q.80.) Finally, the Scriptures themselves make clear how different the Roman virtue of *humanitas* was from the Christian message: "Apparuit benignitas, et humanitas Salvatoris nostri Dei: non ex operibus Justitiae, quae fecimus nos, sed secundum misericordiam salus fecit." (Titus 3. 4–5.)

[20] Karl Marx, *Über die Differenzen der demokritischen und epikureischen Naturphilosophie, Gesamtausgabe*, sec. I, vol. I, pt. I, p. 131. See Chap. X.

revolutions, inspired as they were by the revival of the post-Aristotelian philosophy, retained, Marx observes, the same frustrated spirit of individual revolt that had characterized the a-political post-Aristotelian schools. "None of the pretended rights of man," Marx says of the modern revolutionary theories, "goes beyond the egoistic man, man such as he is . . . that is to say, an individual separated from the community, folded back on himself, uniquely occupied with his own private interests." [21] All the inequalities repudiated "politically" are allowed to subsist in civil society. The final emancipation of man demands "a complete, conscious return, accomplished within the interior of the whole wealth of past development, of *man for himself*, as a social being, that is, insofar as man is human." [22] This final liberation Marx calls "human" rather than "political" because it entails the destruction of every hitherto existing social form and leaves the individual man as the "totality . . . of society thought and felt for itself." [23] The individual thus attains the whole "unity of the species" in "the ensemble of social relations," and the latter ceases to be separable and distinguishable from one's individual life: The individual *is* "socialized humanity." [24] This is indeed the apotheosis and transfiguration of "withdrawal" and "protest," the realization at once of the *political* significance of the early philosophies of conduct and of the *human* significance of the political philosophy of the revolutions of the seventeenth and eighteenth centuries. It is to these conclusions indeed that one is led from those "beginnings of the theory of human nature and society" found in the philosophies of conduct of later Greece and Rome. Scholars working within the Western tradition who have hailed these philosophies as the source of our modern liberties have been misled.

[21] Karl Marx, *Die Judenfrage, Gesamtausgabe*, sec. I, vol. I, pt. I, p. 595.
[22] Karl Marx, *Oekonomische-philosophische Manuskript, Gesamtausgabe*, sec. I, vol. III, p. 114.
[23] *Ibid.*, p. 117.
[24] See Chap. X.

Natural law, law of nations, and civil law

It is in the writings of the great Roman jurists of the second and third centuries that we find some awareness, however inadequate it may have been, of the path along which progress in political and ethical science lay. For here we do find a meaning in the concepts of equality and of the state understood in terms of law that bears some relation to the wisdom of the classical past and which —feeble though it may be—makes an honest effort at intelligibility.

The writings of the great jurists were compiled in the *Digest* (or Pandects) published in 533 by Justinian. The *Digest* formed one part of the Roman *Corpus Juris Civilis* which contained also the code of statutory law of the Empire, the *Institutes* (an elementary textbook of the law by Gaius) and the *Novellae* (statutes of Justinian after 534). The authors of the *Digest* and the *Institutes* distinguish three kinds of right expressed by three kinds of law: Civil Right (*Jus Civile*), expressed by the civil law or enactments of particular states; Right of Nations (*Jus Gentium*), expressed in the Law of Nations; and Natural Right (*Jus Naturale*), expressed by Natural Law.

We shall consider first the distinction between *Jus Gentium* and *Jus Naturale*. We have said that the distinction is not very satisfyingly made by the Roman lawyers. Cicero had indeed used the terms quite synonymously to signify principles of law that were considered universally right as being part of human nature itself, and principles of law that were found commonly in the legal systems of different people. Gaius, in the second century, used the terms interchangeably. Ulpian (the main contributor to the *Digest*), writing in the third century, distinguished the *Jus Naturale* from the *Jus Gentium*: The *Jus Gentium* (or right of nations) falls short of *Jus Naturale* (natural right) in this, that the latter is common to all animals, while the former is common to men only.[25]

---

[25] *Digest*, I, 1,1,3. (Ed. by Theodore Mommsen; revised by Paul Kruger.) Wiedmann, Berlin, 1908.

Historians of political thought have very understandably been at great pains to decipher the terse language of this distinction. A. J. Carlyle, whom most subsequent students have followed, attempted to understand Ulpian's meaning by appealing to later authorities—to Hermogenianus, a fourth-century jurist, to the *Institutes* of Justinian, published in the sixth century, and to the writings of St. Isadore of Seville (seventh century). His understanding of this distinction is further influenced by his reading of the post-Aristotelian philosophies of conduct which interprets the distinction as implying a primitive nature higher and "purer" than that found in the "city." Since Carlyle has appealed outside the texts of Ulpian for light on this matter, and since the distinction in question is contained in many disparate passages of Aristotle's writings, it is indeed altogether justifiable to make an appeal to the great commentator on the philosophy of Aristotle and to examine St. Thomas' remarks both on the Roman lawyers and on Aristotle.

Carlyle's effort to understand the distinction made by Ulpian yields a decidedly simplistic view of the matter. He tends to identify the natural law in man as distinct from the *Jus Gentium* simply with man's animal nature without reference to man's specific nature as a rational animal. Now in traditional psychology man's reason was held to differ from sensible knowledge (which man has in common with other animals) by the capacity to compare one thing with another—to apprehend things in their relations with other things and not merely absolutely in themselves: and this capacity is indeed the source of *Jus Gentium*—a law that introduces what is useful for attaining the ends of human life. But man can also apprehend things absolutely by the nature that is specific to him, namely, his rational nature: He can apprehend things absolutely by his intellect and will. Hence, what belongs to natural law rather than to *Jus Gentium* is to apprehend things absolutely, and among these latter matters, according to traditional psychology, are the first principles of the practical and speculative intellect. The absolute apprehension of things belongs then to all animals, though differently according to the specific difference between the brute and the rational nature.

Although intellect and will set him apart, we must not be abrupt in separating man from nature even with respect to these specific faculties. For intellect and will are also founded upon nature, and all their activity is reducible to a principle which is natural *sicut quod est prioris causae participetur a posteriori*. In the very faculties which are at the root of his freedom we can distinguish an orientation that is physical, determined, necessitated, and even blind in as much as it is indeliberate and not waiting upon choice. This is manifest as regards the intellect which forms its first principles *naturaliter*. But it is no less true of the will. While its proper privilege is to be master of its own act, its first motion in pursuit of its object, *bonum,* is from nature and not within its own power.[26]

By simply identifying the natural law with man's animal nature and the *Jus Gentium* with his rational nature, Carlyle is led to suppose that there is nothing of natural law that is specifically human. He is thus led to the impression that "these writers have present to their minds some primitive circumstances, some primeval or natural institutions of the human race, as distinguished from even the oldest and most universal conventional institutions of human society." In short, Carlyle tells us, what is "natural" for man in the proper sense of the word is simply what is primitive and animal: nakedness, universal freedom, and common possessions. This interpretation of natural law accords well with Carlyle's view that "there is no change in political theory so startling in its completeness as the change from the theory of Aristotle to the later philosophical view represented by Cicero and Seneca" and put into legal form by the jurists; for here "we are indeed at the beginnings of a theory of human nature and society of which the 'Liberty, Equality and Fraternity' of the French Revolution is only the present day expression." [27] Indeed we are here at the foundation of the concept formulated by Rousseau in the eighteenth century —that of the "noble savage" as revealing the fullness of man's natural perfection. Man becomes free in proportion as he is eman-

[26] Joseph V. Dolan, S.J., "Natural Law and Modern Jurisprudence," *Thèse Philosophique de Laval*, no. 1007, pp. 68–69. Laval University, Quebec, 1958.

[27] Carlyle, *op. cit.*, vol. I, p. 9.

cipated from all conventional institutions of society—even the oldest and most universal. We shall have to see that, on the contrary, the *Jus Gentium* was conceived in opposite fashion—as embracing the civilizing institutions that make more easily possible the achievement of the ends of human life appointed by the natural law.

To understand this complex question it will be helpful to recall St. Thomas' description of nature made in the light of Aristotle's demonstration in the second book of the *Physics* that nature acts for an end. St. Thomas defined nature as "a 'reason' put into things by the divine art so that they be moved to a determinate end." [28]

---

[28] *In II Physics* lect.14. It will be well also to heed Aristotle's warning that the term nature is used in many ways. Explaining the multiplicity of meanings and their common note, St. Thomas observes: ". . . the word *nature* is used in a manifold sense. For sometimes it stands for the intrinsic principle in moveable things. In this sense nature is either matter or the material form, as stated in . . . *Physics II.* In another sense nature stands for any substance, or even for any being. And in this sense, that is said to be natural to a thing which benefits it in respect of its substance. And this is that which of itself is in a thing. Now all things that do not of themselves belong to the things in which they are, are reduced to something which belongs of itself to that thing, as to their principle. Wherefore, taking nature in this sense, it is necessary that the principle of whatever belongs to a thing be a natural principle. This is evident in regard to the intellect; for the principles of intellectual knowledge are naturally known. In like manner the principle of voluntary movements must be something naturally willed." (*Summa Theol.* I.II.Q.10 a.1.) Again, speaking of the definition of *person* as "an individual substance of rational nature," St. Thomas observes: "According to [Aristotle] the term *nature* was first used to signify the *generation of living things,* which is called nativity. And because this kind of generation comes from an intrinsic principle, this term is extended to signify the *intrinsic principle of any kind of movement.* In this sense [Aristotle] defines nature (*In Physics* II.192b.14). And since this kind of principle is either formal or material, both matter and form are commonly called nature. And as the essence of anything is completed by the form, for this reason *the essence of anything, signified by the definition, is commonly called nature.* And here nature is taken in that sense. Hence Boethius says that *nature is the specific difference giving its form to each thing;* for the specific difference completes the definition, and is derived from the proper form of a thing." (*Summa Theol.* I.Q.29 a.1 ad 4.)

This inclination inhering in things by virtue of their ordination by the Divine Practical Intellect, is precisely the Natural Law—for "law is something ordained to an end." [29] As wholly measured by the Divine Intellect, the natural universe stands in relation to God as subject to ruler. But nature inclines to things in different ways, because there are specifically different natures to which being is attached in different ways:

> This is evident to anyone who studies the nature of things. For if he will consider carefully he will find that the diversity of things is made up of degrees, since above inanimate bodies he will find plants, and above these, irrational animals, above these intelligent substances, and in each one of these he will find diversity according as some are more perfect than others; so much so that the highest members of a lower genus appear to be close to the higher genus, and conversely, e.g., animals that cannot move are like plants. . . .[30]

Now the rule and measure of the Divine Intellect is found in the rational nature not as determining it without awareness, but in the form of knowledge: There is in man an inclination of the natural law toward the human good ("to its proper act and end") known by the reason. Unlike natures which do not share in an intellectual and rational manner in the law governing them, man has in himself a principle of self-government. As St. Thomas points out, man is a free nature because "the form understood, through which the intellectual substance acts, proceeds from the intellect itself as a thing conceived, and in a way contrived by it; as we see in the case of the artistic form, which the artificer conceives and contrives, and through which he performs his works. Intellectual substances, then, move themselves to act, as having mastery of their own actions." [31] This natural inclination toward the good as apprehended by the reason is the natural law as it exists in man. And this law extends to all other faculties insofar as they come under the direction of the practical reason.

[29] *Summa Theol.* I.II.Q.95 a.3.
[30] *Contra Gentiles* III.chap.97.
[31] *Ibid.* II.chap.47.

Since . . . good has the nature of an end, and evil, the nature of the contrary, hence it is that all those things to which man has a natural inclination are naturally apprehended by reason as being good, and consequently the objects of pursuit, and their contraries as evil, and objects of avoidance. Therefore, the order of the precepts of the natural law is according to the order of natural inclinations. For there is in man, first of all, an inclination to good in accordance with the nature which he has in common with all substances, inasmuch, namely, as every substance seeks the preservation of its own being, according to its nature; and by reason of this inclination, whatever is a means of preserving human life, and of warding off its obstacles, belongs to the natural law. Secondly, there is in man an inclination to things that pertain to him more specially, according to that nature which he has in common with other animals; and in virtue of this inclination, those things are said to belong to the natural law *which nature has taught to all animals,* such as sexual intercourse, the education of offspring and so forth. Thirdly, there is in man an inclination to good according to the nature of his reason, which nature is proper to him. Thus man has a natural inclination to know the truth about God, and to live in society; and in this respect, whatever pertains to this inclination belongs to the natural law: e.g., to shun ignorance, to avoid offending those among whom one has to live, and other such things regarding the above inclination.[32]

The judgments regulating these basic inclinations are precepts of the natural law in its strictest sense—that is, these precepts derive not from individual insight and discursive reasoning, but spontaneously and with necessity from human reason. They are not *products* of practical reason but rather first principles directing practical reason: Both Aristotle and St. Thomas compare them with the first principles of demonstration in the theoretic sciences.[33]

But we must now observe that "from these principles one may proceed in various ways to judge of various matters."[34] For if these principles indeed

[32] *Summa Theol.* I.II.Q.94 a.2.
[33] *Physics* II.200a.21; *Summa Theol.* I.I.Q.82 a.1.
[34] *Summa Theol.* I.II.Q.100 a.1.

are conceived as radiating from the center of nature, we can see how in proportion to their distance from the hard core, the centripetal force of nature trails off and the inclinations become less and less imperious. Other forces arise to block or divert them. . . . Hence there is an inevitable ambiguity in the expression natural law due to the existence of a borderline where nature begins to yield to other forces and manifest its contingency. We cannot draw the exact line of natural law.[35]

There is indeed a difference in degree of imperiousness even in the things that are known naturally—a difference in degree which constitutes the distinction between *natural law* and *Jus Gentium*, which in effect is a distinction between first precepts and secondary precepts of natural law:

. . . whatever renders an action improportionate to the end which nature intends . . . is said to be contrary to the natural law. But an action may be improportionate either to the principal or the secondary end, and in either case this happens in two ways. First, on account of something which wholly hinders the end; for instance a very great excess or a very great deficiency in eating hinders both the health of the body, which is the principal end of food, and aptitude for conducting business, which is its secondary end. Secondly, on account of something that renders the attainment of the principal or secondary end difficult, or less satisfactory, for instance eating inordinately in respect of undue time. Accordingly if an action be improportionate to the end, through altogether hindering the principal end directly, it is forbidden by the first precepts of the natural law, which hold the same place in practical matters as the general concepts of the mind in speculative matters. If, however, it be in any way improportionate to the secondary end, or again to the principal end, as rendering its attainment difficult or less satisfactory, it is forbidden, not indeed by the first precepts of the natural law, but by the second which are derived from the first even as conclusions in speculative matters receive our assent by virtue of self-known principles; and thus the act in question is said to be against the law of nature.[36]

[35] Dolan, *op. cit.*, p. 71.

[36] *Summa Theol.* III (Supplement).Q.65 a.1. The question of plurality of wives, concerning which the above quoted argument is made, will help to elucidate the doctrine of natural law. St. Thomas is here showing that

Natural law in its first precepts (as distinguished, then, from natural law in its secondary precepts—*Jus Gentium*) embraces actions that are naturally known as bearing an *"absolute* natural commensuration with what nature intends for men: for example, to seek good and avoid evil. The matters belonging to *Jus Gentium* on the other hand, are said to bear a *"relative* natural commensuration" with what nature intends for man. These are the civilizing institutions without which the principal ends of human life cannot be attained except with the greatest difficulty. Possession of all things in common and the nonpolitical condition greatly hinder the attainment of the principal end of life, as Aristotle argues in the first and second books of the *Politics*.[37] The introduction, then, of civilizing institutions is indeed natural in the sense that nature inclines thereto; it is the work of man's natural reason. Far from embracing principles of law that are corruptions of an original and "higher law," the *Jus Gentium* embodies legal principles that are perfective of human life. Indeed, the *Jus Gentium*, because it has the force of natural law, is itself part of the "higher law," of which all the different systems of civil law are mere particular determinations.

The *Jus Civile*, the third kind of law mentioned by the Roman jurists, is related to the natural law through the *Jus Gentium*. Gov-

---

plurality of wives is not against the first precepts of the natural law, for the principal end of marriage, the begetting and rearing of children, is neither wholly destroyed nor at all hindered by plurality of wives. Plurality of wives is contrary to the secondary precepts of natural law, for it hinders considerably the secondary end of marriage, which is "the community of works that are a necessity of life." However, it should be noted that if plurality of wives is not contrary to the first precepts of natural law it is, nonetheless, contrary to nature taken as signifying the innate principle of any being (see above, n. 28); for nature's dictate is "to every animal according to the mode befitting its nature," and in the case of man, marriage has "for its secondary end, as [Aristotle] says (*Ethics* VIII.12) the community of works that are a necessity of life. . . . And in reference to this [man and woman] owe one another *fidelity*. . . ." (*Summa Theol.* C. and ad 4.)

[37] It is true that the ancients included slavery along with private property and government among the matters belonging to *Jus Gentium*; but see the discussion of slavery above, p. 55, n. 45.

ernment as such—that is, without reference to the specific form of government—belongs to *Jus Gentium*. For if the political community is one of freemen and equals who are also social beings (since each lacks all that is necessary for human life), the natural reason introduces government for the perfection of man. The *particular form* of government and the laws made in pursuance of it —these make up the *Jus Civile*. This is what Aristotle had called the "legal" part of political justice, as distinguished from the "natural" part, for civil law does not establish natural right; it establishes "that which is originally indifferent, but when it has been laid down is not indifferent, e.g., that a prisoner's ransom shall be a mina, or that a goat and not two sheep shall be sacrificed. . . ." [38] The right in such matters is established by common agreement and, provided it be not in itself contrary to natural law, it has no force other than that of human law. Hence we read in the *Digest* that "it is not possible to give the reason for all the legal enactments of the lawgivers." [39]

Again it is not easy to understand precisely the breach with the past that is so widely attributed by scholars to the Roman lawyers and to Cicero in this matter. If the *De Republica* and the *De Legibus* of Cicero reflect the notion of the test of legality—the presumption "that the state is the creature of law and is to be discussed in terms of legal competence and rights and not merely in terms of ethical fact or social good"—this contribution of the Romans is properly to be understood as a refinement of the Aristotelian doctrine of the rule of law. It is, in fact, the *legal* expression of the philosophical principle of the rule of law by which the political community is distinguished, in Aristotle's teaching, from household and village. Ulpian's famous phrase, "The will of the emperor has the force of law because by the passage of the *lex regia* the people transfers to him and vests in him all its own power and authority" (*Digest* 1, 4, 1), has similarly been widely interpreted as introducing a radically novel notion into political philosophy. To see in Ulpian's statement anything profoundly novel

[38] *Ethics* V.1134b.22.
[39] Cited in *Summa Theol.* I.II.Q.95 a.2 Obj. 4.

—as Carlyle and McIlwain do—is to see it—as indeed these scholars do—as presaging the eighteenth-century doctrine of the State contract, which, taking different forms, sought, by reducing the legal and social order to free individual acts, to restore something of the lost original "independence" of the primitive "natural" man. Despite Aristotle's doctrine that rule of law distinguishes the nature and origin of the political community from household and village, Professor McIlwain can make the unqualified assertion that the Greeks did not understand the State in terms of law but understood law in terms of the State.[40] This view can be meaningful only if we suppose a revolutionary new sense in the dictum of Ulpian—the revolutionary sense precisely of the eighteenth-century reduction of the legal and social order to free individual acts, to a wholly voluntary contractual submission of the governed. That the ambiguity in the Roman lawyers and in Cicero does not argue that either intended so radical a view is somewhat better appreciated by Professor Sabine who observes: "In itself [Ulpian's statement] justifies neither the implication of royal absolutism which was sometimes derived from the first clause, nor of representative government, which the sovereignty of the people came to signify later. . . . The idea behind Ulpian's statement is that expressed by Cicero, that law is the common possession of a people in its corporate capacity."[41] The weakness in Professor Sabine's statement is that it implies that the principle of representative government can be derived only from the modern doctrines of popular sovereignty and social contract and not from the concept of law as the common possession of a people in its corporate capacity. The fact is that the notion of representative government was developed during the Middle Ages, and it was done, as we shall see, in terms of the "common political prudence" of the whole people, whose first act is to set up responsible government.

It is perhaps curious that this very important step of explicating

[40] Charles Howard McIlwain, *Constitutionalism, Ancient and Modern*, Cornell University Press, Ithaca, N.Y., 1940, p. 39.

[41] Sabine, *op. cit.*, p. 172.

IV

Christianity and political philosophy: the relation of Church and State

The rise of the Christian church, as a distinct institution entitled to govern the spiritual concerns of mankind in independence of the state, may not unreasonably be described," says Professor Sabine, "as the most revolutionary event in the history of Western Europe, in respect both to politics and to political philosophy."[1] In view of this assertion it is a bit startling to find Professor Sabine going on to suggest—in common with many others—that it was only with the break-up of this "distinct institution" in the sixteenth century that its revolutionary significance began properly to show itself. "Far beyond the period in which the relation of the two authorities [Church and State] was a chief controversial issue, the belief in spiritual autonomy and the right of spiritual freedom left a residuum without which modern ideas of individual privacy and liberty would be scarcely intelligible."[2] In similar vein Professor D'Entrèves declares that[3]

[1] Sabine, *A History of Political Theory*, p. 180.

[2] *Ibid.*, p. 196.

[3] Reprinted with permission of The Macmillan Company from A. P. D'Entrèves (ed.), *Aquinas: Selected Political Writings*, trans. by J. G. Dawson. First published by Basil Blackwell & Mott, Ltd., Oxford, 1948, p. xxxiii.

"The 'primacy of the spiritual' was perhaps the most important factor of western civilization. But that ideal has lived on through centuries of suffering and hope, and it has come to mean for us something quite different from what it meant for the Middle Ages." What Professors Sabine and D'Entrèves mean is simply that the primacy of the spiritual has come to signify mainly civil and religious liberty—a liberty which, they suggest, is not quite compatible with the original notion of a "distinct institution entitled to govern the spiritual concerns of mankind." Now religious liberty is indeed an important right—and, as we shall see, received a beginning formulation in the jurisprudence of St. Thomas Aquinas in the thirteenth century—but it was not what constituted the revolutionary significance for politics and political philosophy of the rise of the Christian Church—as indeed the authors whom we have cited evidently have some intimation of. If we are to gain an insight into the original revolutionary significance of Christianity, we must examine precisely its claims in reference to the great political doctrines of the Greek and Roman world. In doing so we may advert momentarily—without looking too much ahead—to an important and extraordinary fact: that the primacy of the spiritual in its most characteristically contemporary meaning has come—if on an entirely different plane—much closer to the original revolutionary meaning than is signified by "religious liberty." For this latter, when taken to be the decisive religious attitude, spells not only the separation of the church from the state, but spells the end of any public function for religion. Contrary to this view of religion as a mere private matter, there has arisen in modern times a considerable body of thought whose burden it is to suggest that man's spiritual life has evolved in the course of its domination of material forces in such fashion that an answer, on the plane of the "real life" (the plane of "humanity"), can now be given to the precise question to which Christianity twenty centuries ago offered itself as a solution on the plane of the "ideal life." [4] That question is the one that Aristotle

---

[4] For a penetrating discussion of this matter see William Oliver Martin, "Communism, Religion, and Co-existence," *Religious Education*, vol. 56, no. 4, p. 288, July–August, 1961.

had considered the ultimate public question: that of human happiness, of the last end of human life. It is the Marxist answer to this question that constitutes the contemporary orientation of the "primacy of the spiritual." [5] Far from making freedom of conscience the decisive religious attitude, and thereby relegating religion—as Marx observed of modern Christianity—to the refuse heap of arbitrary private whims, this political philosophy alleges the overcoming of man's "alienation" from himself in the old theologies: It affirms the primacy of the spiritual and does so, as Marx put it, by resolving the religious essence into human essence in affirming that man's spiritual life evolves through his first seeing his nature as if out of himself (in God) and later seeing it as in himself. The concept of God for this philosophy is ". . . an historically conditioned one, in which man has expressed his experience of his higher powers, his longing for truth and for unity at a given historical period. . . . The realm of love, reason and justice exists as a reality only because, and inasmuch as, man has been able to develop these powers in himself throughout the process of his evolution." [6] Nor is this outlook the outlook of single individuals in civil society, of "the individual separated from the community, folded back on himself, uniquely occupied with his own private interests." [7] Rather, Marx tells us, it is the outlook of "social humanity" which is "not an abstraction confronting the individual," but rather is "the objectification of himself . . . that is to say, the object of himself." [8] The characteristically contemporary form of the primacy of the spiritual is not indeed, then, freedom of conscience as the decisive religious attitude; rather it is that "heightened self-consciousness" by which the primacy of the spiritual has again become a social and public force. It is remarkable that this foremost fact in the whole consideration of

---

[5] We have already said that the profoundly spiritual root of the concept of political common good does not at the moment play an effective role in the political life of the West, and that it has been "restored" in profoundly perverted form in the Marxist concept of man's "generic being." Above, p. 51.

[6] Fromm, *The Art of Loving*, p. 72. See Chap. IX, for a detailed critique of this Marxist position.

[7] Marx, *Die Judenfrage*, p. 595.

[8] Marx, *Oekonomische-philosophische Manuskript*, pp. 116, 119.

the question of Church and State as it bears on the character of civilization seems scarcely to have been noticed by those who are today conspicuously concerned with that question.

Greek political philosophy and Christian theology

The important element of truth in the observations of Professors Sabine and D'Entrèves concerning the revolutionary significance of Christianity for politics is that prior to the appearance of the Christian Church the State had been considered to have an important role to play in the spiritual concerns of mankind. Aristotle had declared politics to be "the master art . . . for it is this that ordains which of the sciences should be studied in a state and which each class of citizens should learn and up to what point they should learn them." [9] And of all the forms of knowledge "wisdom must plainly be the most finished. . . ." [10] Wisdom is knowledge of the "highest objects," and life according to this wisdom is "divine" rather than "human": "But we must not follow those who advise us, being men, to think of human things, and, being mortal, of mortal things, but must, so far as we can, make ourselves immortal, and strain every nerve to live in accordance with the best thing in us; for even if it be small in bulk, much more does it in power and worth surpass everything." [11] Although the State is the highest society that Aristotle knows, the political life is explicitly declared to be less good than the contemplative life: that is to say, there is a common good knowable by man (the extrinsic common good of the universe, God) that is better than the political common good. If then the State is the highest society, and politics the master art, the highest care of this art is the cultivation of wisdom in its citizens.

We must observe more closely the nature of the State's authoritative role in the task of cultivating wisdom in its citizens. As the promoter and guardian of truth (which is the good of the

[9] *Ethics* I.1094a.27–1094b.3.
[10] *Ibid.* 1141a.20.
[11] *Ibid.* X.1177b.27–1178a.

speculative intellect and the object of theoretic science) the State may not interfere with its free determination.[12] The reason for this is that such matters are not subject to the human will: In theoretic knowledge the intelligence is measured by its object, not the other way round. And therefore when it is said that the State may not interfere with the free determination of truth, it should be carefully noticed that the freedom here asserted is primarily in behalf of truth itself and only consequently in behalf of man. We may note in passing that the Marxist concept of the primacy of the spiritual, to which we alluded above, is perforce totalitarian in character: for if "the realm of love, reason and justice exists . . . only because, and inasmuch as, man has been able to develop these powers in himself . . . ," then the human reason is the measure of every truth—not merely of those matters which properly fall under human art and practical science, but of the whole order of things that Aristotle had reserved to the theoretic intellect and had safeguarded from any interference by the political art.

It is truth, then, that is sovereignly free, and man becomes free in proportion as he knows the truth and the highest truth. For, as St. Thomas says, by this good of the speculative intellect, "if [it] be perfect, the whole man is perfected and made good thereby." [13] Hence politics serves this good and "is not *supreme over philosophic wisdom . . . any more than the art of medicine is over health; for it does not use it but provides for its coming into being; it issues orders, then, for its sake, but not to it.* Further, to maintain its supremacy would be like saying that the art of politics rules the gods because it issues orders about all the affairs of the state." [14] And so St. Thomas remarks: "And [thus] political prudence does not *use* philosophic wisdom, telling it how it ought to judge concerning divine things, but prescribes for it, ordaining how men can come to wisdom." [15] It is by providing for the communication of the wisdom of its wise men that the State is able to

---

[12] *Ibid.* I.1094a.28–1094b.7. See *In I Ethics* lect.2.
[13] *Summa Theol.* I.II.Q.3 a.5 ad 2.
[14] *Ethics* VI.1145a.7–12. (Italics added.)
[15] *In VI Ethics* lect.11. (Italics in original.)

fulfill its obligation to profess the truth and the highest truth; for the State makes this profession by respecting the freedom of truth —that is, by not entering into the interior truth of the speculative sciences but, by a prudential judgment, prescribing for wisdom precisely under the formality of the good of the speculative intellect—a good which the political community seeks from its wise men, and which, as such, political prudence is competent to prescribe for.

We must next notice that however solicitous the State may be both for the attainment of truth and its freedom, the likelihood of reaching the highest truths is not very great. For human nature "is in many ways in bondage," so that "the possession of (wisdom) might be justly regarded as beyond human power." [16] If perfect happiness consists, as Aristotle avers, in the operation of the speculative intellect according to its highest virtue (wisdom), such a life is nevertheless declared to be "too high for man"; he must "strain every nerve to live in accordance with it." [17] The truths about the highest objects are not to be had by many and are had by the few with the admixture, often, of many errors and with much uncertainty. The State, then, even when it most rigorously protects freedom of inquiry, is seriously handicapped in its highest care by the very condition of human nature. Now this fact suggests that the knowledge about God acquired by demonstration and held by natural wisdom cannot be the perfect happiness that all men seek. Not denying that happiness consists in the operation of the speculative intellect according to its highest virtue, St. Thomas is saying, in accordance with the teaching laid down in the second book of the *Physics* (as well as the first book of the *Ethics*), that since things belonging to a species attain for the most part to the end of that species (because nature achieves its purpose always or for the most part and fails in only a few instances because of some corruption), the happiness that all men naturally seek as their final perfection cannot consist in that which is attained only by a very few.[18] But further, even if all or

[16] *Metaph.* I.982b.28.
[17] *Ethics* X.1177b.26–35.
[18] *Contra Gentiles* III.chap.39. Cf. *Ethics* I.1099b.15–20.

most men were to attain wisdom, this wisdom is itself insufficient
for constituting the perfect happiness that men seek: Again without abandoning the view that happiness consists in the operation
of the speculative intellect according to its highest virtue, St.
Thomas points out that in the present life the operation of the
speculative intellect is very unsatisfactory—it is neither continuous nor one, but multiplied and discontinuous.[19] If indeed, as
Aristotle says, "we can contemplate truth more continuously than
we can *do* anything," it is nonetheless the case that—as he also
says—"the future is obscure to us, while happiness, we claim, is
an end and something in every way final."[20] And "if so," he concludes, we may call men happy but only as men—that is, as fall-
ing short of possessing perfect happiness.

But we must observe that this imperfect happiness, although
the best that can reasonably be looked for in this life, does not remove the fact that man's natural desire is not at rest in this life:
it is only at rest with respect to what is *possible in this life*. It is
for this reason that St. Thomas draws our attention to the fact
that Aristotle's explanation does not remove Aristotle's own arguments to the effect that man seeks a happiness "in every way final"
and that "nature does nothing in vain." Pursuing this point, St.
Thomas observes that although man is below the "separate substances" (in whom, according to Aristotle's doctrine, the intellectual nature is perfect) he is above irrational creatures, and so

he attains his ultimate end in a more perfect way than they. Now
these attain their last end so perfectly that they seek nothing further.
Thus . . . when an animal enjoys sensible pleasure, its natural desire
is at rest. Much more, therefore, when man has obtained his last end,
must his natural desire be at rest. But this cannot happen in this life.
Therefore in this life man does not obtain happiness considered as his
proper end, . . . Therefore he must obtain it after this life.

Again, natural desire cannot be empty, since "nature does nothing
in vain." (Aristotle *De Caelo* II, XI, 291b, 13.) But nature's desire
would be empty if it could never be fulfilled. Therefore man's natural

[19] *Summa Theol.* I.II.Q.3 a.2 ad 4. Cf. *Ethics* X.1177a.23–24.
[20] *Ethics* I.1191a.18, X.1177a.23.

desire can be fulfilled. But not in this life. Therefore man's ultimate happiness is after this life.[21]

Final happiness can consist in nothing else than the vision of God in His essence, a vision which surpasses altogether the grasp of man's natural reason.[22] The Sacred Scriptures contain the revealed word of God in whose intellect are the principles of that sacred science whereby "saving faith is begotten." These instruct us concerning our final end: " 'The eye hath not seen, besides thee, O God, what things Thou hast prepared for them that wait for Thee.' " [23] The final aim of social life is, then[24]

not merely to live in virtue, but rather through virtuous life to attain to the enjoyment of God. If, indeed, it were possible to attain this

[21] *Contra Gentiles* III.chap.48.

[22] *Summa Theol.* I.II.Q.3 a.8. Aristotle had himself said that the perfection of the power of the intellect is determined by the nature of the object, which is *what a thing is*, i.e., the essence of a thing, and that man is not perfectly happy so long as something remains for him to desire and seek. "Consequently," St. Thomas argues, "when a man knows an effect, and knows that it has a cause, there naturally remains in man the desire to know about that cause, *what it is*. And this desire is one of wonder, and causes inquiry, as is stated in the beginning of the *Metaphysics*. For instance, if a man, knowing the eclipse of the sun, consider that it must be due to some cause, and know not what that cause is, he wonders about it, and from wondering proceeds to inquire. Nor does this inquiry cease until he arrive at a knowledge of the essence of the cause.

"If therefore the human intellect, knowing the essence of some created effect, knows no more of God than *that* He is; the perfection of that intellect does not yet reach simply the First Cause, but there remains in it the natural desire to seek the cause. Wherefore it is not yet perfectly happy. Consequently, for perfect happiness the intellect needs to reach the very Essence of the First Cause. And thus it will have its perfection through union with God as with that object, in which alone man's happiness consists. . . ." (*Ibid.*)

As to how God may be seen in His essence, if it is indeed impossible to see His essence in this life, cf. *Contra Gentiles* III.chaps.47 and 51.

[23] Citing *Isaias* 64:4; *Summa Theol.* I.Q.1 a.1; also *ibid.* I.II.Q.3 a.8.

[24] *On Princely Government*, xiv. Reprinted with permission of The Macmillan Company from D'Entrèves, *op. cit.*, pp. 75–77.

object by natural human virtue, it would, in consequence, be the duty of kings to guide men to this end. . . . But the enjoyment of God is an aim which cannot be attained by human virtue alone, but only through divine grace. . . . Only a divine rule, then, and not human government, can lead us to this end. Such government belongs only to that King who is both man, and also God: that is to Jesus Christ, our Lord, Who, making men to be Sons of God has led them to the glory of heaven.

This, then, is the government entrusted to Him: a dominion which shall never pass away, and in virtue of which He is called in the Holy Scriptures, not only a priest, but a king: as *Jeremias* says (XXIII, 5): 'A king shall reign and shall be wise.' It is from Him that the royal priesthood derives; and, what is more, all the Faithful of Christ, being members of Him, become thus, priests and kings. The ministry of this kingdom is entrusted not to the rulers of this earth but to priests, so that temporal affairs may remain distinct from those spiritual: and, in particular, it is delegated to the High Priest, the successor of Peter and Vicar of Christ, the Roman Pontiff; to whom all kings in Christendom should be subject, as to the Lord Jesus Christ Himself. For those who are concerned with the subordinate ends of life must be subject to him who is concerned with the supreme end and be directed by his command.

The theory of Church and State

The effective spread of Christianity throughout the Mediterranean world began with the ministry of St. Paul. From the time of St. Paul's martyrdom (about A.D. 67) in Rome until the reign of the Emperor Constantine (sole emperor 324–327), Christianity was an illegal sect, subject to severe persecution and in competition with the cult of emperor worship to which the official religions of the Empire had yielded. The Church was a new society, claiming divine institution, whose mission was to bring men to a good which altogether surpasses the present state of life, a supernatural society. Although from the standpoint of the imperial concept of political obligation the Christian church was treasonable (for, as we have said, the native cults of Greece and Rome had yielded to a common religion of empire, and the Emperor was a "present and corporeal god" as well as supreme civil ruler), the new religion recognized the State as ordained by God. "Let every soul," wrote St. Paul, "be subject to the higher powers. For there is no power but of God: the powers that be are ordained of God." [25] Had not Christ clearly repudiated the designing Pharisees with the simple command: "Render . . . to Caesar the things that are Caesar's and to God the things that are God's?" [26] Christianity affirmed the existence of two distinct societies with separate but related jurisdictions: a natural, temporal, and perfect society in its own order—the State, and a supernatural, spiritual, and perfect society—the Church. It was the relation between the religious and political institutions that created the new problem for the Roman world.

St. Augustine: The City of God

The Christian philosophy of politics that was implied in the relation of the two societies received its first and most comprehensive statement in the writings of St. Augustine, the fourth-century Bishop of Hippo. *The City of God,* the great work which contains the political thought of St. Augustine, is not at all a systematic treatise in political philosophy.[27] Acknowledged to be the greatest of the Saint's writings (and so acknowledged by Augustine himself), *The City of God* presents a picture of the Christian "world view" that is extremely detailed for all its panoramic character. Begun in 413 and completed only in 426, its composition

---

[25] Romans 13:1.

[26] Matthew 22:21.

[27] The Latin text, *De Civitate Dei,* edited by the Benedictines of St. Maur, will be found in *Patrologia Latina* 41.11–804. An acceptable text, with notes in English, is S. Aurelii Augustini, *De Civitate Dei contra Paganos,* J. E. C. Welldon (ed.), 2 vols., London, 1924. In the present study all references are to the English version by J. Healey (London, 1610), *St. Augustine: The City of God,* R. V. G. Tasker (ed.), with an introduction by Sir Ernest Barker, 2 vols., E. P. Dutton & Co., Inc., New York, 1945.

was directly inspired by the need St. Augustine felt to defend the Christian religion against the charge that it was responsible for the fall of Rome at the hands of Alaric in 410. The defense is divided into two parts: In the first ten books, which make up Part One, St. Augustine is concerned with the polemical task of refuting the pagan charge. Taking note of the curious blindness to the fact that Rome was not protected by the pagan gods during the sack of 410, St. Augustine proceeds in the first ten books to describe the spiritual and moral evils of paganism and to put the pagan theology under some degree of pressure. The second half of St. Augustine's work is given over to an altogether original task —that of constructing a Christian philosophy of society: That is to say, matters that belong to the separate philosophical sciences (such as ethics and politics) are given a higher unity by reason of the more universal formality under which they are regarded, namely, Divine Revelation. Because sacred science considers things precisely under the formality of being divinely revealed, whatever has been divinely revealed—though it may also be the matter of other disciplines—possesses the one precise formality of the object of sacred science. And just as certain human sciences proceed from principles known by the light of a higher science (e.g., the science of perspective proceeds from principles established by geometry and the science of music from principles established by arithmetic), so sacred science proceeds from principles established by the light of a higher science, namely, the science of God in Whose Intellect are the principles of this science. And because this is the case, because sacred science is established on principles revealed by God, "to this science alone," St. Augustine observes, "belongs that whereby saving faith is begotten, nourished, protected, and strengthened." [28] The fundamental point for understanding *The City of God* is the fact that it is under the formality of sacred doctrine that St. Augustine treats of history and politics.

The pertinence of this consideration becomes clear when we inquire how the central idea of St. Augustine's *City of God* is re-

[28] 14 *De Trin.* (c.l.a).

lated to the past teaching in political philosophy. If, for the moment, we take the fundamental teaching in St. Augustine's political philosophy to be simply that no man owes an unqualified allegiance to any earthly society, then it is clear that this idea was not entirely new to the world. It is to be found in Aristotle's injunction to pursue the life that is more divine than human and in his view that political science is not the highest wisdom, nor man the best thing in the universe.[29] The same idea is to be found in Plato's teaching that there is a "better life than that of politics." [30] The central idea of St. Augustine, on the contrary, emerges only after this very noble and right teaching of the philosophers is subjected to a critique in the light of the higher principles of sacred doctrine.

It is the sacred Scriptures that instruct man concerning the supreme good and the supreme evil, and instruct him unerringly: "Eternal life is the perfection of good, and eternal death the consummation of evil; and the aim of our life must be to avoid the one, and to attain the other. Therefore it is written: 'The just shall live by faith.' " [31] As for the philosophers:

Their studies seemed wholly to aim at the attainment of beatitude [but] what course, what act can mortal misery perform to the obtaining of true blessedness . . . ? For who can discourse exactly of the miseries of this life? Tully, upon his daughter's death, did what he could. But what could he do? In what person can the first objects of nature be found without alteration? What, have not sorrow and disquiet full power to disturb the pleasure and quiet of the wisest? Even so, strength, beauty, health, vigor, and activity, are all subverted by their contraries. . . . And then the first gifts of nature, whereof sense and reason are the two first, because of the apprehension of truth, how easily are they lost! . . . So then far be it from us ever to think that we have attained the true happiness whilst we live here.[32]

---

[29] *Ethics* X.1177b.26–35, VI.1141a.20.

[30] *Republic* VII.514–521.

[31] *The City of God*, XIX.chap.4; vol. II, p. 237. (Volume and page numbers refer to the Healey version.)

[32] *Ibid.* XVIII.chap.41; vol. II, p. 214; XIX.chap.4; vol. II, pp. 237–238.

Without divine instruction there is indeed neither goal nor path to man's strivings.

> Let one look amongst all the multitude of philosophers' writings, and if he find two that tell both one tale in all respects, it may be registered for a rarity. . . . The prophet laughs at them, saying: "The Lord knoweth the thoughts of men" (or, as St. Paul has it, "of the wise") "that they are vain." But the people, state, nation and city of Israel, to whom God's holy laws were left, did not confound with that licentious confusion the false prophets with the true, but all in one consent held and acknowledged the latter for the true authors recording God's testimonies. . . . He that lived after their rules, followed not man, but God, who spake in them. The sacrilege forbidden there, God forbids. The commandment of "Honor thy father and mother" God commands. "Thou shalt not commit adultery, nor murder, nor shalt steal," God's wisdom pronounces this, not the wit of man. For what truth soever the philosophers attained and disputed of amidst their falsehood, as namely, that God framed the world, and governed it most excellently; the honesty of virtue; the love of country; the faith of friendship; just dealing, and all the things belonging to good manners —they knew not to what end the whole was to be referred.[33]

> But Israel, the keeper of God's testimonies, knew: "And then it happened as it was prophesized: 'The law shall go forth from Sion, and the word of the Lord from Jerusalem'": The Church founded by Christ fulfills the ancient prophecies: their witness "'in Jerusalem, and in all Judea, and in Samaria, and unto the utmost part of the earth.'"[34]

We find in these considerations the essential elements for understanding the four basic concepts of St. Augustine's philosophy of politics: the concepts of Church, State, Heavenly City, and Earthly City. It is the relationship of these concepts that will lead us to St. Augustine's central idea.

The Church, a divinely established society, is the guardian of the sacred Scriptures, of the law of the Old and the New Testa-

---

[33] *Ibid.* XVII.chap.41; vol. II, p. 215.
[34] *Ibid.* XVIII.chap.50; vol. II, p. 224.

ments by which men are directed to eternal beatitude in the
vision of God, Whom St. Augustine calls the Common Good of
the universe. The State is concerned with "just dealing and all
the things belonging to good manners": In the measure that men
organize for a life of the political virtues as well as the virtues of
the mind ("what truth soever the philosophers attained. . . ."),
they compose the political community, the State. The Church and
the State are thus recognizable, "visible" societies for the good.
But since indeed God alone sounds the heart and plumbs the
depths of the mind, there are two invisible "cities": the Heavenly
City of the predestined and the Earthly City of the damned. Those
who, availing themselves as far as possible of the grace given
through the Church, direct their just dealings and all the things
belonging to good manners to final beatitude, are, the world over,
members of the Heavenly City. Finally, those who seek no good
beyond the present life, or on the other hand, seeking this good
contemn the other, that is, "the honesty of virtue, the love of country, the faith of friendship, just dealing and all the things belonging to good manners" are, the world over, members of the Earthly
City and destined to eternal death. Indeed, as we shall presently
see, the very virtues of those who seek no good beyond the present life are vices; but more often than not such men are without
virtue, and their vices are "a harvest of variable impiety." Their
fortitude and their patience find expression in suicide; the rule
of their prudence is marked by "ambition" and "proud sovereignty."

We are now in a position to see what the central idea of St.
Augustine's political philosophy is. "Ambition" and "proud sovereignty" are indeed precisely the wound of sin inflicted by the
Earthly City on the State. The State, whose rule is that of freemen over freemen—embracing "the love of country, the honesty
of virtue, the faith of friendship, just dealing, and all the things
belonging to good manners"—is required by the very order of
nature. The order of nature is not destroyed by sin, but it has
been weakened: It is too commonly marked by ambition and
proud sovereignty. It is this rule—of masters, as it were, over
slaves—to which "guilt and not nature gave origin." But the do-

minion of freemen over freemen, which is not by domineering but
by the service of counsel—this rule is both the prescription of
nature itself and the rule established at the moment of creation:
"But in the family of the faithful man . . . there the commanders
are indeed the servants of those they seem to command; ruling
not in ambition, but being bound by careful duty; not in proud
sovereignty, but in nourishing pity. Thus has nature's order prescribed, and man by God was thus created." [35] Political authority
indeed there is, but its rule is in the service of freedom, and its
perfection in proportion to its movement away from mastership,
from proud sovereignty, from ambition and the quality of "au-
thoritarianism." It is the members of the Heavenly City who ought
to perfect the State, healing its wounded nature and restoring the
free character of its rule. If, to be sure, while here on earth the
celestial society "increases itself out of all languages, being un-
concerned by the different temporal laws that are made," it nonetheless "observes . . . the coherence of men's wills in honest
morality . . . not breaking but observing their diversity in divers
nations." [36] For everything that a citizen of the Heavenly City
does, he refers both "unto God and his neighbour, because being
a citizen, he must not be all for himself, but sociable in his life and
actions." Again, if the members of the Heavenly City must refer
the "temporal conveniences" of the State to an eternal end, it is
indeed nonetheless precisely they alone who may be said to be
made happy by these temporal conveniences: "Yet he that has the
latter in possession, and applies it all with reference to his hope's
firm and faithful object, may not unfitly be called happy already.
. . ." [37] For such a man there is nothing false about earthly happiness: It is the very beginning of beatitude. On the other hand,
"this present possession without the other hope is a false beatitude" and we must "avouch [such an estate] to be most miserable,
were it never so well fraught with temporal conveniences. . . .
For herein is no use of the mind's truest good, because there is
lacking the true wisdom, which in the prudent discretion, resolute

[35] *Ibid.* XIX.chaps.14, 15; vol. II, pp. 252–253.
[36] *Ibid.* chap.17; vol. II, p. 255.
[37] *Ibid.* chap.20; vol. II, p. 257.

performance, temperate restraint, and just distribution of (these temporal conveniences) should refer his intent in all these unto that end, where God shall be all in all, where eternity shall be firm, and peace most perfect and absolute." [38] For St. Augustine, then, social justice should receive its initial movement from the most final of causes, eternal beatitude, the just distribution of temporal goods making us proportionately like God, "the most just Disposer . . . of all the adjuncts of [temporal peace]—the visible light, the breathable air, the potable water, and all the other necessaries of meat, drink, and clothing." [39] This is the root of Christian social justice.

Far from eliminating the State by referring its temporal peace to eternal peace, St. Augustine's thought rather would reestablish the State's integrity both in the mode of its operation (which is free) and in the order to its end (which is the temporal human common good). And if it is to St. Augustine "more than (to) any other individual [that] we owe the characteristically western ideal of the Church as a dynamic social power," [40] it is by this very same ideal that St. Augustine seeks to preserve the State from the inordinateness of that "variable impiety" by which it aims at something more than "the coherence of men's wills in honest morality." For in the law of the Old and New Testaments, by which God instructs man, the Church supplies the doctrinal rectitude concerning man's final end; and in the grace by which God heals human nature, the Church supplies the means for moral rectitude. Here the Church and the Heavenly City do indeed touch and blend.

For we must now note that if the political philosophy of Plato and Aristotle had taught that there is a dimension of life beyond the political, which sets limits to political authority, this philosophy had gone much beyond the common thought of Greece and had gone altogether beyond classical Greek and Roman

---

[38] *Ibid.* chap.20; vol. II, p. 257.

[39] *Ibid.* chap.13; vol. II, p. 251.

[40] Christopher Dawson, "St. Augustine and His Age" in M. C. D'Arcy and others, *A Monument to St. Augustine,* Meridian Books, Inc., New York, 1957, p. 76.

practice. The common practice had recognized no distinction between secular and religious spheres. We have already seen that beginning with Octavius Augustus in 27 B.C., the native cults of Greece and Rome, fostered for political purposes, yielded to a common religion of empire. The cult of Isis, brought to Rome from Egypt, and that of Mithra, brought from Persia, had such great influence on the growing absolutism of the emperor as to transform his rule from something political and legal into something metaphysical and transcendent. Now what needs to be most carefully noticed is that in St. Augustine's view, this "ambition" and "proud sovereignty" have their very root in the natural virtue that does not refer itself to the true God. This very virtue is a vice. Here the State and the Earthly City do indeed touch and blend. For if indeed natural justice is "generally found wanting . . . where God does not govern and men do not obey by sacrificing unto Him alone," it is also true that even where this justice is found not wanting, it is rather a vice than a virtue: "No, those things which [the soul] seems to account virtues . . . if they be not all referred unto God, are indeed rather vices than virtues. For although some hold them to be real virtues, when they are desired only for their own account, and nothing else; yet even so they incur vainglory and so lose their true goodness." [41] We must try to understand how this is the case.

Desiring the virtues for their own account and not referring them to God is not "honest morality" because the mean of virtue is taken according to various circumstances. Nothing hinders something from being extreme (either by defect or by excess) in a particular virtue according to one circumstance while the same thing is a mean according to other circumstances, through its conformity with reason. This may be seen in the case of the virtues of magnanimity and magnificence: If we look at the absolute quantity of the respective objects of these virtues, we shall call it an extreme and a maximum; but if we consider the quantity in relation to other circumstances, then it has the character of a mean, since these virtues tend to this maximum in accordance with the

---

[41] *The City of God* XIX.chap.25; vol. II, p. 265.

rule of reason, i.e., *where* it is right, *when* it is right, and for an *end* that is right. There will be excess if one tends to this maximum *when* it is not right, or *where* it is not right, or for an undue *end*. All virtue, then, St. Augustine is saying, when not referred to God is vice by excess: being sought on its own account it is sought as an undue end. As St. Augustine puts it: "For as that is not of the flesh, but above the flesh, that animates the body; so that is not of man, but above man, which beatifies the mind of man. . . ." [42] It is vainglorious and excessive to seek virtue without referring it to God, "since" (as Aristotle himself had put it) "man is not the best thing in the world." Sought on its own account, all virtue is itself "ambition" and "proud sovereignty," the beginning of "variable impiety."

It is this precise consideration that leads St. Augustine to remove "justice" from Cicero's definition of an organized people as "a union of a number of men associated by the two bonds of common acknowledgment of right (*jus*) and common pursuit of interest." St. Augustine's purpose is not to show that justice is not necessary to a state; it is to show that the justice by which Cicero defines the *res publica* does not make a true *res publica* because the circumstance of its not being referred to God makes it inordinate and therefore not just. And further, since this precise inordinateness is of the essence of variable impiety, a good definition of the State must include even those states that are most impious. As Professor McIlwain well says, this is a *reductio ad absurdum*, but it is not so much the absurdity of Cicero's definition as it is of heathenism.[43] The inordinateness of seeking virtue on its own account is of the essence of variable impiety because the frustration of man's final end (eternal beatitude) leads to an insane search for a substitute infinity—as in emperor worship—and destroys the proper forms by which human life is well lived on this earth.

For St. Augustine wishes us to see that it is only the well-in-

---

[42] *Ibid.* chap.25; vol. II, p. 265.
[43] Charles Howard McIlwain, *The Growth of Political Thought in the West,* The Macmillan Company, New York, 1932, p. 157.

structed pursuit of the Heavenly City that makes it possible for man to hold in their proper order the temporal conveniences of earthly peace. "In contemplation one may not seek for idleness, but for truth; . . . and not to grudge to impart it unto others"; and in the civil life, the life of action, "one may not aim at power or honor . . . but unto the benefit of the subject." [44] Asking why God punishes the good as well as the evil in this life, St. Augustine answers by saying that the good, while indeed turning away from the conduct of the wicked, are blameworthy in "keeping aloof, [forbearing] to give [the wicked] due instructions, admonitions, or reprehensions . . . [eschewing] their hate for [their own] greater temporal preferment, [winking] at their . . . exorbitances because they fear to lose by them their own vain temporalities. . . ." [45] If the citizens of the Heavenly City neglect the duty laid upon them in this world by its temporal exigencies, they are not without fault: "wholly abhorring the course of the wicked, they yet spare to tax others' sins . . . because they fear to . . . be hurt in their possession of those things whose use is lawful . . . desiring temporalities . . . far more greedily than is fit. . . ." For it should be carefully understood that if indeed it is only the saints who, having temporal conveniences in possession, "may not unfitly be called happy already," by the same token "the saints in their loss of things temporal lose not anything at all." [46] The fall of Rome is a very small matter. The large matter is the Heavenly City's continuing task of "laying up . . . a good foundation against the time to come" by "the honesty of virtue, the love of country, the faith of friendship, just dealing, and all the things belonging to good manners." Thus it becomes saints—as it becomes none others—to effect the good of earthly peace itself. This is the central idea, the chief significance for politics and political philosophy of *The City of God*. And this was the original and true revolutionary significance of Christianity for politics and political philosophy. "They that follow the Lord's counsel . . . 'Lay not

[44] *The City of God* XIX.chap.19; vol. II, pp. 256–257.
[45] *Ibid*. I.chap.8; vol. I, pp. 10–11.
[46] *Ibid*. chap.9; vol. I, p. 12.

up treasures for yourselves upon the earth where the moth and
rust corrupt, or where thieves dig through and steal, but lay up
treasures for yourselves in heaven, where neither rust nor moth
corrupt, nor thieves dig through and steal' "—they alone know
how to make a just distribution of temporal conveniences in imitation of "the most just Disposer of all the adjuncts of temporal
peace." They have the needed mandate and the only mandate:
" 'Charge them that are rich in this world that they be not high-
minded, and that they trust not in their uncertain wealth, but in
the living God, who giveth us plentifully all things to enjoy: that
they do good and be rich in good works, ready to distribute and
communicate: laying up in store for themselves a good foundation
against the time to come, that they may obtain the true life.' " [47]

St. Thomas Aquinas: Church and State

This true life, to which the Church leads men, is in itself superior
to the political. The roles of State and Church vis-à-vis each other
are determined by this hierarchy. The function of the State with
respect to wisdom is tutelary, that is, the State has the obligation
to protect and encourage the wisdom of its wise men. Vis-à-vis the
State, the role of the Church, as guardian of the law of the Old
and New Testaments whereby man is directed to the ultimate end
of eternal beatitude, is as St. Thomas puts it, to keep "the business
of [the State] what we believe [it] is, supreme direction of temporal affairs." [48] For indeed, the "Divine law which is the law of
grace, does not do away with human law which is the law of
natural reason," and therefore it is necessary in strictly civil matters to obey the secular rather than the spiritual authority. [49]

But to "keep the business of (the State) what we believe (it)
is" implies the right of the Church in certain circumstances to

---

[47] I *Timothy* 6:17–19; cited in *The City of God* I.chap.9; vol. I, p. 13.

[48] *On Princely Government*, xiv. In D'Entrèves, *op. cit.*, p. 75.

[49] *Summa Theol.* II.II.Q.10 a.10. Cf. *Commentary on the Sentences of
Peter Lombard* bk.II.dist.44.Q.3. In D'Entrèves, *op. cit.*, p. 187.

intervene in temporal affairs. For although temporal authority "preceded the distinction of faithful from unbelievers" so that this distinction, *considered in itself*, does not do away with the authority of human law, this authority—which, indeed, it is necessary "in strictly civil matters to obey"—may be "justly done away with by the sentence or ordination of the Church who has the authority of God. . . ." [50] What circumstances, then, account for the possibility of this extraordinary exception, of the Pope's doing away with the authority of human law? The civil authority, which in strictly civil matters is supreme, may be done away with by the Pope where the civil power exceeds its jurisdiction, which is over the matter of the practical sciences, i.e., the sciences concerned with human affairs.[51] To understand the force here of the phrase "human affairs," we may recall the classical definition given by Aristotle to political justice: "Of political justice part is natural, part legal—natural, that which everywhere has the same force and does not exist by people's thinking this or that; legal, that which is originally indifferent, but when it has been laid down is not indifferent. . . ." [52] It is part of the limited or constitutional character of government that it may not legislate contrary to the ends appointed by the natural law: The natural part of political justice belongs to the divine-natural law and is not a "strictly civil" matter. It is not a "human affair," for it "does not exist by people's thinking this or that." The legal part of political justice prescribes "that which is originally indifferent"; it is of "strictly civil matters." This means that the civil law may not prescribe what is of itself contrary to natural justice, for this is not a matter of indifference. Aristotle had given an excellent example of this latter kind of thing in speaking of the practice of abortion. While recommending abortion in certain circumstances, he insists that it should be ". . . procured before life and sense have begun," and adds: "what may or may not be lawfully done in these cases depends on the question of life and sensation." [53] What may or

[50] *Summa Theol.* II.II.Q.10 a.10.C.
[51] Cf. *In I Ethics* lect.1.
[52] *Ethics* V.1134b.18–20.
[53] *Politics* VII.1335b.24–26.

may not be "lawfully done" in these cases is not a matter of indifference: It is prescribed by the natural law which is the divine law as it appears in man as measured and ruled by the divine government. This natural law is prior to any civil jurisdiction, and its general principles must be observed by every civil authority in its proper enactments: It may issue orders for its sake, but not to it. The Church, as the guardian of the divine law, claims the right to decide such cases in the light indeed of theological science served by all the theoretic sciences.

The second class of cases in which the Church may touch the civil law at the point where the civil law itself touches matters that are not "indifferent," has to do with all matters that concern the Faith and the law of the Church itself. The deposition of heretical rulers was a lively question in the Middle Ages. In asking whether a ruler forfeits his authority over his subjects on account of apostasy from the Faith, St. Thomas answers as follows:

> As stated above, unbelief, in itself, is not inconsistent with dominion, since dominion is a device of the law of nations which is a human law: whereas the distinction between believers and unbelievers is of Divine right, which does not annul human right. Nevertheless a man who sins by unbelief may be sentenced to the loss of his right of dominion, as also, sometimes, on account of other sins.
>
> Now it is not within the competency of the Church to punish unbelief in those who have never received the Faith. . . . She can, however, pass sentence of punishment on the unbelief of those who have received the Faith: and it is *fitting* that they should be punished by being deprived of the allegiance of their subjects: for this same allegiance might conduce to great corruption of the Faith. . . . Consequently, as soon as sentence of excommunication is passed on a man on account of apostasy from the Faith, his subjects are *ipso facto* absolved from his authority and from the oath of allegiance whereby they were bound to him.[54]

In virtue of the same principle, the Church may ask the aid of the State in curbing heresy. St. Thomas expresses the view that

[54] *Summa Theol.* II.II.Q.12 a.2.C. Italics added. It is not within the competence of the State to depose a person for heresy.

persons who at some time have accepted the Faith should be compelled to "fulfill what they promised"—on the ground that if
the acceptance of the Faith is indeed a matter of freedom of conscience, its retention is a matter of contract, which should be enforced.[55] On the other hand, "those who have never received the
faith . . . are by no means to be compelled to the faith" because
to believe depends on the will. Further, the rites of unbelievers
who are neither formal heretics nor apostates ought to be tolerated
by the State: for human government is derived from the Divine
government and should imitate it in permitting things that are
"quite inferior" and indeed in permitting things that are evil; lest
by preventing them, "greater good might be forfeited or greater
evils ensue." [56]

For indeed, as we have seen, "dominion and authority are institutions of human law [and] the Divine law which is the law of
grace, does not do away with human law which is the law of
natural reason." And since law "as a measure and rule of human
acts . . . should be homogeneous with that which it measures
. . . laws imposed on men should . . . be in keeping with their
condition, for . . . law should be possible both according to
nature, and according to the customs of the country." As we shall
presently see when we consider St. Thomas' theory of constitutional government, "consent" and "possibility" are intrinsic de-
terminants of the power of human law. The law, while aiming always at the good and avoiding evil, must consider the interior
habits of a people, which in turn depend on their internal natural
liberty: For the appetitive part of the soul obeys the reason not
instantaneously, but with a certain natural right of opposition. For
this reason both Aristotle and St. Thomas say that the reason commands the appetitive part by a *political* rule, whereby a man rules
over subjects that are free, having a certain right of opposition.
And thus the factors of consent and possibility are present both
in the attainment of the perfection of man's liberty—in the discovery of wisdom—and in the attainment of something "quite in-

---

[55] *Ibid.* Q.10 a.8.C. This distinction suggests a reservation in behalf of
higher and more universal norms. See immediately below.
[56] *Ibid.* a.11.

ferior." This doctrine of tolerance has its root in St. Thomas' jurisprudence and belongs to his theory of constitutional government,
to which we shall turn our attention in the next chapter.

Egidius Colonna—John of Paris—Marsilius of Padua

At the very beginning of the century following the death of St.
Thomas (1274) the subtlety and exactness that belong to the
proper principles of this question of Church and State were lost
in the polemic heat of the struggle between Pope Boniface VIII
(1294–1303) and Philip the Fair, King of France (1285–1314).
We cannot be concerned here with the details of that bitter controversy. It is sufficient to note that the principal matters in question—the need for Papal consent to royal taxes on the clergy and
the immunity of clerics from the royal courts—were rights that
had long been acknowledged. There was imprudence on the part
of both Pope and King in the struggle between them, but the
King's behavior was outrageous by any standards. Boniface con-
voked a synod at Rome on All Saints Day, November 18, 1302,
and issued the famous bull *Unam Sanctam*. It was the strongest
statement of papal claims that had hitherto been made. The
strength, however, was in the style of the pronouncement rather
than in its substance. Professor McIlwain states that "In the first
place . . . not a single assertion or claim made in the bull is new.
. . . In the second place, however sweeping its demands, there
is in the bull no explicit claim to a direct power in temporal matters. . . . In the third place, if Boniface's claim to forty years' experience in the canon law was true—and it was—he well knew
that the canonists insisted on a papal power far stronger than the
one he put forth in the bull." [57] It is this view of the canonists
which we must briefly examine.

The most notable exponent of the canonists' view was Egidius

[57] Reprinted with permission of the publisher from *The Growth of Political
Thought in the West* by Charles Howard McIlwain. Copyright 1932 by The
Macmillan Company. Copyright 1960 by James McIlwain, p. 246.

Colonna (Giles of Rome), a doctor of both canon and civil law, Archbishop of Bourges and head of the Augustinian Order. In the *De Ecclesiastica Potestate*, which appeared in 1301, Egidius presented what has come to be known as the theocratic or hierocratic doctrine of Church and State. The essential contention of Egidius was that temporal authority is derived directly from the Pope. All temporal power belongs of right to the Pope, for it has its origin in the papal *plenitudo potestatis*, within which all authority, spiritual and temporal, is contained. Central to the position of Egidius is the subjection of the principle of the hierarchy of ends to a *Respublica Christiana* viewed as a *simple unity* under the hegemony of the Pope. We will recall that in any whole that has a simple unity, the parts have no function independently of the function of the whole.[58] If this conception be applied to a whole that has in reality a mere unity of order the result must be the dissolution of the parts. Egidius' theory would in practice entail a dissolution of political society much as Plato's "too simple unity" of the *Republic* entailed the destruction of the family.

St. Thomas, who acknowledged an independent origin for the temporal power, was not himself forgetful of the *plenitudo potestatis* of the Pope. He had said that secular and spiritual power are joined in the Pope who stands at the top of both.[59] But because "the authority of Caesar (that is secular authority) preceded the distinction of faithful from unbelievers," the *plenitudo potestatis* of the Pope, considered in itself, does not do away with secular authority. Since, then, the simple fact of the Pope having both secular and spiritual authority does not abrogate the temporal power, this latter can be exercised by the Pope only indirectly—when, as we have seen, the civil authority jeopardizes the divine law.

If Egidius' claims in behalf of the papacy were palpably beyond any that had hitherto been made, the view of the King's principal defender, the French Dominican John of Paris, was an ingenious

---

[58] See above, p. 53.

[59] *Commentary on the Sentences of Peter Lombard*, dist.44, Q.3 a.4. Cited in D'Entrèves, *op. cit.*, p. 187.

"marking down" of the authentic thing. The authentic thing is the principle of the two independent powers related by a unity of order through the principle of the hierarchy of ends. In the *De Potestate Regia et Papali* (1302–1303) John sought to keep the unity of order by interpreting the principle of the hierarchy of ends as implying merely a gradation of dignity but not of power. John of course maintained the primacy of dignity of the spiritual because of the primacy of its end—eternal (final) beatitude. Examining the spiritual power in its component parts—consecration and absolution, teaching, and the power of judgment in the external forum—he distinguished, in the case of the last, the right of moral judgment from the right of imposing sanctions to enforce judgment. Although he allowed the right of the Church to pronounce judgment in temporal matters where the sin involved could be reduced to a spiritual or ecclesiastical crime,[60] he denied that the Church had any right to enforce its judgments in the temporal order. Despite his ardent Aristotelianism, he refused to accept Aristotle's principle that the "master art" plays an architectonic role with respect to the subordinate arts. The right of the Pope to depose a king is of no more legal value, he held, than the right of the king to depose a Pope; this right belongs only to those in the state who are duly authorized to elect the king. Papal warning, excommunication and direct spiritual action on the peo-

---

[60] ". . . if the concept of fault is analyzed, this case should not be considered an exception to our rule, since the church has cognizance of no fault except as it is reduced to a spiritual or ecclesiastical matter. For there are two kinds of sin in temporals. One kind is the sin of contradiction or error, as when it is maintained that usury is not a mortal sin, or that one can claim another's property by any title whatever, or when someone doubts whether such things are permitted or forbidden by God. Since all such questions are determined by divine law, which is the law used by the ecclesiastical judge, there is no doubt that the cognizance of such cases belongs only to the ecclesiastical judge. The other kind of sin in temporals is that of retaining something that belongs to another, or of using another's property as one's own; and the cognizance of such cases belongs only to the secular judge, who judges according to human, or civil, laws. . . ." (*De Potestate Regia et Papali,* chap. XII., trans. by Mrs. Ewart Lewis, in *Mediaeval Political Ideas,* Alfred A. Knopf, Inc., New York, 1954, vol. II, p. 587.)

ple may have the effect of bringing about the king's deposition by the properly constituted political authority that elected him. It is only in this way that the Pope may be said to have indirectly a power in temporal affairs—the exercise of his spiritual power having merely an influence on the duly constituted temporal authorities. For St. Thomas, on the contrary, the Pope's indirect power in temporal affairs touches the very substance of temporal matters—but indirectly because it touches the civil law only at the point where the civil law itself touches matters that are not "indifferent"—the divine-natural law and the divine-positive law. In St. Thomas' view, then, papal excommunication either carried or could be made to carry with it *ipso facto* deposition.

I have called John's theory "ingenious" because it gives the appearance of saving the "indirect power" of the Pope while more perfectly securing the proper autonomy of the political order. His theory was based on the expectation that only after the papal pronouncement of excommunication would the political authorities proceed to depose the heretical ruler; in this way John thought that he had preserved intact both papal and secular rights. A closer examination of his position will show that, on the contrary, it effectively removes the indirect power and goes very far—in an opposite way from Egidius—toward obliterating the distinction between the two orders. In effect it puts the care of the divine law of the Church in the hands of the State: for the theory does nothing less, in effect, than confer on the properly constituted political authorities a right to depose a king for heresy—an incredible impertinence on the part of a purely civil power. I say "a right of their own," for in John's view the Pope's excommunication cannot carry an *ipso facto* deposition, and there is no legal obligation whatsoever upon the duly constituted political authorities to proceed to depose the king for a heresy defined by the Pope. Deposition follows, then, the definition of heresy by the political authorities charged with the king's election; for these authorities are in effect (if not in principle) quite free to decide either that the alleged heresy is not heretical, or that it is heretical and the ruler should be deposed, or that it is heretical, but that heresy is a matter of public and political indifference. In any case the spiritual authority is effectively put into the hands of the secular power which now defines truth in theological matters; and if heresy is taken cognizance of at all, it is reduced to a political crime—a state of things that would bring politics back to the times of emperor worship or ahead to the times of Hitler and Khrushchev.

The consequences which John's theory implied were asserted in principle within the next quarter century by Marsilius of Padua. In the *Defensor Pacis*,[61] written in 1324 in defense of Lewis of Bavaria against Pope John XXII, we have the fourth of the major mediaeval theories on Church and State, and the one that is at the opposite extreme from that of Egidius Colonna. Marsilius' arguments are a kind of extrapolation of the thesis of John of Paris: The dignity of the spiritual power comes from its authority in matters relating to the next world. Since, then, the Church's authority carries with it no sanctions in the present world, its authority is not a genuine power at all. The only authority worthy of the name in this world is one whose commands are validated by coercive power. And this is the authority of the political community. This authority is expressed through the civil law, which Marsilius understands to be simply the command of the whole people or its "prevailing part" (*pars valentior*). The "prevailing part" (not a numerical majority but the part that carries the greatest weight) delegates authority to the executive part (*pars principans*) whose duty it is to see that every part of the state performs its function for the good of the whole. This authority must be simple and unified and absolutely supreme. It is not that Marsilius, any more than John, denies that society is a *Respublica Christiana,* a Christian Commonwealth comprising both Empire and Church. But he finds the source of this Christian Commonwealth's authority to be simple and unified in the people who are at once citizens and Christians. The Church he defines as "the body of faithful believing in and calling upon the name of Christ," and from this people all power—political and ecclesiastical—is derived. The

[61] C. W. Previte-Orton (ed.), *The Defensor Pacis of Marsilius of Padua,* Cambridge, 1928.

Pope is merely an administrative head of the Church. Heresy may indeed be punished, but it is punishable by the community or by the emperor who has his authority from the people; and it is punished as a civil offense. Indeed the Pope himself may be deposed by the secular authority.

The philosophical basis for Marsilius' theory was the Aristotelianism of the celebrated Arabian commentator, Averroes. Professor Sabine writes:

> The essential characteristics of Latin Averroism were its thoroughgoing naturalism and rationalism. It admitted, indeed, the absolute truth of Christian revelation but it divorced this entirely from philosophy, and unlike St. Thomas, held that the rational conclusions of the latter might be quite contrary to the truths of faith. It was responsible therefore for the doctrine of a two-fold truth. With this tendency the separation in the *Defensor Pacis* of reason from revelation, "which we believe by pure faith," is quite in accord.[62]

If we are to understand the implications of Averroistic Aristotelianism for political philosophy in general and for the Church-State question in particular, we must take careful note of this: The doctrine of the twofold truth operated at a deeper level than that of the Church-State question or of the relation between Faith and Philosophy. It operated within the realm of philosophy itself where it set up an opposition between what had always been considered to be the rule and measure of human reason (namely, the truth of things—*rerum veritas*) and the human reason. We have already had occasion to observe that the principles of Faith are in the Divine Intellect rather than in human science[63] (so that we do not see them as self-evident, nor can we demonstrate them) and that the principles of philosophical science are in the human intellect. In both cases—that of the principles of Faith and of the principles of philosophical science —the source of truth is that Prime Intellect upon which "depend the heavens and the world of nature." As we have said, in theoretic

[62] Sabine, *op. cit.*, pp. 291–292.
[63] See above.

science the human intellect is measured by its object—not the other way round. That is why, too, as we have noted, freedom in the determination of theoretic truth is asserted primarily in behalf of truth itself and only consequently in behalf of man. Now the Christian Averroists sought to render innocuous the truths of Faith (and the authority of the Church in the temporal order) precisely by affirming—not indeed philosophy, but the freedom of human reason from what had always been considered its rule and measure—the truth of things (*rerum veritas*). This emancipation from "the truth of things" as the measure of the human reason was done, very curiously indeed, by appealing to the absolute authority of the letter of Aristotle as the incarnation of human reason. I say "very curiously" because, as Professor Alan Gewirth has amply shown,[64] Marsilius wrought a complete reorientation of the whole political philosophy of Aristotle: which indeed he could do since even the thought and reason of Aristotle himself are excluded by the arbitrary acceptance of the letter of Aristotle![65] Thus the core of the Marsilian theory of Church and State

---

[64] Gewirth, *Marsilius of Padua, The Defender of the Peace*, Columbia University Press, New York, 1951.

[65] "I believe," Averroes writes, "that this man (Aristotle) was the rule and measure in nature, and indeed the exemplar which nature invented to demonstrate final human perfection in all matters . . . we praise God who separated this man from all others in perfection and gave to him the ultimate human dignity, which no other man will ever be able to attain in any age whatever." (Cited in Pierre Mandonnet, O.P., *Siger de Brabant et l'Averroisme Latin au XIII siecle*, 2d ed., in the collection *Les Philosophes Belges*, Louvain, part I, pp. 153–154.) Commenting on this passage, Pierre Conway, O.P., writes: "To what St. Thomas calls reason, that reason which is either the 'why' of things, or our own reason which is posterior to things and prior to Aristotle, the Averroists substitute the primacy of the letter. St. Thomas supposes that even in reading an author such as Aristotle, reason comes first. The author's positions are to be judged in the light of truth. *Studium philosophiae non est ad hoc quod sciatur quid homines senserint, sed qualiter se habeat veritas rerum.* (*In I de Caelo*, lect.22, n. 8.) To this is opposed the notion of the authority of the philosopher, and in particular Aristotle, by Siger and Averroes. *Quaerendo intentionem philosophorum in hoc, magis quam veritatem, cum philosophice procedamus.* (In Mandonnet, *op. cit.*, p. 145). . . . We insist upon the unity of truth, which is the measure

is now before us: It was not merely the supposed power and right of reason to contradict the truths of Faith; rather the possibility of such a contradiction was rooted in the power and the right of reason to contradict the truth of things. In political science this meant denying that "law is . . . defined by justice, by its relation to the . . . rational structure of natural law; instead, it is sharply differentiated from . . . these and is defined simply as a coercive command." [66] Just as in theoretical truth the human intellect precedes, for the Averroists, the "why" of things, so in politics there is no "why" by which the law can be tested: It is the authority of its letter, written by the people or the "weightier part," that is the sole measure of right.

We are confronted, once again, with that effort at emancipation from the human condition that is a recurrent note throughout the history of Western thought. The character of this emancipation is well established by Professor Gewirth. He has shown that the "natural" for Marsilius is always identified with man's material endowment—his biological nature:

---

of the intellect in speculative matters. The divine intellect is the cause of truth of things and it is one. Our intellect, however, is subject to opinion. For the Averroist, human reason is one and it shines forth so completely in Aristotle that what the letter of Aristotle says becomes the authority for all future thought. Aristotle's letter becomes as the temporal measure for all human learning. Thus, the human intellect becomes prior to the things themselves from which knowledge should come to us, and its unity is substituted for the unity of truth. In making this *rapprochement* between the divine unity of truth and the unity of the Averroistic intellect, one is only drawing the very conclusion that St. Thomas drew in his Opusculum, namely, that the Averroistic intellect is not only separated but is God himself." (Keeler, ed., *De Unitate intellectus contra Averroistas parisienses,* Rome, 1936, pp. 69–70; "The Emancipation of Man in Latin Averroism," *Laval Théologique et Philosophique,* vol. 1, no. 2, pp. 126–127, 1946.)

[66] Gewirth, *op. cit.,* p. 47. Since I have called attention earlier to the Marxist view of the public and social efficacy of the concept of the primacy of the spiritual in which reason and justice have meaning only as powers of man himself, of "social humanity," it might be instructive at this point to direct attention to the kind of intervention in the international legal order implied by the Marxist concept. See Chap. X, especially pp. 299–301, on the Soviet pronouncement on the seizure of Goa in December, 1961.

Marsilius departs completely from [Aristotle's and St. Thomas'] view of human nature . . . the "natural" as he conceives it is always the primitive, not the perfected; it consists in man's material endowment, physical and biological, not in his rational powers or virtues . . . when the state is itself based upon "natural desire" in the sense of an exclusively biological desire, the norms which were integral to the preceding doctrines suffer a corresponding reduction. The standard of reference and evaluation no longer consists in ideal ends, as with the other Aristotelians, but rather in original potentialities and desires. Thus where "natural" law in the sense of a standard of justice equivalent to or deduced from reason had been of controlling importance in the antecedent tradition, Marsilius' interpretation of the "natural" enables him to deny the existence or political relevance of such law. Instead, he refers to a primitive "quasi-natural law" which is below rather than above positive enactments.[67]

And since, as Aristotle says, the natural is that which happens always or for the most part and is equated by Marsilius with the biological and physical, it follows that, as Professor Gewirth points out, supreme political power is no longer "delegated" by the whole people to the most prudent and just and temperate and rational of men, but is "willed" by the whole people taken "collectively"— or by "the most part" who are not "deformed or otherwise impeded" (for as Aristotle says, nature fails in a few instances). Since for Marsilius that which makes life perfectly desirable and lacking in nothing (to use Aristotle's phrase describing the sufficiency of happiness) is constituted by biological desire, all the values of the antecedent tradition are not only leveled but indeed reversed: "for [Marsilius] is so far from regarding theoretic activity as an end in itself, in the manner of Aristotle, that he rather treats it in the same fashion as the practical, as instrumental to all the needs of life. . . ." [68] Thus, indeed, Marsilius' attempt to overthrow the traditional claims of the Church had its source in the uprooting of the whole natural order of things, of the whole structure of ethical and political thought.

[67] *Ibid.*, p. 55.
[68] *Ibid.*, p. 65.

When Marsilius wrote the *Defensor Pacis* the papacy had already succumbed to the power of the new France. The successor of Boniface VIII was Benedict XI who died in mysterious circumstances after a reign of one year. His successor, Clement V, was a Frenchman, Archbishop of Bordeaux. At the urging of Philip the Fair, Clement never went to Rome. He established his residence at Avignon in 1309. From this date the papal residence was away from Rome for almost seventy years. The mischievous French influence blossomed in the Great Schism (1379–1417). The attempt of the new national states to control the papacy resulted in the scandalous contention of two, and later of three claimants to the See of Peter. Within a century the Church, weakened by that long struggle and caught up in the new worldly spirit of the Renaissance, witnessed the breakup of the spiritual unity of Europe in the Reformation. The immediate effect of this disruption of Christendom was to increase enormously the power of the secular rulers, both Catholic and Protestant. As Professor Sabine remarks, ". . . whoever lost, the kings won, and the absolute monarchy . . . was in the first instance its chief political beneficiary." [69] The question of what was to be its subsequent political beneficiary had to await, for answer, what Ernst Cassirer calls the ultimate validation of Protestantism's "ideal significance." [70] Both matters—the immediate effect of Protestantism and its "ideal significance," its "true nature and substance"—must await consideration in a later chapter.

[69] Sabine, *op. cit.*, p. 356.
[70] Cassirer, *The Philosophy of the Enlightenment,* Beacon Press, Boston, 1955, p. 160.

V

Christianity and political philosophy:
the theory of constitutional government

If we ask ourselves," Professor Barker writes, ". . . what . . . is the nature of the legacy which [Aristotle's *Politics*] bequeathed to the common thought of Europe? the answer may almost be compressed in a single word. The word is 'constitutionalism.'" [1] Christian Europe, freed from the almost pathological efforts at the spurious freedom that had marked the philosophies of conduct of later Greece and Rome, directed its attention to explaining and perfecting the classical Greek notion of the political community as a community of freemen living under the rule of law. The sustained attention to this question and its successful exploration were indeed consequent upon the tranquility of mind brought by Christianity's solution to the problem of final happiness.

All that I have said on Aristotle's political doctrine is not only substantially adopted by St. Thomas Aquinas, but indeed that doctrine is greatly in debt to the extraordinarily profound and thorough explication made of it by St. Thomas—particularly in the Commentaries on the *Ethics* and that portion of the Com-

[1] Barker, *The Politics of Aristotle*, p. lxi.

133

mentary on the *Politics* of which St. Thomas was the author.[2] On the question of constitutional government and the rule of law, while remaining faithful to Aristotle's principles, St. Thomas goes beyond the letter of his master's thought. St. Thomas' teaching on this matter has to be constructed from the many different passages which touch upon it and which are found scattered throughout the following: the *Summa Theologica,* the *Summa Contra Gentiles,* and the treatise *On the Rule of Princes* (*De Regimine Principum*).

The political community: the law of the constitution

In treating the *Jus Gentium* in an earlier chapter, it was pointed out that government as such—that is, without reference to the specific form that it may take—belongs to the *Jus Gentium* and has the force of the natural law itself: For if the political community is one of freemen and equals who are also social beings, the natural reason introduces government for the perfection of man. ". . . since man is a part of the home and state, he must needs consider what is good for him by being prudent about the good of the many."[3] A social life cannot exist among a number of people unless under a government to look after the common good: "Hence the Philosopher says, in the beginning of the *Politics,* that wherever many things are directed to one, we shall always find one at the head directing them."[4] Just as the inclination inhering in all the species of natural things is toward the common order and good of the universe, so man in his self-government must imitate the rule of the universe by appointing an authority to administer the community.

---

[2] St. Thomas was the author of the Commentary on the *Politics* as far as Book III, chap. VI; the remainder was the work of St. Thomas' pupil, Peter of Auvergne.

[3] *Summa Theol.* II.II.Q.47 a.10 ad 2.

[4] *Ibid.* I.Q.96 a.7.

Now in nature there is to be found both a universal and a particular form of government. The universal is that by which all things find their place under the direction of God, who, by His providence, governs the universe. The particular is very similar to this divine control, and is found within man himself; who, for this reason, is called a microcosm, because he provides an example of universal government . . . so in a certain sense, reason is to man what God is to the universe.[5]

The political community is, then, one of self-governing men. Since law as a measure and rule must be homogeneous with what it measures, the homogeneity of human law with the community whose acts it rules is found initially in the derivation itself of the *specific form* of constitution from the community of freemen: For freemen, who are equal in having the disposal of themselves, are of such nature as to make it impossible that any one of them in particular should have a natural right to rule over others; and therefore the specific form of government (as distinguished from government *as such*—which has the necessity of natural law) is a matter of free choice. And because the individual good is impossible without the common good of all, this good is an end that belongs to all, and therefore it is within the competence of the whole multitude to make the very first law—that of the constitution by which the government (whatever its form) is set up. And if any one person or group of persons should presume to found a State, this action is justifiable only on the ground of their representing the will of the whole people. As St. Thomas puts it:

A law properly speaking, regards first and foremost the order to the common good. Now to order anything to the common good belongs either to the whole people or to someone who is the vicegerent of the whole people . . . for in all other matters the direction of anything to the end concerns him to whom the end belongs.[6]

[5] *On Princely Government,* I. xii. Reprinted with permission of The Macmillan Company from D'Entrèves, *Aquinas: Selected Political Writings,* p. 67.

[6] *Summa Theol.* I.II.Q.90 a.3.C.

Two elements of constitutional government thus emerge: The first is the element of consent, based on man's moral freedom. The second is the principle of rule to which consent is given:

> In whatever things are constituted of many parts there is found a ruling and a subject element. But a multitude of men is constituted from a number of individuals; and therefore among men it is natural that one should rule and another be subject. . . . He (Aristotle) says therefore . . . that whatever things are constituted from many in such a way that from this many a community results, whether the parts are continuous, as are the members of the body which are joined in the constitution of the whole, or whether they are discrete, as from many soldiers one army is constituted, in all of these there is found a ruling and a subject element. And this is both natural and expedient, as will be apparent from any example.[7]

In a natural composite the ruling and subject parts are brought in by nature itself, and the commensuration of one with respect to the other is natural by an "absolute" commensuration. Thus, St. Thomas says, the intellect is by its very nature, considered absolutely, commensurate with the sense appetites to regulate them; and the male by its very nature is commensurate with the female to beget offspring by her, and the parent with the child to nourish it. But in a community where ordering to the common good is among persons in whom there is found no absolute commensuration of one as ruler with the other as subject, this relation is introduced by the natural reason in imitation of what nature brings in elsewhere.

There is, finally, a third element of constitutionalism: The element of possibility, which corresponds to man's physical freedom. Comparing the art of gymnastics with that of politics, Aristotle had observed that a man may not desire the best habit of body even though this be physically possible to him; and a man for whom there is a physical impediment to acquiring the best habit of body may desire what the circumstances permit, or he may desire something even less than the circumstances permit. "The same

---

[7] *In I Politics* lect.3.

principle equally holds in medicine and ship-building, and making of clothes, and in the arts generally." [8] On the basis of that comparison, Aristotle had argued that political science "has to consider what government is best and of what sort it must be, to be most in accordance with our aspirations, if there were no external impediment, and also what kind of government is adapted to particular states." [9] Thus political science will deal even with states that are "neither . . . the best under the circumstances, but of an inferior type," much as medicine is concerned to know to what degree a person can in fact attain health. And since the moral sciences bear on the contraries of good and evil only in the sense that they pursue the one and avoid the other, a constitutional government cannot be one that is simply bad, though it may be neither the best absolutely nor best as what is best suited to the majority of states, nor even best in the circumstances. But it cannot be simply bad, for the "rule of law" that Aristotle had required of all good government requires a *right* consent: "The tyranny that is the counterpart of perfect monarchy . . . no freeman, if he can escape from it, will endure." [10] The element of possibility allows for the choice of a government that may indeed be "quite inferior" and less good even than the circumstances permit; but it does not extend to permitting what of itself would be contrary to natural law—the tyranny that no freeman, if he can escape from it, will endure. The incompetence of a primitive people is analogous to the incompetence of a corrupt people, and, as St. Thomas points out, where a people are thoroughly corrupt and entrust the government to scoundrels and criminals, "the right of appointing their public officials is rightly forfeit to such a people and the choice devolves upon a few good men." [11] Such a people do not, then, have a constitutional government that is properly political, for they are not competent to share in government. Politically immature or corrupt, they may be likened to brute natures, for like nonrational nature they need to be directed to

[8] *Politics* IV.1288b.19–20.
[9] *Ibid.*
[10] *Ibid.* 1295a.24.
[11] *Summa Theol.* I.II.Q.97 a.2.C.

their proper end by an intelligence extrinsic to them. But the seeds of political life are there: They have the kind of government that their nature and condition require for growth in political maturity. As St. Thomas says, different things are expedient to different men because of the differences of their condition. If, then, a people originally incompetent by reason either of corruption or immaturity come to "have a sense of moderation and responsibility and are most careful guardians of the common welfare, it is right to enact a law allowing such people to choose their own magistrates for the government of the commonweal." [12] And indeed, along with growing maturity in political virtue, there is advancement in the science of government:

. . . it seems natural to human reason to advance gradually from the imperfect to the perfect. Hence in the speculative sciences, we see that the teaching of the early philosophers was imperfect, and that it was afterwards perfected by those who succeeded them. So also in practical matters, for those who first endeavored to discover something useful for the human community, not being able themselves to take everything into consideration, set up certain institutions which were deficient in many ways; and these were changed by subsequent lawgivers who made institutions that might prove less frequently deficient in relation to the common welfare.[13]

The best form of government

The problem of the best constitution is that of combining the elements of consent and possibility with the perfection of the governing principle—the unity, effectiveness, and stability of the form of government. Aristotle had found each of the simple forms of good government defective in relation to the common welfare on the score either of inadequate allowance for the elements of consent and possibility or of inadequate provision for effectiveness in the governmental structure—the two aspects of constitutional

[12] *Ibid.*
[13] *Ibid.*

government. The simple form of monarchy—which Aristotle considered, absolutely speaking, the best form because it best imitates the perfection of the governing principle of the rational soul over the "free" appetites—has the curious disadvantage that there are no citizens in such a state—neither the ruler nor the subjects are true citizens, "for the virtue of a citizen includes ruling and obeying." [14] Despite its acknowledged primacy from the point of view of the perfection of the governing principle, this form, if it be transferred to a community where the ideal prerequisites for it are lacking, loses its advantage of unity of rule, St. Thomas points out, by a lack of interest in the common welfare on the part of the members of the community, who do not share in the government.[15] On the other hand, democracy, the simple "political" form, in which citizens rule and are ruled in turn, has for Aristotle the more serious disadvantage that by dividing political authority among equals it tends to ostracize the better element and to seek equality in everything.

To retain the democratic principle of ruling and being ruled in turn—without, however, retaining the democratic principle of absolute equality and the social instability that it entails—Aristotle had suggested a substitute for absolute kingship modeled on the substitute that the continent man employs for true virtue. The kind of consent to true rule and the possibility of it that are found in the average (continent) man were made to serve as the model for the average political community. The unity of rule that is

[14] In the Commentary on the *Politics* St. Thomas explains the consistency of Aristotle's absolute preference for this form of government. "Nor is there validity to the objection that such a ruler is not a citizen: for what is true is that just as he who rules by reason of exceeding all others in virtue is not a citizen but above citizenship, so in the same way we recognize the excellence of any citizen by the way he relates himself to the law (for he who obeys virtuously is a good man and above being merely a good citizen); but the assumption that only a citizen may rule does not hold for the royal polity, which is that which is best simply speaking." (*In III Politics* lect.12.)

[15] *On Princely Government,* I.iv. In D'Entrèves, *op. cit.,* p. 21. Further, of course, where there is no one man whose virtue ("heroic," "godlike") exceeds that of the whole people, it would be contrary to simple justice "that [he] should be lord of all." (*Politics* III.1288a.1–3.)

exemplified in the virtuous man's government of himself is imitated in the continent man by a somewhat precarious combination of the two extremes that lie outside the intermediate of true virtue: The man who is overindulgent by nature, moves toward the opposite extreme of total abstention and thus by a combination of the two extremes imitates the intermediate condition of true temperance. In similar fashion the extremes of freedom and equality on the one hand and wealth on the other are brought together in a large middle class by a wide distribution of property; and this large middle class is capable of a unity of action that imitates the unity of absolute kingship: for just as the continent man does not live by virtue precisely, but by something less, so the middle-class Polity lives by the steadying effects of property values.

St. Thomas does not disagree with this diagnosis and prescription. Speaking of the various kinds of law that are distinguished in reference to the various kinds of government, he observes that the best form of government is made up of all the good forms together with the forms of government that are not altogether corrupt—of monarchy, aristocracy, democracy, and oligarchy.[16] He shows himself sensitive, too, to the importance of property distribution in creating a stable and enduring society:

As the Philosopher says, the regulation of possessions conduces much to the preservation of a state or nation. Consequently, as he himself observes, it was forbidden by the law in some of the pagan states that anyone should sell his possessions, except to avoid manifest loss. For if possessions were to be sold indiscriminately, they might happen to come into the hands of a few, so that it might become necessary for a state . . . to become void of inhabitants.[17]

We must note, however, that Aristotle's solution to the problem of combining consent and possibility with unity of rule achieves the latter in regard to the stability of unified rule but not in regard to effectiveness of legislative prudence (what we today would call policy-making authority). For if the stability that is lacking in

[16] *Summa Theol.* I.II.Q.95 a.4.C.
[17] *Summa Theol.* I.II.Q.105 a.2 ad 3.

the simple democratic principle of freedom and equality is achieved through the middle-class character of the government, the democratic principle of rule by turns retains the need for a fixed order both of succession and of power of legislation. For where the citizen at times rules and at other times is ruled, the government is carried out *in eodem modo*—that is, in conformity with restrictions upon the policy-making authority.[18] Thus the purely "political" principle, though "corrected" in the direction of stability, retains the weakness of constricting legislative prudence. Instead of the full capacity to proceed in the manner of genuine government, there is a restriction that tends to convert the government into a mere administrator of the *status quo*. Stability is indeed a peculiar and special need for the "art" of politics, but it must not exclude the need for change in law—a need which springs, as we have noticed, partly from men's changed condition and partly from advance in the science of government. St. Thomas' task was to devise on the basis of Aristotle's principles a form of government that would combine stability of middle-class government with the need for change in law. St. Thomas was well aware of the paralyzing effect of concretizing political prudence in existing property relations: The feudal system of the Middle Ages stood as eloquent testimony to this consequence. Indeed, as Mrs. Ewart Lewis says, "feudalism tended to dissolve governmental functions themselves into forms of property," and "in the context of the mediaeval problem one of the most important strands of

---

[18] Discussing the difference between this "political" principle and the "royal" principle, St. Thomas writes: "But the state can be ruled by a two-fold government: namely, political and royal. The regime is royal indeed when he who is head of the state has a plenitude of power. But the government is political when he who is the ruler has power which is constricted by certain laws of the State. . . .

"For when one man rules simply and with respect to everything, the regime is royal. But when, according to the principles of this science, he rules only over certain things—that is, according to laws laid down according to the science of politics—the regime is political; for he rules in part—with respect to those matters which fall under his authority; and in part he is subject—with respect to the things concerning which he himself is under the law." (*In I Politics* lect.1. See *In III Politics* lect.15.)

thought was . . . the gradual emancipation of an effective public authority from the bonds of feudal traditions." [19] St. Thomas' theory of constitutional government represents this most important strand of thought.

To the device of middle-class government (which for Aristotle combines the elements of consent and possibility—the "political" elements of constitutional government—with stability—one of the two elements of "royal" rule) St. Thomas adds the second element of "royal" rule, namely, effective leadership. And he does this by restoring the exercise of government to the one best qualified man conceived now, by the tying of the instruments of his power, as representative of the people. It is this latter conception that is the "political" element in St. Thomas' theory.[20]

St. Thomas' theory of the "mixed monarchy" has been the subject of a good deal of misunderstanding. The key to the theory is to be found in his concept of the people sharing in rule without dividing the government, of introducing the "political" element through the concept of representation. If we suppose—as, for example, Professor McIlwain does—that a genuinely "mixed monarchy" cannot be had without the existence of two independent and competing organs of government, then we would be justified in declaring St. Thomas' mixed monarchy no different from pure monarchy.[21] But if we consider the possibility of pure monarchy being "tempered" [22] by "tying the instruments it was to act by," [23] then this monarchy, while retaining the purity of the form

[19] *Mediaeval Political Ideas*, p. 88; Mrs. Ewart Lewis, "The Contribution of Mediaeval Thought to the American Political Tradition," *American Political Science Review*, vol. 50, no. 2, p. 463, June, 1956.

[20] *Summa Theol.* I.II.Q.90 a.3.C. Aristotle's "royal rule" was indeed, as we have seen St. Thomas call it, "supra-political." See above, p. 68, n. 56.

[21] "On the whole," says Professor McIlwain, "it is pure monarchy, whether elective or not, which seems to me to be St. Thomas' mature choice as the general form of royal government best adapted to the needs of Europe in the Thirteenth Century." (McIlwain, *The Growth of Political Thought in the West*, p. 331, n. 1, p. 332.)

[22] *On Princely Government*, I.vi. In D'Entrèves, *op. cit.*, pp. 28–29.

[23] Sir Roger Twysden, *Certayne Considerations upon the Government of England*, Camden Society, p. 111. Cited in McIlwain, *op. cit.*, p. 366.

(for the authority is not divided), is "mixed" with the political element; it is in this way distinguished from the "pure monarchy" which signifies simply the form as such of monarchial government untempered. This latter was called simply "royal," while the former was called "royal and political." St. Thomas' "mixed monarchy" is not, then, identical with pure monarchy, although it does indeed retain the *form* of pure monarchy; it is not, as is pure monarchy, "supra-political."

The English monarchy of the late Middle Ages amply illustrates these principles of constitutionalism. Sir John Fortescue, Chief Justice of the Court of King's Bench under Henry VI (1422–1461), was the author probably most relied upon in the constitutional struggles of the seventeenth century. He was among the greatest of the mediaeval English writers on law and politics. In the *De Natura Legis Naturae,* in the *De Laudibus Legum Angliae,* and in *The Governance of England* Fortescue speaks of two kinds of regime—a *dominium regale* (royal rule) and a *dominium politicum et regale* (royal and political rule). In support of this distinction he calls upon the authority of St. Thomas. The editor of *The Governance of England,* Mr. Charles Plummer, equates Fortescue's *dominium regale* with "absolute monarchy," and the *dominium politicum et regale* with "constitutional monarchy." [24] Fortescue describes *dominium regale* as a government in which the king "may rule his peple bi suche lawes as he makyth hymself"; and a *dominium politicum et regale* as a government in which the king "may not rule his peple bi other lawes than such as thai assenten unto." [25] In the *De Natura Legis Naturae* Fortescue clarifies the nature of the limits put on the exercise of the king's authority in the *dominium politicum et regale* by saying that the king rules *secundum leges quas cives instituerunt* (according to laws which the citizens have instituted).[26] The past tense of *instituerunt* suggests, as Professor McIlwain rightly avers, that the laws

[24] Charles Plummer (ed.), *The Governance of England,* Oxford, 1885, p. 83.

[25] *Ibid.,* p. 109. Cited in McIlwain, *op. cit.,* p. 358.

[26] Thomas (Fortescue) Lord Clermont (ed.), *The Works of Sir John Fortescue, Knight,* London, 1869, vol. I, pt. I, chap. XVI, p. 77.

according to which the king rules are constitutional laws—laws tying the instruments by which the king acts.[27]

Not only is the constitutional form of the "mixed monarchy" designed to achieve effective leadership as well as stability; it is, in St. Thomas' view, the best safeguard against tyranny—better, of course, than monarchy not tempered, but a better safeguard too than the rule of the many. This latter position might appear implausible in view of the fact that the rule of the many, when perverted, goes into what St. Thomas himself agrees is the least bad of the bad forms of government—extreme democracy. And monarchy, when it becomes perverted, goes into what St. Thomas admits is the worst of the bad forms of government—tyranny. But it is precisely the mixture of the "royal" and "political" elements

---

[27] Professor McIlwain evidently had some misgivings on this point, for earlier in his book he had remarked that the "political" element in the mixed monarchy only substituted "the directive force of law for the king's unbridled will." (McIlwain, *op. cit.*, p. 362.) Subsequently, however, he acknowledges that the limitations on the king's will "were considered to be, and actually were in some degree legal and practical and not merely 'moral,' truly coercive and not simply a 'bridle.'" (*Ibid.*, pp. 365–366.) Indeed, he then proceeds to give as excellent an account of the legal character of these restraints as could be wished for: "One of the best proofs that these limitations . . . actually were legal . . . and not merely 'moral' . . . is the fact that the sanction of these limitations did not rest in 'legalized rebellion' alone, but often lay to some extent also within the power of the officials of the state and was actually exercised by them in cases where they were convinced that the 'absolute' power of the king in administration had exceeded its bound and trenched upon the customary rights of the people. This would naturally appear most clearly in a control over royal enactments actually exercised by those officials or bodies whose participation was a regular and necessary part of the formalities of promulgation. In this way monarchy was more or less restricted 'by tying the instruments it was to act by.' In England, for example, this 'tying' was ultimately brought about by the requirement that all 'statutes' must be made by the king with the cooperation of the Lords and Commons. In France, we have numerous proofs of the practical effectiveness of such checks, in the refusal of the Parliament of Paris and of other *Parlements* in the realm to register ordinances of the king. Without registration, it was held, no royal ordinance was binding. . . . This requirement of registration was a very real, even though incomplete check upon the king, a check that was external and even 'constitutional' in character." (*Ibid.*)

that gives the mixed regime its peculiar advantage. In the first place, St. Thomas argues, monarchy, even when not tempered, does not proceed at once to tyranny, and if, indeed, the final consequences of its degeneration are worse than those of a degenerate democracy, its first effects are not. In the first stage of tyranny some particular good of the subjects is affected, but the general good of the peace of the community is not destroyed; whereas when a democracy degenerates it very soon is marked by dissensions that disrupt the good of peace. The chance of avoiding the path to tyranny under a mixed monarchy is enhanced by the presence of the "political" element, and indeed is greater than the simple democratic form provides: A government of the many degenerates into tyranny not less but perhaps more frequently than a monarchy. When on account of there being many rulers, dissensions arise in such a government, it often happens that the power of one preponderates, and he then usurps the government of the multitude for himself.[28] This has its explanation fundamentally in the peculiarly fragile and substitute character of the rule of law as it is specifically embodied in the simple democratic principle—which, as we saw in our consideration of Aristotle's doctrine, is relied upon in the most superficial and legalistic fashion to preserve the good of society. Aristotle specially designates the rule of the many as "the rule of law" precisely to indicate that law is present in such a community not as in one who rules and measures but as in one who needs to be ruled and measured. And indeed it is a modern fact that totalitarian governments have had a broadly popular base.[29] On the other hand, the true spirit

---

[28] *De Regimine Principum*, v. In D'Entrèves, *op. cit.*, p. 25.

[29] See Carlton J. H. Hayes, "The Novelty of Totalitarianism in the History of Western Civilization," *Proceedings of the American Philosophical Society*, vol. 82, no. 1, 1940. Prof. John H. Hallowell observes appositely of the point we are dealing with that "The Nazi regime was sometimes described in the early days of the regime, as a personal dictatorship and it was thought that if Hitler could be eliminated the regime would collapse. . . . This explanation . . . was a gross oversimplification of reality. It ignored the fact that despite the personal magnetism and daemonic energy of Hitler the Nazi movement rested upon a broad base. We refused for a long time to recognize the popularity of the movement since, consciously or sub-con-

of modern representative government is rather to be traced not to the simple principle of the rule of the many, but to the principles of Aristotle's middle-class government and St. Thomas' mixed regime. As Prof. Ernest Barker has acutely observed, the means devised by England in the seventeenth and eighteenth centuries to ensure greater responsibility to national opinion ought to be looked upon as "a lesson in the art of preserving monarchy" [30]—intending not so much the literal sense of the word as the proper Aristotelian sense of "royal" which signifies the perfection of the governing principle among freemen.

This becomes clear if we examine the philosophical roots of the doctrine of the mixed monarchy. We should recall that Aristotle had himself described the virtuous man's rule over himself as "royal *and* political." This he did by way of indicating the relatively "free" nature of the sense appetites that are ruled by the reason. But the "justice" that may be said to be established by the virtuous man's rule over himself is merely "metaphorical": Justice, properly speaking, because it implies some equality and independence, denotes the relation of one thing to another and must needs be between beings capable of action.[31] Hence justice, properly speaking, is only in one man toward another. Now freemen— as distinguished, in Aristotle's doctrine, from the so-called natural slave—are not instruments of another but are fitted by nature to have the disposal of themselves; and so there can be justice be-

---

sciously, we suspected that if true it would challenge one of our most cherished illusions, namely, that a government founded upon the consent of the governed could never be inhuman, illiberal, or dictatorial. The optimistic conception of human nature upon which this illusion was based would be severely challenged if we had to admit that large numbers of people could willingly condone the brutal things which the Nazi regime did. But the facts we soon came to realize were otherwise. . . . Technically, the Nazi regime was legally voted into power which vividly illustrates that legal barriers, contrary to the nineteenth-century liberal belief, are no bulwark against tyranny." (*Main Currents in Modern Political Thought*, Holt, Rinehart and Winston, Inc., New York, 1950, pp. 596–597.)

[30] Barker, *Essays on Government*, Oxford, 1951, p. 2.

[31] *Summa Theol.* II.II.Q.58. a.2.C.

tween them not merely as men but as freemen, that is to say, as belonging to the political community: For the freeman, as a subject, is not the instrument of the ruler.[32] Because they have the disposal of themselves, the rule that they introduce among themselves is—as we have seen—not accomplished without their taking counsel among themselves and is not continued without their being taken into counsel by the government that they establish. A slave, to be sure, is not capable of being taken into counsel insofar as he is a slave (for thus he is the instrument of his master), but a freeman must be taken into counsel because as a subject he is not the instrument of the ruler. Thus the free subject by virtue of the free nature which gives him disposal of himself shares in the prudence of the *ruler as such* by being taken into counsel in the formulating of law, in the determining of policy: He is "re-presented" by the ruler as the slave is not by the master. We distinguish, as both St. Thomas and Aristotle do, between "common political prudence," which is in all subjects and enables them to govern themselves in their own individual acts in accordance with the governance of the ruler, and "legislative" or "reignative" prudence, which is the virtue proper to the ruler.[33] St. Thomas' teaching is that more than common political prudence is required of the free subject, for as a freeman having the disposal of himself, he shares in the legislative prudence of the ruler by being taken into counsel in the formulating of law. Indeed, a free people, St. Thomas tells us, are capable of legislating for themselves, but— for reasons that we have observed—the purely democratic or political form is defective in legislative prudence; it is perfected in the degree to which it is made to share in "kingly" government.[34] Thus it is that St. Thomas concludes:

[32] See *Summa Theol.* I.Q.96 a.4, II.II.Q.57 a.4 ad. 1,2.

[33] "Of wisdom concerned with the city, the practical wisdom which plays a controlling part is legislative wisdom, while that which is related to this as particulars to their universal is known by the general name 'political wisdom'; this has to do with action and deliberation, for a decree is a thing to be carried out in the form of an individual act." (*Ethics* VI.1141b.24–26. Cf. *Politics* III.1277b.28; and *In III Politics* lect.3.)

[34] *Summa Theol.* II.II.Q.50 a.1.C ad. 2,3.

Two points are to be observed concerning the right ordering of rulers in a state or nation. One is that all should take some share in the government. . . . The other point is to be observed in respect of the kinds of government, or the different ways in which the constitutions are established. For whereas these differ in kind, as the Philosopher states, nevertheless, the first place is held by a *kingdom,* where the power of government is vested in one, and *aristocracy,* which signifies government by the best, where the power of government is vested in a few. Accordingly, the best form of government is in a state or kingdom, wherein one is given the power to preside over all, while under him are others having governing powers. And yet a government of this kind is shared by all, both because all are eligible to govern, and because the rulers are chosen by all. For this is the best form of polity, being partly kingdom, since there is one at the head of all; partly aristocracy, insofar as a number of persons are set in authority; partly democracy, i.e., government by the people, insofar as the rulers can be chosen from the people, and the people have the right to choose their rulers.[35]

In this passage St. Thomas speaks of tempering the rule of the one best qualified man, first by making him responsible to the people through the elective process, and secondly by setting up a political body having governing powers under the one who "presides over all." And in another passage he specifies this second means: The ruler is to be responsible to the people through the ratifying process—"of law sanctioned by the Lords and Commons," which, he says, is the law proper to "the best form of government." [36]

[35] *Ibid.* Q.105 a.1.C.

[36] *Ibid.* Q.95 a.4.C. We have alluded to the uncertainty that Professor McIlwain experiences with the notion of the "mixed regime" of St. Thomas. In one place McIlwain says that "the political" element in mixed monarchy only substituted "the directive force of law for the king's unbridled will" (McIlwain, *op. cit.,* p. 362.), while in another place he admits that the limitations on the king's will in medieval monarchy "were considered to be, and actually were in some degree legal and practical and not merely 'moral,' truly coercive and not simply a 'bridle.'" (*Ibid.,* pp. 365–366.) Professor McIlwain's uncertainty here comes from an original failure to see that in the virtuous man's "royal and political" rule over himself, the independence

The weakness of medieval constitutionalization did not lie in its refusal to divide governmental authority. The room it left for improvement was rather in the area of responsibility of the unified government to the consensus of the community. This may be seen from a consideration of the kind of situation created by a conflict between the king's absolute administrative authority and the procedural rights of the Parliament. In such an event the king's authority prevailed, but even here the assent of Parliament could not be dispensed with and was obtained—however much under formal protest—by the command of the king in person and by virtue of his supreme governmental authority. The disadvantage of this scheme was that the only way in which national opinion could ultimately assert itself when the king's policy was widely opposed was by rebellion or revolution. That is why, indeed, Professor Barker made the observation to which we have alluded —that the means devised by England in the seventeenth and eighteenth centuries to ensure greater responsibility to national opinion ought to be looked upon as "a lesson in the art of preserving monarchy." The parliamentary and cabinet system can be considered—if certain modifications were to be allowed for—as the lineal development of the medieval theory of constitutional government; for that system preserves the essential principle of undivided government directed by the best qualified man while making that government sensitive to popular consensus.

---

of the "free" appetites in relation to the governing reason comes precisely from the fact that the power and operation of the sense appetites do not derive from the governing (rational) principle but from the law of man's nature as *rational animal,* from the way he is constituted by nature. Similarly, the right of freemen to share in the government is not derived from the government: It derives from the constitution of a community of freemen, whose participation in "legislative prudence" is incorporated in the positive law of the constitution. Nor does this sharing divide the exercise of governmental authority: The king, in the mixed monarchy, as in the unmixed, is *legibus solutus* with respect to the civil law; but in the mixed monarchy he is under not merely the natural moral law but under the positive law of the constitution which fixes the mode of exercise of his authority by establishing the participation of the citizens in formulating the civil law.

Consent and possibility:
intrinsic limits on positive law

We must notice finally that the canon of consent, based on man's moral freedom, and the canon of possibility, based on his physical freedom, carry intrinsic limitations on positive law. Aristotle had defined positive law as the "legal part" of political justice, of which the other part is natural—"having the same force everywhere and . . . not such by people thinking this or that." [37] Positive law does indeed, as part of its function, declare natural right, but it does not establish it.[38] Its main function is to declare the "legal just," that "which is originally indifferent, but when it has been laid down is not indifferent, *e.g.*, that a prisoner's ransom shall be a mina, or that a goat and not two sheep shall be sacrificed. . . ." [39] For positive law derives from the natural law not in the way of conclusions from its first principles, but by way of determination of these common notions.[40] It derives from the natural law in such fashion simply that what it prescribes may not of itself be contrary to natural right. In its function of establishing the legal just, human law is a *product* of the practical reason

---

[37] *Ethics* V.1134b.18.

[38] ". . . a thing becomes just in two ways: first by the very nature of the case, and this is called *natural right*, secondly by some agreement between men, and this is called *positive right*. Now laws are written for the purpose of manifesting both these rights, but in different ways. For the written law does indeed contain natural right, but it does not establish it, for the latter derives its force, not from the law but from nature: whereas the written law both contains positive right, and establishes it by giving it force of authority." (*Summa Theol.* II.II.Q.60 a.5.C.)

[39] *Ethics* V.1134b.22.

[40] "But it must be noted that something may be derived from the natural law in two ways: first, as a conclusion from principles; secondly, by way of a determination of certain common notions. The first way is like to that by which, in the sciences, demonstrated conclusions are drawn from the principles; while the second is likened to that whereby, in the arts, common forms are determined to some particular. Thus, the craftsman needs to determine the common form of a house to the shape of this or that particular house. . . ." (*Summa Theol.* I.II.Q.95 a.2.C.)

and its dependence on natural law is only one of the properties that its structure must take account of. Human law falls short of the natural law's participation in the objective order of essences that is the natural law,[41] for it is applied to very refractory material, to the common condition of men. As we have seen, law as a measure and rule must be homogeneous with what it measures, and human law as a work of the practical reason ought to be imposed on men according to their condition:

Now human law is framed for the multitude of human beings, the majority of whom are not perfect in virtue. Therefore human laws do not forbid all vices, from which the virtuous abstain, but only the more grievous vices, from which it is possible for the majority to abstain; and chiefly those that are injurious to others, without the prohibition of which human society could not be maintained. Thus human law prohibits murder, theft, and the like.[42]

The purpose of human law is to lead men to virtue, not suddenly, but gradually. Therefore it does not lay upon the multitude of imperfect men the burdens of those who are already virtuous, *viz.*, that they should abstain from all evil. Otherwise these imperfect ones, being unable to bear such precepts, would break out into yet greater evil.[43]

There is, then, for St. Thomas a distinction between the juridical order and the moral order. The purpose of law is indeed, as he says, "to make men good," but the good which the law can achieve is the human good of a multitude of persons the majority of whom are not perfect in virtue.[44] It is enough, then, for the com-

---

[41] *Summa Theol.* I.II.Q.96 a.2. ad 3.

[42] *Ibid.* a.2.C.

[43] *Ibid.* ad 2.

[44] "Human law aims at one part of the moral order, the good of justice, whereby is furthered the good of political society. It is through man's social nature that law connects with the moral order, regulating him with respect to other individuals and the common good. His own moral integrity is of no *immediate* interest to the law except as it touches on justice. The law will not bother him be he ever so concupiscent until he upsets the common life. The legislator does not seek an individual's moral virtue as the good of that individual in the way a parent seeks the moral good of his child. If the

mon good of the state "that the citizens (other than the rulers) be so far virtuous that they obey the commands of their rulers." [45] It is enough—that is, *more does not come under the precept of the law*. But it is not the end at which the law aims: for the virtuous performance of virtuous acts "is the end at which every lawgiver aims." [46] St. Thomas is not saying, then, that the common good is subordinate to the private good of the individual, as if one's private good consisted in the virtuous performance of acts of virtue. On the contrary, he is saying that the end which the law seeks is a common good predicated not on force and fear of the law but on a free advancing to the perfection of the virtues directed to the common good of each and all. What law accomplishes is an extrinsic and remote disposing of the citizen for inward growth in the virtues; force and fear only supply motives for regulating the passions and developing true virtue. The ultimate aim of the law is accomplished only through one's interior freedom. That a whole people have "a sense of moderation and responsibility" [47] depends essentially on a free commitment to the ends appointed by the natural law.

The divine positive law and constitutional liberty

We have seen that beyond the first common principles of natural law, certainty in the mind's grasp of its precepts cannot be de-

---

law aims to make Socrates temperate and brave, it is not with a view to his own everlasting crown. It is so that he will not become publicly drunk or panic in battle. All the virtues admit some connection with legal justice and the law wants them not as goods for Socrates (which they are) but for the common good in which Socrates shares." (Dolan, "Natural Law and Modern Jurisprudence," p. 232.) (Italics added.)

[45] *Summa Theol.* I.II.Q.92 a.1 ad 3.

[46] *Ibid.* Q.96 a.3 ad 2. Indeed, of the ruler true virtue is required. See *Ibid.* Q.92 a.1 ad 3.

[47] *Ibid.* I.II.Q.97 a.1.C.

pended upon. And the common principles themselves, as applied to particular action, can be blotted out of the conscience.[48] If then, as we have been saying, it is part of the very structure of human law, in its declaring of natural law principles, to fall short of the natural law's participation in the objective order of essences that is the natural law, and if the natural law itself is uncertain as regards the mind's grasp of those precepts that are not naturally known though objectively certain, it follows that neither the positive law nor the natural law are effective norms for liberty. The end of a political community, the end at which "every lawgiver aims" (but which does not come under the precept of human law) can be adequately assured only with the help of a law which does not suffer the deficiencies of human and natural law— the divine positive law. Hence St. Thomas:

Besides the natural and the human law it was necessary for the directing of human conduct to have a divine law . . . because by reason of the uncertainty of human judgment . . . different people form different judgments on human acts. . . . In order, therefore, that man may know without any doubt what he ought to do and what he ought to avoid, it was necessary for man to be directed in his proper acts by a law given by God, for it is certain that such a law cannot err.

[Again] because man can make laws in those matters of which he is competent to judge. But man is not competent to judge of interior movements, that are hidden, but only of exterior acts which are observable; and yet for the perfection of virtue it is necessary for man to conduct himself rightly in both kinds of acts. Consequently, human law could not sufficiently curb and direct interior acts, and it was necessary for this purpose that a divine law should supervene.

[Again] because as Augustine says, human law cannot punish or forbid all evil deeds, since, while aiming at doing away with all evils, it would do away with many good things, and would hinder the advance of the common good, which is necessary for human living. In order, therefore, that no evil might remain unforbidden and unpunished, it was necessary for the divine law to supervene, whereby all sins are forbidden.[49]

[48] *Ibid.* Q.94 a.6.C.
[49] *Ibid.* Q.91 a.4.C.

These considerations of the role of divine positive law in preserving the structure of constitutional rule by supplying the deficiencies of both natural and human law as norms for liberty, bring us, as it were, full circle in the appreciation of the significance that St. Thomas attributes to Christianity in politics and political philosophy. The analysis of constitutional liberty showed that the civil law may not force the highest virtues on men nor force men to perform virtuously the acts which it prescribes: The perfection of liberty must come through a law that, by reaching the interior movements of the soul, forbids and prescribes, rewards and punishes without compelling. And this perfection of freedom is the end at which every lawgiver aims. Fortunate then, St. Thomas says, is the community that comes by this wisdom. It will "issue orders . . . for its sake, but not to it," determining nothing and compelling no one. Indeed Aristotle had called the political life "god-like" and had done so by reason of the measure in which it imitates the Divine freedom which freely causes the goodness of order in the whole universe and which draws all things to itself, the ultimate essential goodness. Now it is this goodness of order (which defines the common good) that the divine positive law alone can bring to perfection: for the good to which this law directs man is that "supereminent principle of wisdom" by which "the whole man is perfected and made good." It alone reaches the individual in that which is most determinate and proper, most profound and obscure in him—the interior movements of the soul. Unlike civil law which, finding the common denominator, extends indifferently to all (*communiter proponitur*)[50] and unlike the natural law, which reflects an objective order of essences, the divine positive law brings the perfect order of the common good by extending to individuals in their very diversity, in their being not all alike. In St. Thomas' doctrine, the divine law, by providing the ultimate safeguard against mere conformity and conventionality, makes possible the ultimate verification of the meaning of constitutional liberty.

[50] *In X Ethics* lect.14.

part two

the modern theory of politics

In things that relate to defect, intensity depends not on approach to something supreme, but in receding from that which is perfect; because therein consists the very notion of privation and defect. Wherefore the less a thing recedes from that which stands first, the less intense it is; and the result is that at first we always find some small defect, which afterwards increases as it goes on.

St. Thomas Aquinas

VI

Machiavelli and the new politics:
the primacy of art

The structure of political thought in the Greek-medieval tradition was built on the subordination of practical science to theoretic science and, within the sphere of practical science, on the subordination of art to prudence. The very essence of constitutional liberty was held to depend on the maintenance of these relations. The modern theory of politics begins by reversing the order between prudence and art: It will seek a liberty that is proper not to prudence but to art, and it will define the good by a judgment proper to art—by conformity simply of what the prince actually produces with what he intends to produce. The opening phase of modern political thought avows an indifference to the morally good; it frees man from an obligation to a moral order founded on man's given nature. But it does not yet think of creating a new morality. When Niccolo Machiavelli, the father of modern politics, "writes that the prince must learn how not to be good, he is perfectly aware that not to be good is to be bad." [1] Indeed the success of the new artist-prince

[1] Maritain, "The End of Machiavellianism," *The Review of Politics,* vol. 4, no. 1, p. 7, January, 1942.

was very largely made to depend on his opportunity to operate on and to exploit the given moral basis of civilized tradition. But if Machiavelli does not think of creating a new morality, independent of past tradition, he anticipates this task of the second phase of modern political thought. For if he knows that not to be good is to be bad, he nonetheless thinks that goodness, as traditionally understood, has been the cause of political debility. It is precisely the ultimate task of the "good" artist-prince to shape the matter of the given moral basis of civilized tradition into a new morality. The second phase of modern political thought begins when this objective is seen not as something to be imposed by the wielder of arbitrary power but rather as springing from a new sense of nature: Nature itself will be freed from all past metaphysical and theological conceptions. This second phase seeks a new moral basis for society and does so by reversing the order between theoretic science and practical science (in which art already has the ascendancy). It will seek a liberty that is proper neither to prudence nor to human art but to divine art (for divine art had always been considered the ultimate principle of the works of nature); and it will define the good in terms not of an end which man seeks but rather in terms of the very *being* of man which becomes the principle from which all things are made—all things humanly significant, which becomes the totality of significance. It will become impossible—as Halévy says in speaking of nineteenth-century philosophic radicalism—for the individual not to act morally. Of the many spokesmen for the new morality, none will give it so final and clear a voice as Karl Marx: "Socialism," he will proclaim, "takes its departure from the *theoretically and practically sensible conscience* of man, in nature, considered as *being*." [2]

Machiavelli and the Renaissance

That the Renaissance is not a mere *flatus vocis*, that the term corresponds to a historical reality, is undeniable. If we were in need of

---

[2] Marx, *Oekonomische-philosophische Manuskript*, p. 125.

proving this reality it would be enough to summon two classical witnesses and to point to two works: Galileo's *Dialogues Concerning Two
New Sciences* and Machiavelli's *Prince*. To connect these two works
may, at first sight, appear to be very arbitrary. They deal with entirely
diverse subjects. . . . Nevertheless the two books have something in
common. In both of them we find a certain trend of thought which
marks them as two great and crucial events in the history of modern
civilization. . . . What Galileo gave in his *Dialogues* and what Machiavelli gave in his *Prince* were really "new sciences." "My purpose,"
said Galileo, "is to set forth a very new science dealing with a very
ancient subject. . . ." Machiavelli would have been perfectly entitled
to speak of his book in the same way. Just as Galileo's Dynamics became the foundation of our modern science of nature, so Machiavelli
paved a new way to political science.[3]

What is the trend of thought that Cassirer says is common to
Galileo and Machiavelli? What was the novelty common to the
new sciences of physics and politics? If we wish to find this common element we must consider the fact that the revival of learning
in the fifteenth century differed from its predecessors in that it
was an artistic rather than a philosophical movement. To connect
the new physics with art may indeed appear as arbitrary as con-
necting the new physics with the new politics. But this *is* their
connection: The new politics is related to the new physics by
their common relation to art. Once we understand that the primacy accorded art in the fifteenth-century revival of learning was
itself a radically new philosophical position, we shall begin to
have an insight into the trend of thought which marks the works
of both Galileo and Machiavelli as crucial events in the history
of modern civilization.

Art and the new physics

In his preface to the second edition of the *Critque of Pure
Reason*, Immanuel Kant, speaking of the new physics, says:

---

[3] Cassirer, *The Myth of the State*, pp. 129–30.

When Galileo experimented with balls of a definite weight on the inclined plane, when Torricelli caused air to sustain a weight which he had calculated beforehand to be equal to that of a definite column of water, or when Stahl, at a later period, converted metals into lime, and reconverted lime into metal, by the addition and subtraction of certain elements; a light broke upon all natural philosophers. They learned that reason only perceives that which it produces after its own design; that it must not be content to follow as it were, in the leading-strings of nature, but must proceed in advance with principles of judgment according to unvarying laws, and compel nature to reply to its questions. For accidental observations, made according to no preconceived plan, cannot be united under a necessary law. But it is this that reason seeks for and requires. It is only the principles of reason which can give to concordant phenomena the validity of laws, and it is only when experiment is directed by these rational principles that it can have any real utility. Reason must approach nature with the view, indeed, of receiving information from it, not, however, in the character of a pupil, who listens to all that his master chooses to tell him, but in that of a judge, who compels the witnesses to reply to those questions which he himself thinks fit to propose. To this single idea must the revolution be ascribed, by which, after groping in the dark for so many centuries, natural science was at length conducted into the path of certain progress.[4]

To the "single idea" that "reason only perceives [in nature] that which it produces after its own design" must be ascribed, Kant points out, the emancipation of the new physics. Now the explanation of this "single idea" lies indeed in the distinction that Aristotle had made between the kind of knowledge that we have in the philosophy of nature and the kind that is acquired in "dialectical" knowledge, or what we today call the experimental natural sciences. For Aristotle the philosophy of nature is only the first part of natural doctrine. As St. Thomas warns us, Aristotle's *Physics* and his treatise *On the Soul* constitute only a very general introduction to the more detailed studies of nature.[5] The concept

[4] Immanuel Kant, *Critique of Pure Reason*, 2d ed., trans. by N. K. Smith, Macmillan & Co., Ltd., London, 1933, pref., p. 20.

[5] *In I Meteorol.* lect.1.

of motion, for example, in the *Physics*, however certain it is, is extremely general and indeterminate: It does not account for the motion of the elephant. The treatment of color in no way accounts for the whiteness of snow. Beyond even the "dialectical" questions of Aristotle's specialized treatises in natural science lies the domain of the experimental sciences which complete our knowledge of nature. Now the kind of knowledge obtained in the experimental sciences Aristotle called "dialectical" because it never reveals a necessary connection between the terms of its propositions: The information nature gives us here is not given us, as Kant puts it, "in the character of a pupil who listens to all that his master chooses to tell him." Nature tells us that snow and white are presented together to the senses, but if nature chooses to tell us (as she appears to do) that all snow must necessarily be white, we must not listen to her. The proposition "snow is white" is not for us a real universal, for it cannot go beyond the particular sense experience of the fact.

. . . to the extent that natural doctrine approaches things in their concrete natures we depend more and more upon sensible experience. The propositions acquired . . . announce only what appears to sense. Snow and white are presented together to the sense but we do not see why the whiteness should be a property of snow. Even though all the snow which is presented in our experience is white, we do not see *by this experience* that black snow would be something contradictory in itself. Even supposing that black snow is a contradiction in nature, experience could never show this. We should have to prove it by something other than experience. Thus we see that the proposition "snow is white" is not for us a real universal because it remains tied up essentially with the sense experience of the fact. . . .

A proposition is universal only if it can be seen by the intellect as universal. This means that we must know why it is, and why it cannot be otherwise than it is.[6]

Experimental science, then, has no concern with the truly universal propositions that are proper to the philosophy of nature, the

[6] R. A. Kocourek, *An Introduction to the Philosophy of Nature,* North Central Publishing Co., St. Paul, Minn., 1948, pp. 174–175.

first part of natural doctrine. The regularity, however, of our experience of the whiteness of snow suggests certainly that there is some determinate reason for its being white. We use this regularity as a substitute for a real "why," a real universal, and we posit the whiteness of snow *as if* it were a universal. We may then proceed to use such a proposition in searching for the real cause of the connection between "snow" and "white." This search is now carried on with the aid of "hypotheses" formulated to "save the appearances"—the domain understood by our sensible impressions. These hypotheses, St. Thomas points out in speaking of hypotheses of Aristotle in astronomy, "are not necessarily true, because although by making such suppositions we save the appearances, it is not necessary to say that these suppositions are true. Perhaps the appearances about the stars can be saved in some other way not yet understood by men." [7] It is hypotheses, then, that "our reason produces after its own design," as Kant says, and compels nature to reply to. When experiment confirms our hypotheses, we are flattered to find ourselves "artists," as it were, who have made the "designs" which we recognize in nature. But the reason for this is that we increasingly share in the divine art by which the universe is made. The fundamental reason for the dialectical character of natural science is given by St. Thomas in his Prologue to the Commentary on the *Politics*.[8]

[7] *In II De Caelo* lect.17.

[8] "As the Philosopher teaches in Book II of the *Physics,* art imitates nature. The reason for this is that actions and their effects stand in the same relationship to one another as do principles among themselves. Now the human intellect is the principle of all things created by art, and, at the same time, itself derives in a certain sense from the divine intellect which is the principle of natural things. So works of art necessarily imitate the works of nature, and the processes of art are modeled upon those found in nature. . . . So the human intellect, which obtains the light of intelligence from the divine intellect, must go for inspiration in what it does to the architecture of nature, and imitate that as its model. So the Philosopher says that if art were to succeed in creating the things that are in nature, it would have to operate in the same way as nature itself; and conversely if nature were to create things which are proper to art, it would act according to the model of the latter." (In *Aquinas: Selected Political Writings,* D'Entrèves, p. 195.)

Nature itself is said to be an *opus intelligentiae* (a work of intelligence), and, as we have had occasion to note, St. Thomas defines nature as *ratio cuiusdam artis, scilicet divinae, indita rebus, qua ipsae res moventur ad finem determinatum* (the reason of a certain art, namely, the divine, written into things, whereby they are moved to a determinate end).[9] Experimental science is a getting closer to the art of Him who made the universe. It is because the structure of the universe depends upon the art of Him who made it that experimental science gets away from the "givenness" of things as "formed" to things as "formable." There is a parallel in the case of our knowledge of a work of architecture: The more we get away from generalities of the structure, e.g., that a house will have roof, walls, entrance, the more our knowledge depends on the freedom of the architect. There is obscurity concerning the particulars of the house because of the liberty of the architect. This is why, as we have already had occasion to observe, in *The Parts of Animals* Aristotle speaks of physics as a *practical* science, for in the experimental sciences we see the universe as something "constructed" by the divine art.[10] That we are not ourselves the artists and masters of nature is clear from the following considerations: First, that the hypotheses which we formulate to discover the "why" of the sensible phenomena are themselves suggested by the regularity of nature which conveys some "reason." Secondly, the hypotheses are designed to explain "the domain understood by the sensible impressions" and must conform to these.[11] We ourselves do not determine the resem-

[9] *In II Physics* lect.14.

[10] I.640a. See above, p. 36, n. 13.

[11] "Physical concepts are free creations of the human mind, and are not, however it may seem, *uniquely* determined by the external world. In our endeavor to understand reality we are somewhat like a man trying to understand the mechanism of a closed watch. He sees the face and the moving hands, even hears its ticking, but he has no way of opening the case. If he is ingenious he may form some picture of a mechanism which would be responsible for all the things he observes, but he may never be quite sure his picture is the only one which could explain his observations. He will never be able to compare his picture with the real mechanism and he cannot even imagine the possibility or the meaning of such a comparison. But he cer-

blance that the hypotheses bear to the truth. Thirdly, even when a hypothesis is confirmed by experiment, it is not thereby "true" rather than "false," but "good" rather than "bad": for while it saves the sensible appearances, other hypotheses might do so as well.[12] It is not by the hypotheses of the botanist that vegetables are made. The botanist must always come to the gardener for the carrots that he wants to eat. The carrots of scientific botany are not edible. The physicist, too, for whom the only "real" world is the world of protons, neutrons, and "mostly emptiness," will never succeed in exorcising the familiar world: "The frank realization that physical science is concerned with a world of shadows is one of the most significant of recent advances." [13]

Now what the universal principles and common notions of the philosophy of nature are to natural science, the "ends" of human life are to practical science.[14] So that an experimental science of politics would proceed as do the experimental natural sciences, from first common principles.[15] Aristotle's *Constitution of Athens*

---

tainly believes that, as his knowledge increases, his picture of reality will become simpler and simpler and will explain a wider and wider range of his sensuous impressions." (Albert Einstein and Leopold Infeld, *The Evolution of Physics*, Simon and Schuster, Inc., New York, 1942, p. 33.)

[12] "The goal of the physical sciences is in no sense to attain to an absolute truth: on the contrary, the progress of these sciences has more and more shown the provisionary, approximative, and to a high degree arbitrary character of all scientific construction. The physical sciences do not, then, constitute a 'science' in the Aristotelian sense of the word, but only a 'dialectical knowledge,' that is to say, the discussion of consequences of certain principles posed as having verisimilitude. However, if one may not say that a physical theory is 'true' or 'false' in the philosophic sense, it remains nonetheless true that there are 'good' and 'bad' theories. The first are those whose consequences are not contradicted by experience. . . ." (Franco Rasetti, *La Méthode des science physiques*, Laval University, Quebec, 1942, p. 10.)

[13] Eddington, *The Nature of the Physical World*, p. xiv.

[14] *Physics* II.200a.21; *Summa Theol.* I.Q.82. a.1.

[15] We may observe with Eddington that ". . . the whole scientific inquiry starts from the familiar world and in the end it must return to the familiar world; but the part of the journey over which the physicist has charge is in foreign territory." (Eddington, *The Nature of the Physical World*, p. xiii.) ". . . although we try to make a clean start, rejecting instinctive or tradi-

is a kind of beginning at an experimental political science; it does not ignore the general principles of his *Politics*. But we must note that there is a compelling reason why practical science should have its first principles always in mind: The physicist can safely and properly ignore the "familiar world" in his quest for knowledge of its construction for the simple reason that the physical universe is already made. But the world of human culture and civilization—the object of practical science—is, on the contrary, a world that has to be constructed: not from nothing, but, unlike the familiar world of physics, there is nothing there that cannot be exorcised. What is there are the ends of human life (including, incidentally, truth, which is the end of the theoretic intellect), and the natural associations that help guarantee the ends of living. These first principles of practical science are unchangeable in the sense that the liberty of contrariety whereby they can be exorcised is not a mark of the perfection of human nature. Indeed, as Aristotle says, it is vice that exorcises them. "Virtue and vice respectively preserve and destroy the first principles, and in actions the final cause is the first principle as the hypotheses are in mathematics." [16] Now then, when Machiavelli lays it down as the cardinal rule of successful politics that the prince must know how to be bad as well as how to be good, he is removing from the experimental part of the science the common experience of first principles, from which like common experience in natural doctrine, the physicist never frees himself—though the physicist is properly not directly concerned with it. The illusion of the pro-

---

tional interpretations of experience and accepting only the kind of knowledge which can be inferred by strictly scientific methods, we cannot cut ourselves loose altogether from the familiar story teller. We lay down the principle that he is always to be mistrusted; but we cannot do without him in science. What I mean is this: we rig up some delicate physical experiment with galvanometers, micrometers, etc., specially designed to eliminate the fallibility of human perceptions; but in the end we must trust to our perceptions to tell us the result of the experiment. Even if the apparatus is self-recording we employ our senses to read the records." (Sir Arthur Eddington, *New Pathways in Science*, Cambridge University Press, New York, 1935, pp. 2–3.)

[16] *Ethics* VII.1151a.15.

priety of this same indifference to common experience in the moral world is due to Machiavelli's failure to notice the profound difference between the world of theoretic science and that of practical science. We see, then, that the ultimate point in common between the new physics and the new politics is their unconcern, in their aspect of arts, for the familiar world of common experience. This unconcern, proper enough for experimental natural science, is improperly carried over by Machiavelli as part of the experimental character of political science. But to pursue a systematic indifference to moral ends and purposes means the impossibility of constructing our moral and political life. Much as Professor Cassirer admires Machiavelli as a "liberator" of the human spirit, he is compelled to take notice of this crucial point and to enter a caveat in the course of praising him; a caveat for which he does not feel the same need in his praise of Galileo. Speaking of the immediate outcome of the new politics, he writes:

With Machiavelli we stand at the gateway of the modern world. The desired end is attained; the state has won its full autonomy. Yet this result has had to be bought dearly. The state is entirely independent; but at the same time it is completely isolated. The sharp knife of Machiavelli's thought has cut off all the threads by which in former generations the state was fastened to the organic whole of human existence. The political world has lost its connection not only with religion or metaphysics but also with all the other forms of man's ethical and cultural life. It stands alone—in an empty space.[17]

To speak—as many scholars do—about the primacy of the political common good in Machiavelli, is indeed almost to talk about "empty space," for it is drained of the intelligible content that common moral experience, credited by all past thought, had given it.[18]

[17] Cassirer, *The Myth of the State,* p. 140.
[18] See J. W. Allen, *A History of Political Thought in the Sixteenth Century,* The Dial Press, Inc., New York, 1928, pp. 464–465; Allen H. Gilbert (ed.), *Machiavelli, The Prince and Other Works,* Packard & Co., Chicago, 1941, p. 15. Professor Gilbert writes of Machiavelli that "the chief of his political ideas is to be found in the traditional political conception of the common good."

The political thought of Machiavelli

Since more than a century ago the study of Machiavelli's writings has issued in a sharp reaction against the early conception of him as a purveyor of Medicean poison. The new estimate has been reached by an examination not of *The Prince* alone, but of all Machiavelli's works, and particularly by reading *The Prince* in the light of his *Discourses on Livy*.[19] The judgment that *The Prince* must be interpreted in the light of the *Discourses* is very sound; for, as Professor Allen has said, "the reverse process can lead to nothing but confusion."[20] *The Prince* is essentially a manual for tyrants, replete with the sagest observations on the stakes of the political game and with the nicest insights into the ways of success—from deceit and treachery to the uses, indeed, of classical virtue "carried about in its case like the fiddle of a virtuoso." The *Discourses,* while by no means lacking the deep cynicism of *The Prince,* is chiefly devoted to the history of the expansion of the Roman Republic and is distinguished by an unexpected enthusiasm for republican government and for the classical sense of the common good. It is obvious then that the *Discourses* would be quite unintelligible were *The Prince* to be taken as expressing the whole thought of Machiavelli. But if we read *The Prince* in the light of the *Discourses,* we can find a certain degree of intelligibility in Machiavelli's thought. The conclusion that modern scholarship has reached by this comparison of texts is that Machiavelli valued above all things the "common good" realized by a "free" people, and that his *Prince* was written with the objective of eliciting the aid of a strong man in bringing the Italian people out of their condition of political "corruption."

There can be no quarrel with this conclusion *as it is drawn:* for

[19] For both the *Discourses on the First Ten Books of Titus Livius* and *The Prince* I have used the translation by Luigi Ricci, revised by E. R. P. Vincent. These are printed in the "Modern Library, 1940" (edited by Max Lerner). Page references are to this edition.

[20] Allen, *op. cit.,* p. 464.

it is drawn by doing one's best with Machiavelli's texts. The point
for quarreling with the conclusion is its ignoring of grave difficulties about which nothing can be done so long as the investigator
confines himself to the texts of Machiavelli. A genuine understanding of Machiavelli's place in the history of political thought
can be had only by comparing his use of terms common to the
past tradition of political thought with their use by preceding
writers in the tradition. The essential difficulty in the way of
accepting the rehabilitated Machiavelli for the "old Nick" is
Machiavelli's basic and pervading notion of man's nature as
essentially antisocial and anarchical. After remarking that
"Machiavelli's sympathies were wholly republican," and that "one
of the finer traits in his cynical and repellent character is his faith
in the people," Professor Hearnshaw proceeds to obscure considerably his vindication by adding: "a faith . . . not very easy to
reconcile with his pessimistic estimate of individual human nature." [21] It is in the *Discourses* that Machiavelli gives as his own
the view of the origin and nature of society expressed in antiquity
by the sophists Thrasymachus and Glaucon: "Men act right only
upon compulsion, but from the moment they have the option and
liberty to commit wrong with impunity, then they never fail to
carry confusion and disorder everywhere." [22]

Now these "basic premises," as Professor Allen calls them, are
overlooked in the work of rehabilitating Machiavelli; and sound
scholarship is perfectly justified in omitting them for the simple
reason that if they are taken into account it is impossible to make
anything out of the *Discourses*. That is why I have said that one
can agree with the conclusion of modern scholarship about
Machiavelli *as that conclusion is drawn:* for again, it is drawn
only by doing one's best with Machiavelli's texts. But if we ask
ourselves in what this rehabilitation essentially consists, the answer can only be that it consists in a residue of traditional con-

---

[21] F. J. C. Hearnshaw, *The Social and Political Ideas of Some Great
Thinkers of the Renaissance and Reformation,* Barnes & Noble, Inc., New
York, 1932, p. 107. More than this, of course, Machiavelli insists that evil
is radical in man. (*Discourses,* bk. I, chap. 3; *The Prince,* chap. 23.)

[22] *Discourses,* bk. I, chap. 3, p. 118.

cepts which in Machiavelli are drained of their intelligible content. For if in one sense Machiavelli must be interpreted as espousing liberty, virtue, justice, and the common good, there remains the fact that these terms receive their worth and significance from nothing that Machiavelli wrote. Their value in the rehabilitated Machiavelli rests on the assumption (which in the conclusion of modern scholarship is left unexamined) that these terms retain in some way their traditional force when they have lost their traditional meaning. Modern scholarship stops short just at the point where it can say something significant about Machiavelli. Having extracted from his works the only reading that allows all of his writings to make sense together, and having observed that this reading of Machiavelli depends on traditional notions which Machiavelli merely employed without discussing, the inquirer is obligated to two further steps: first, to make an examination of the traditionally accepted sense of such terms as common good, virtue, liberty, etc., and secondly, to return for a final reading of Machiavelli with the intention (and now the ability) of discovering from all that Machiavelli had to say whether his verbal adherence to the traditional concepts carries with it an intelligibility equal to that attaching to these concepts as they were traditionally taken. There can be no legitimate protest against such a procedure, for it merely suggests that we should discover whether that is in fact true which has in fact been assumed.

Machiavelli himself is in no doubt about his break with the whole past tradition in political thought. It is his intention, he tells us, "to open a new route, which has not yet been followed by anyone." [23] Machiavelli's politics will reveal its true novelty, as I have suggested, at the point of its similarity with the new physics. For the Greek-Medieval tradition, nature is encountered in political and moral philosophy at two extremes: in the nature of man as rational animal and in the natural associations. It is between these two extremes that the field of voluntary action lies: The subject matter of moral and political philosophy is found in the actions, habits, and institutions which perfect and guarantee

---

[23] *Discourses*, bk. I, p. 103.

the ends of life. In the spirit of the new physics, Machiavelli adopts a systematic indifference to these manifestations of nature and the ends appointed by the natural reason, the securing of which by good acts, habits, and institutions had always been thought to constitute the legitimate "art" of politics. Ignoring the first principles of the science, Machiavelli's politics takes as its point of departure the power and passions of man considered not only in their original indetermination with respect to good and evil (Aristotle's liberty of contrariety) but as not being presupposed to an end that is truly good. Machiavelli takes the indetermination of the liberty of contrariety as constituting the essence of liberty, a liberty whereby man decides for himself the limits of his nature and the ends he will pursue.[24] Where Aristotle had said that the state does not make man, but taking him from nature, perfects him, Machiavelli proposes a political art that will extend to setting the limits of human nature, instructing man in the art of knowing how to be both good and bad. To see this clearly we have only to study Machiavelli's remarks on the relation between reason and the passions in man.

The traditional construction of the political virtues was founded, as we have seen, on the natural ordering of the sense appetites to the governing principle in man, which is his reason. Now for Machiavelli man's animal nature and his rational nature are considered to be two unrelated principles of action:

You must realize that there are two ways to fight. In one kind the laws are used, in the other force. The first is suitable to man, the

[24] This theme is expressed in the celebrated "Oration on the Dignity of Man," composed by Pico della Mirandola (1463–1494): In addressing man, God says: "The nature of all other beings is limited and constrained within the bounds of laws prescribed by Us. Thou, constrained by no limits, in accordance with thine own free will, shalt ordain for thyself the limits of thy nature. . . . With freedom of choice and with honor, as though the maker and molder of thyself, thou mayest fashion thyself in whatever shape thou shalt prefer. Thou shalt have the power to degenerate into the lower forms of life, which are brutish. Thou shalt have the power . . . to be reborn into the higher forms, which are divine." In *The Renaissance Philosophy of Man*, Ernst Cassirer, P. O. Kristeller, and J. H. Randall, Jr. (eds.) (Copyright, 1948, by The University of Chicago), p. 225.

second to animals. But because the first often falls short, one has to turn to the second. Hence a prince must know perfectly how to act like a beast and like a man. . . . To have as teacher one who is half beast and half man . . . means nothing else than that a prince needs to know how to use the qualities of both creatures.[25]

We must be careful to notice the implications of this view. By man's animal nature man acts like a beast, and by his rational nature he acts like a man. And "the one will not last long without the other." Man acts like a beast by virtue of his animal nature. But *to know how* to act like a beast requires more than mere animal nature. To have knowledge of how to act like a beast is to be clever at being a beast, to be more beastly than any beast: It is precisely to know how to act like a man. This is why Machiavelli's prince can have the qualities of several beasts at once: He can be lion and fox precisely because he is a man. Thus if it is by man's animal nature that he acts like a beast, he acts like a man by virtue of his capacity to make prudent use of the conduct of animals. This is inevitable in Machiavelli. Failing to perceive that man is substantially *rational animal*, he fails to see that the animal passions and appetites which are in man are ordered under the rational principle. He fails to see that there is a *right* desire, a *right* fear, a *right* use of force, all of which are properly attributable to man as man. Machiavelli thinks that to be forceful and to be fearful is to act in a mode suitable not to man but to beasts; and recognizing that force and fear are necessary, he advises his prince to know how to put the rational principle in the service of animal passion.[26]

All this is confirmed by what he has to say about the relation

[25] *The Prince*, chap. 18.

[26] There is to be noted here that complication which Jacques Maritain has pointed out. It is the complication arising from Machiavelli's "rough and elementary idea of moral science," which makes him fail to understand its "realist, experiential . . . character. Accordingly, what he calls vice and evil, and considers to be contrary to virtue and morality, may sometimes be only the authentically moral behavior of a just man engaged in the complexities of human life and of true ethics. . . ." (Maritain, "The End of Machiavellianism," p. 5.)

of law to force. Law, he tells us, is an instrument proper to man, and force is an instrument proper to animals.[27] But if law is proper to man, and if man acts like a man by virtue of his ability to make prudent use of animal conduct, it should follow that law is nothing more than a superior kind of force. And it does follow: for Machiavelli clearly establishes the essence of law in force when he says that law is one of the two ways of fighting, of which force is the other. ". . . there are two ways to fight, in one kind the laws are used and in the other force." [28] Therefore law, which, according to Machiavelli, is the product of man and not of animal, is one way of fighting. Here we see Machiavelli's sophistical notion of the foundation of society in a coercive contract entered into for the purpose of forcibly preventing man's natural tendency toward anarchy from expressing itself. The element of force is the essential element in law, which is to say that it is the determining element in man qua man and not merely in man qua animal. And we have just observed that as force is made the determining element of the rational principle, the rational principle is put at the service of force as exemplified by man's animal nature: What is Machiavelli's fox but the "virtue" of prudence put in the service of the lion?

It is evident how the traditional concept of virtue undergoes a transmutation into Machiavelli's *virtù* the new habit of skillful force proper to the "lion-fox." In the common tradition, moral virtue was understood as being constituted in its species by its position as an intermediate between the extremes of excess and defect; courage, for example, was opposed to both rashness and cowardice. With respect to courage one can be morally bad by being either rash or cowardly, for these two contraries constitute a single opposite to the kind of goodness in question. Now in what does Machiavelli's *virtù* consist? It consists in a habit of mind that enables one skillfully to turn "in whatever direction the winds of Fortune and variations of affairs require." [29] Indeed, "if

[27] *The Prince,* chap. 18.
[28] *Ibid.*
[29] *Ibid.*

one could change one's nature with time and circumstances fortune would never change." [30] This is the ideal "limit" toward which the prince tends in the mastery of both nature and chance. The artistic aspect of the prince's imitation of virtue is seen in his ability to practice now one extreme and now the other lying outside the intermediate, as when one would be rash and audacious at one moment and cowardly at another.[31] It is by art that he extends the limits of human nature. It is the irrelevance of "character" in the classical sense that fixes with absolute clarity the prince's virtue as being art and not prudence, of its resembling the intellectual habits of the theoretic sciences. Art is like the habits of the theoretic intellect, St. Thomas observes, because it is concerned simply with "the disposition of things considered by [it]" and not with the good perfective of man himself.[32]

As long as the geometrician demonstrates the truth, it matters not how his appetite is disposed, whether he be joyful or angry; . . . neither does this matter in a craftsman. And so art has the nature of a virtue in the same way as the speculative habits, insofar, namely, as neither art nor a speculative habit makes a good work as regards the use of the habit, which is distinctive of a virtue that perfects the appetite, but only as regards the ability to work well.[33]

What interests Machiavelli in Cesare Borgia is nothing in his character; it is simply the "ability to work well." As Cassirer has said, "the real source of Machiavelli's admiration was not the man himself but the structure of the new state that had been created by him." [34] He finds nothing to reprehend in the ruthlessness, the deceit, and cruelty of Borgia. What he deplores is simply the speculative error, the failure of the product to conform to the intention of the artist—the grave error of permitting Julius II,

---

[30] *Ibid.*, chap. 25.

[31] Machiavelli insists that the prince guard above all against a *reputation* for cowardice. (*Ibid.*, chap. 19.) I have said that the successful prince will carry classical virtue "in its case like the fiddle of a virtuoso."

[32] See *Summa Theol.* I.II.Q.57 as.3,4.

[33] *Ibid.*

[34] Cassirer, *The Myth of the State,* p. 167.

Borgia's chief enemy, to be chosen Pope after the death of Alexander VI. In his analysis of political actions, Machiavelli, as Spinoza says of him indeed, speaks as if human affairs were lines, planes, or solids. Like the physicist and the geometrician in their constructions, Machiavelli is interested only in the disposition of things and not at all in the disposition and habits that form character. Talleyrand—that practiced Machiavellian—in his celebrated comment on the execution of the Duke of Enghein by Napoleon Bonaparte spoke as a faithful disciple of Machiavelli: "It is more than a crime; it is a mistake." Machiavelli is indeed the father of the bewildering spectacle of the twentieth-century political trials with their curious "confessions"—curious because the crimes that are punished have nothing to do with moral culpability but with mistakes, with technical errors, judged as errors by the political art.[35] The new theory of politics is consistent with

[35] Cassirer, for reasons that we shall presently examine, considers Machiavelli to have been a liberator of the human spirit, and suggests that ". . . if *The Prince* is anything but a moral . . . treatise, it does not follow that, for this reason, it is an immoral book. Both judgments are equally wrong. *The Prince* is neither a moral nor an immoral book: it is simply a technical book. In a technical book we do not seek for rules of ethical conduct, of good or evil. It is enough if we are told what is useful or useless. . . . Machiavelli studied political actions in the same way as a chemist studies chemical reactions. . . . Vice and virtue are products like vitriol and sugar, and we should deal with them in the same cool and detached scientific spirit. That was exactly the method of Machiavelli." (*Ibid.*, pp. 153–155.) But if this method is not "immoral" for political science, Cassirer is nonetheless prompted to obscure his vindication of it by the following remarks: "That this complete isolation (from all the forms of man's ethical life) was pregnant with the most dangerous consequences should not be denied. There is no point in overlooking or minimizing these consequences. We must see them face to face. I do not mean to say that Machiavelli was fully aware of all the implications of his political theory. . . . He spoke and judged from his own personal experience, the experience of a secretary of the State of Florence. He had studied with the keenest interest the rise and fall of the 'new principalities." But what were the small Italian tyrannies of the Cinquecento when compared to the absolute monarchies of the seventeenth century and with our modern forms of dictatorship? Machiavelli highly admired the methods used by Cesare Borgia to liquidate his adversaries. Yet in comparison with the later much more developed technique of political crimes these

itself in its concept of political crime, for as St. Thomas points out, blame is more to be attributed to a craftsman who is unwillingly at fault than to one who is willingly at fault since rectitude of the will is not essential to art as it is to prudence.[36] The new politics "[casts] a cold eye on life, on death."

Machiavelli is not redeemed by saying that in *The Prince* he "expresses in terms of the ruler alone what he intends to apply to the whole people," and that "the chief of his political ideas is to be found in the traditional political conception of the common good."[37] On the contrary, as Cassirer rightly says, "if the common good could justify all those things that are recommended in Machiavelli's book, . . . it would hardly be distinguishable from the common evil."[38] Machiavelli is in the tradition of treatises *de regimine principum* only in the sense that his prince is the exemplar of his people's good: He quite naturally has the exemplary quality of his prince consist in knowing how not to be good because his prince is the exemplar of a common good predicated on the judgment that man by nature radically tends not to be good. In Machiavelli the notion of common good is exemplified for us in the prince who is its exemplar: It is the same *virtù* which society naturally and the prince artistically produces. A "people's democracy" modeled on the exemplar of a prince who is half-man and half-beast is the ultimate issue—the "absolute Machiavel-

---

methods appear to be only child's play. Machiavellianism showed its true face and its real danger when its principles were later applied to a larger scene and to entirely new political conditions. In this sense we may say that the consequences of Machiavelli's theory were not brought to light until our own age. Now we can, as it were, study Machiavellianism in a magnifying glass." (*Ibid.*, pp. 140–141.) It is true, of course, that if a treatise is anything but a moral treatise, it does not follow that, *for this reason,* it is an immoral book: A treatise on chemistry is neither a moral nor an immoral book. But —as Cassirer is forced amply to acknowledge—when a general treatise on politics is anything but a moral book it *is* an immoral book.

[36] *Summa Theol.* I.II.Q.57 a.4.c.

[37] In Gilbert, *op. cit.*, pp. 19, 15.

[38] Cassirer, *The Myth of the State*, p. 145. Note that Cassirer says this despite his assertion, just alluded to, that "*The Prince* is neither a moral nor an immoral book. . . ." (*Ibid.*, p. 153.)

lianism" of the twentieth-century totalitarian regimes. The redeeming value which modern scholarship has attached to Machiavelli's subordinating the prince's activity to the "common good" rests on an ambiguity which deceives precisely because of the moral quality traditionally attached to the term. Once that ambiguity is removed, it becomes evident that the concepts "common good," "virtue," "liberty" can have for Machiavelli only an ornamental value—can serve in the *Discourses* only as a sign or symbol. It is precisely this kind of value that is indispensable to the pure political artist; as we today indeed know.

The *Discourses*, with their concern for the common good and republican government, do not in any way show a modification of Machiavelli's basic premises. Indeed the Machiavellian notion of *virtù* informs all the specific virtues in much the same way as Aristotle's prudence informs the other virtues. Throughout the *Discourses* the one factor which Machiavelli insists on as the basis for the common good of a whole people is that combination of boldness, desperate will, and intelligence which signify *virtù*. "Lack of public spirit appears to be the chief symptom of what (Machiavelli) calls corruption." [39] What was it that Machiavelli thought distinguished the ancient lovers of liberty? It was their spirit and vigor of action; indeed the mark of a free man is a spirit of savagery. Speaking of the value of religion in inculcating a free spirit, Machiavelli says of the ancients that their acts of sacrifice, "full of blood and ferocity" were savage spectacles and made men become similarly savage.[40] "Ancient religion made [the highest good] consist in greatness of spirit, strength of body, and in all other things likely to make men very courageous." [41] Speculatively he does not deny Christianity (indeed he says that it "showed us the truth and the true way");[42] nor does he rest the chief blame

[39] Allen, *op. cit.*, p. 457.

[40] *Discourses*, bk. II, p. 2.

[41] *Ibid.*

[42] What Machiavelli meant here is at best doubtful, but perhaps the meaning is that which is conveyed in the following extract from one of his letters: "For years I have never said what I believed, nor ever believed what I have said; and if it sometimes happens that I tell the truth, I conceal it among

for the destruction of republics on Christianity but on the power of the Roman Empire. What then, is his argument? It is that the failure of freedom has been due to the failure to inculcate *in the people* a fighting spirit. And to what end is this liberty? It is ordained to the acquisition of power, but power for the people; for "it is easy . . . to see whence the love of liberty has sprung, since states have never increased in dominions or in wealth save while they lived in liberty." [43] In the light of the *Discourses* Machiavelli's prince is clearly seen as an artist whose work it is to bring the people out of their lethargic state, out of their weak corruption; and as an artist the prince imitates nature: The virtues of the prince are the *virtù* which Machiavelli conceives as the desirable thing in a whole people. For are not the people weak and corrupt because they do not know how to play the part of lion and fox? The "bad" prince takes advantage of their weakness and plays the role of lion and fox for his own benefit; the "good" prince assumes the role of lion and fox for the sake of the "common good," for the instruction and education of the people in *virtù*.

Professor Allen's statement of the verdict of modern scholarship on the problem of understanding Machiavelli is enlightening. He declares: "If we assume that, in the *Discorsi*, Machiavelli expressed, however fragmentarily, his real views, we can understand the *principe* and see it as, at bottom, consistent with those views." [44] It should be noticed, as Professor Allen indicates, that Machiavelli's real views are expressed fragmentarily in the *Discourses*, and that *The Prince* is at bottom consistent with those views. What Professor Allen means, of course, is simply that "Machiavelli conceived of 'popular' government as a character of the healthiest, most vigorous and lasting type of State and of arbitrary government of a Prince as a desperate remedy for corruption." [45] There is no reason for denying that conclusion. But

---

so many lies that it is hard to find it." (*Familiar Letters* in Gilbert, *op. cit.*, p. 260.)

[43] *Discourses*, bk. II, p. 2.

[44] Allen, *op. cit.*, p. 464.

[45] *Ibid.*, p. 465.

if we carry out the work of interpreting Machiavelli's writings from the point where modern scholarship leaves off, and attempt to see the value of this conclusion in the light of the past tradition in political philosophy, Professor Allen's observation that *The Prince* is at bottom consistent with the views expressed in the *Discourses* takes on another and a truer significance. For it then becomes unmistakably clear that *The Prince* is not only at bottom consistent with the views expressed in the *Discourses,* but indeed that *The Prince* is at the bottom of the views expressed in the *Discourses.* The evil in Machiavelli is not, as was long commonly thought, that he favored the rule of a despot; it is that the rule of a republic which he favored was no different from the rule of a despot. The aura of virtue which surrounds his discussion of republics is merely the reflection of the antique past, a past whose intellectual and moral tradition had no real meaning for Machiavelli. This is not to say that the classical aspects of political virtue were uninfluential with Machiavelli. It was precisely as something influential, as bringing themselves to bear, that the virtues of Republican Rome, like stars in some ethical firmament, held Machiavelli fascinated, his cap in his hand, his mouth open, himself for once understanding nothing—nothing except (counselor, strategist, teller of fortune that he was) politico-astrological signs indicating a "return to the future" for his beloved Italy.

We must try finally to fix as precisely as possible the place that Machiavelli occupies in the development of the modern theory of politics. Professor Cassirer had found it "one of the great puzzles in the history of human civilization how a man like Machiavelli, a great and noble mind, could become the advocate of 'splendid wickedness.'" [46] That Machiavelli was a "great and noble mind" is clear to Cassirer upon consideration of what he supposes to have been Machiavelli's role as liberator of the human spirit—precisely, as a liberator of man from theology and metaphysics to which, in the past, man's ethical and cultural life had been tied. But if, indeed, "the sharp knife of Machiavelli's thought had cut off all the threads by which in former generations the state was

[46] Cassirer, *The Myth of the State*, p. 145.

tied to the organic whole of human existence," his knife was not
sharp enough: It was not so sharp nor did it cut so closely as to
save the forms of man's ethical and cultural life other than religion and metaphysics from the scrap-heap. It had cut *"all* the
threads." The intention—so runs Cassirer's thought on the matter
—was good: The state had won its full autonomy, it is entirely
independent. But "this result had to be bought dearly." It had to
be bought at the price of "splendid wickedness," at the cost of
all the forms of man's ethical and cultural life. Not having been
sharp enough simply to remove the extraneous "growth" of theology and metaphysics from nature and to preserve the intrinsic
and autonomous principle of nature itself, Machiavelli, by the
same stroke by which he cut man off from the ends appointed by
the Divine Reason, cut him off from the possibility of a morality
based on the "reason" that is nature itself, considered as an original, formative, and sufficient principle. Like Pico della Mirandola,
Machiavelli could praise God that He had arranged the passions
and powers of man's nature in such fashion that they were not
presupposed to any proper end; and hence the ends of human life
are brought within the sphere of human art which operates upon
man's original indetermination to good and evil as upon unformed
and homogeneous matter. But if Machiavelli prescinded from fixed
ends in the way in which the new physics prescinded from final
and formal causes in nature, he failed to perceive (after all, he
was not a philosopher) that the new physics was discovering that
nature was itself perfectly capable of giving adequate reasons for
the order in the universe. It was not necessary for the new physics
to consider the divine art as the principle of the works of nature.
Galileo had asserted the supremacy of mathematics, by which, he
said, man can have a knowledge of the universe that is not inferior
to that of the Divine Intellect. The laws of nature will find their
very model in the laws of man's reason, and the autonomy of
intellect will correspond to the pure autonomy of nature; nature
will no longer stand as a barrier between man and his liberty. It
is on the basis of an autonomous nature that the second phase of
the modern theory of politics will secure the independence and
autonomy of the state, while restoring the connection between the

state and morality. The new morality, based on an autonomous nature, will define the good not in terms of an end which men seek but in terms of man's very being, whose laws are increasingly understood by him.

The Protestant Reformation and political philosophy

It is impossible to state fully the causes of events so complex and varied as those involved in the Protestant Reformation. The difficulty of assessing the significance for political philosophy of the breakup of the Christian unity of Europe is increased by the fact indeed that, as Professor Sabine says, the Protestant Reformation "produced no such thing as a Protestant political theory . . . nor . . . even an Anglican or Presbyterian or a Lutheran theory that had any close dependence upon the theologies of these Protestant churches." [47] It is true that certain teachings of Luther (the doctrine of justification by Faith alone) and of Calvin (the doctrine of nonresistance) may be said to have favored the development of absolutism and secularism; but the point of general importance, rather, is that the success of any religious party—Catholic or Protestant—depended on the circumstance of its being allied with the secular power and being subjected to its control. If the enhancement of secular power was not then due to any specifically Protestant political theory—and if indeed the weakness of the Catholic Church under the worldly Renaissance papacy considerably contributed to this development—it was the revolt itself against the Church, as a mere fact, and more profoundly, in its spirit and nature, that was the crucial element abetting the growth of the new political principles announced by Machiavelli. Ernst Troeltsch remarks that although "the Protestant theory of the State is . . . based on that very same Christian 'Law of Nature' [of the] Middle Ages" . . . nonetheless by delivering the state from the guidance of the Church as a divinely established society, its effect was such that "the principles which Machiavelli . . .

[47] Sabine, *A History of Political Theory*, p. 354.

developed in opposition to the Christian consciousness . . . became capable of combining with [that consciousness] and being strengthened by it." [48] As a mere fact, the revolt against the Catholic Church meant that the State took over the task of deciding what was and what was not true doctrine. "Everyone assumed, with what now seems incredible naiveté, that agreement about religious truth was possible or even certain, if only the blindness of their opponents could be removed." [49] But in fact "where the government of the Roman Church was broken, the maintenance of the faith became a charge on the civil authorities. . . ." [50] John of Paris, Marsilius of Padua, and Machiavelli were all vindicated in this new freedom of the State which, because it had been achieved in fact, was proclaimed, in the spirit of the new politics, as incontestably juridical. In England and Germany Protestantism was under the control of the princes. Under Henry VIII and Elizabeth I the Church of England was under the Crown. In Germany the Lutheran movement came to be allied with the princes after the Peasants' Revolt. The Peace of Augsburg in 1555 adopted the principle *"cujus regio ejus religio":* The religion of the prince determines the religion of the people. The protest of Pope Innocent X (1644–1655) against the Treaty of Westphalia (1648) which had incorporated the Augsburg principle was of no avail. Catholic and Protestant princes alike effected a "union" of Church and State, of religion and politics precisely as Machiavelli had recommended: Christianity was made a tool in the hands of the

---

[48] Ernst Troeltsch, *Protestantism and Progress: A Historical Study of the Relation of Protestantism to the Modern World,* trans. by W. Montgomery, Beacon Press, Boston, 1958, pp. 107–108.

[49] Sabine, *op. cit.,* p. 355.

[50] "As supra-national and supernatural as the essential Christian teachings were, taken by themselves they would not have been sufficient to challenge and curb Caesar. With any body of teachings, two elements must be balanced. The one is the teachings themselves, and the other is the interpretation and application of those teachings. Where the function of interpreting and applying Christ's teachings remained finally in the hands of government officials, God meant, for practical purposes, what the rulers said He meant, in a particular case." (W. Y. Elliott and N. A. McDonald, *Western Political Heritage,* Prentice-Hall, Inc., Englewood Cliffs, N.J., 1959, p. 293.)

political masters. Unfortunately, it is this spurious "confessional" state that is today the image commonly held of the "traditional" relation of Church and State. But, indeed, the treaties incorporating the Augsburg principle

> . . . mark the end of an epoch, or rather they are a definite sign that the ages in which the Catholic Church, through its head the pope, was a recognized force in the public life of Europe, had finally come to an end. After more than a thousand years the State was once more to transact its business as though the Church did not exist, and the Church would now . . . be considered—by Catholic powers, too— as simply a collective association of those who held like beliefs in religious matters. . . . The next hundred and forty years, from the Treaties of Westphalia to the French Revolution, are dominated by the development of this new, anti-Catholic principle, and in virtue of it, by virtue of the denial implicit in it of the Church's authority as a moral guide in public affairs, the Catholic princes tended once more to enslave Catholicism, to stifle its own independent voice and, breaking the Church into a series of national bodies, make it, each in his own dominions, a mere organ of the State. There is no denial of the classic Catholic doctrines of the Incarnation, the Redemption. . . . But in this other field, this practical denial of the Church's right to teach and make herself heard, they are as dangerous to her existence as any Protestant.[51]

It is in the basic principle of the sixteenth-century Reformers that we find the fundamental ground of alliance between the Reformation and the new humanism of the Renaissance. At first sight it may appear just as arbitrary to connect such different movements as to connect such different works as those of Galileo and Machiavelli. Indeed, in a very basic respect the Reformation is deeply at odds with the Renaissance. The religious individualism of the Reformers affirms the objective reality of the supernatural world. Dogmatic theology retains its primacy among the sciences. But if the Reformers did not reject the life that is

[51] Philip Hughes, *A Popular History of the Catholic Church*, The Macmillan Company, New York, 1954, pp. 192–193.

"more divine than human," their basic principle—the right of private judgment—was founded on a presumption which in effect denied the existence of truths too high for man. Revealed doctrine came to be subject to the infallible authority of every and any individual. This position contradicted the highest natural wisdom: If in the order of natural knowledge very few, as Aristotle had taught, attain to the knowledge of divine things—and then only with uncertainty and the admixture of many errors—it is to be expected that truths which altogether surpass the grasp of the natural intelligence should be presented to man through a divinely instituted teacher. The act of Faith, which is an intellectual assent to truths revealed by God and on the authority of God revealing, does not violate nature—"grace supposes nature." In speaking earlier of Aristotle's excluding theoretic truth from the domain of human art—political or otherwise—attention was called to the fact that the freedom asserted here is asserted primarily on behalf of truth itself and secondarily on behalf of man. Theoretic truth is not subject to human determination: The intelligence is here measured by its object, and not the other way round. The immediate effect of the revolutionary Protestant principle was, as we have said, that the secular rulers—Catholic and Protestant alike—took over the task of defining religious truth. But this outcome was to give way to a profounder expression of the new freedom. As Machiavellianism itself was to give way to the second phase of modern political theory whose vision of an enlargement of freedom and rational direction of human life would be based on the correspondence of the autonomy of intellect with the pure autonomy of nature (the intellect "perceiving in nature only that which it produces after its own design"), so Protestantism was to fall in with the new freedom as, by the inevitable tendency of its inner principle, its theology came to consider the individual right to freedom of conscience to be itself the decisive religious attitude. As Troeltsch says, "the possibility of the change was inherent in Protestantism." [52] And with what consequences, he makes clear:

[52] Troeltsch, *op. cit.,* p. 161.

". . . once the point was reached in the development of Protestantism at which the 'way' of personal conviction became more important than the goal of supernatural salvation, religious conviction could not remain wholly unrelated to scientific conviction. The former had to take on the experimental character of the latter, while the latter assumed the character of a sacred religious duty which belongs to the former." [53] Protestantism was welded into "modern, completely self-directing science"; and this was accomplished mainly under the influence of the German Enlightenment, the great directive force of modern Protestantism.[54] Speaking of the Protestant conception of original sin, Cassirer writes:

The rejection of this dogma is the typical indication of the basic direction of the theology of the Enlightenment, especially as it develops in Germany where it has its most important representatives. These advocates of the new theology all consider the idea of original sin . . . as absolutely absurd. . . . Even where the attempt is made to retain the fundamental ingredients of dogmatics with a few modifications and reinterpretations, the opinion that man through the fall has lost all his ability to attain the good and the true without divine grace is most emphatically rejected. . . . With this reasoning an important change takes place in the inner development of Protestantism. For now the controversy between Luther and Erasmus arises again, but this time it is decided in favor of the latter. The deep gulf between the Renaissance and the Reformation . . . has now been bridged. The epoch of the Enlightenment ventures to go back to those basic postulates from which the Renaissance struggle against the fetters of the mediaeval system had arisen. That conception of Protestantism has now been reached whose true substance Hegel expresses in his philosophy of history. In its reconciliation with humanism, Protestantism became the religion of freedom. . . . the idea of Protestantism in Germany proved capable of such a transformation that it was able to absorb the fresh trends of thought and the attitude from which they had sprung, and to abandon the previous historical form of Protestant-

[53] *Ibid.*, pp. 200–201.
[54] *Ibid.*, pp. 161, 185.

ism in order the more effectively to validate its ideal significance.[55] The ultimate validation of Protestantism's "ideal significance" coincides with the anthropocentric humanism of the Renaissance; the way will be fully cleared for the progress of the new independent morality on which modern politics will be based.

[55] Cassirer, *The Philosophy of the Enlightenment,* Princeton University Press, Princeton, N.J., pp. 159–160.

VII

The modernized theory of natural law and the enlightenment

Speaking of the new intellectual climate of seventeenth-century Europe, Professor Sabine observes that

> . . . vast changes . . . in philosophy and science demanded equally drastic changes in political theory. More than a century before the English civil wars, Machiavelli had stated with brutal clearness the fact that European politics rested in the main on force and selfishness, either national or individual, but he had supplied little interpretation of the fact.[1]

It is the interpretation of this fact that will constitute the modern theory of politics.

Jean Bodin (1530–1596)

When Jean Bodin, writing in the midst of the religious wars in France, sought in his *Six Books of the Republic* to establish the

[1] Sabine, *A History of Political Theory*, p. 455.

ground of right for the political community on the basis of physical force—on the mere fact of subjection of the citizen to the ruler—he was attempting to find a *raison d'être* for the state other than the human common good which had traditionally been its *raison d'être*. He was trying to explore and understand the way which Machiavelli had opened to the modern mind. The attainment of this objective called for an intellectual position lying altogether outside the moral orbit of good and evil. The mere transposition, within the practical order, of prudence to art was not enough. What had to be overcome was the whole traditional notion of an end to be pursued for the perfection of man, and the substitution of the idea of human perfection ontologically rather than morally established: Bodin's theory of sovereignty was in substance and intention an effort to provide a system which would reconcile things as they are in fact with things as they ought to be.

The theory of sovereignty has always been something of a riddle to students of political thought. Bodin's great treatise is celebrated for its confusions, but its riddle is not the product of these confusions; rather the riddle is the explanation of the confusions. It is essentially this: how to reconcile a theory of sovereignty as "supreme power over citizen and subject unrestrained by law" with Bodin's acknowledgment of natural law as the foundation of the structure of the State. As Professor Sabine says, ". . . Bodin's system was not a philosophical structure of the first rank. Its two sides—constitutionalism and centralized power —were not really drawn together. Natural law . . . was accepted as a tradition and was never analyzed or solidly based. The theory of sovereignty . . . floats in the air, a feat of definition rather than an explanation." [2] However, if Bodin's theory of sovereignty "floats in the air," we must see that this is what it was meant to do, what it had to do if a new political science was to establish itself outside the moral orbit of the medieval world.

The riddle of Bodin is brought a long way toward solution if we keep in mind what his purpose was and how appropriately this purpose was served by the device which he employed. The pur-

[2] *Ibid.*, pp. 413–414.

pose was to find grounds for political unity and peace in a France torn apart by the religious wars of the sixteenth century. The device employed was this: to acknowledge natural law so far as the rights of family and private property are concerned, and, with regard to the political order, to acknowledge it only as it bears on the *form* of that society, which is sufficiently understood in terms of guaranteeing the chief objective of the family community—physical well-being. We must recall that for Aristotle the family association was distinguished from the polis in terms of the *being* and the *end* of man: If the family, to be sure, initiates the work of education in the virtues, its specific task is with reference to the generation and preservation of the species. The State comes into existence for the sake of a sufficiency of material goods, but it continues in existence for the sake of the good life—the life of the virtues.[3] Now with regard to the ends of human life Bodin had curiously found Aristotle to be a not reliable guide; hence, while not denying the moral ends of the state, Bodin held that happiness, or life according to virtue, is not a practicable end for the State. As Professor J. W. Allen remarks:[4]

[3] It has been profoundly observed that "when political society concerns itself in an exaggerated way with the propagation of the species—for example, in the dominating intention to maintain the purity of the race or blood, it avows at bottom its powerlessness, it diminishes itself as a *political* society. . . . This is not to say that political society ought to be entirely uninterested in the matter of physical generation; on the contrary, it must concern itself with mere human existence; but this is done by assuring the family its power to survive; the state, in the line of its proper formality, has a different object." (De Monléon, "Petites notes autour de la famille et de la cité," pp. 278–279.)

[4] J. W. Allen, *A History of Political Thought in the Sixteenth Century*, pp. 411–412. (By permission of Barnes and Noble, Inc., New York.) Bodin's confusions even jeopardize the natural rights of the family. "In this case," says Professor Sabine, "the confusion amounts to a flat contradiction. . . . The right of property he considered to be an indefeasible attribute of the family, and the family is an independently existing unit out of which the state is constructed. A well-ordered state, however, requires a sovereign whose legal power is unlimited. Thus Bodin's state contained two absolutes: the indefeasible rights of the family and the unlimited legislative power of the sovereign. . . . Logically his thought breaks in two at this point where

. . . wherever there is "puissance souveraine" there is a State. . . .
It is clear [then] that when a State is . . . established by conquest,
the process involves no recognition of what Bodin describes as the
ends of the State. The State may exist without any reference to its
ends! This, in fact, is precisely what Bodin did think. All that is
necessary to constitute a State is the acceptance of "puissance
souveraine," and the "ends" Bodin speaks of are not those of the State
as such, but those of the "République bien ordonée."

This prescinding from the consideration of the ends of the State
in setting up the formal notion of political society, was a truncating of natural law that admirably suited Bodin's immediate purpose. The conflicting claims of the different religious bodies to
represent the true religion could all of them together be unim-
peachably repudiated by asserting the absence of any natural
ends for political society. The claim of a supernatural society,
based on the order of nature and grace in the hierarchy of ends,
to exercise a certain supervision over temporal affairs would be
cut at its strongest link. Bodin's advocacy, indeed, of religious tol-
eration was based neither on the medieval distinction between
what the natural law imposes and what, within the limits of consent and possibility, the positive law can enforce; nor upon any
doctrine whatever of freedom of conscience. It was based simply
on the irrelevance for political unity of the ends of human life.
With Bodin we are at the beginning of a genuine possibility for a
natural law which will be nonteleological and in which the idea
of political excellence will be established independently of all
consideration of ends.

But Bodin brings us only to the threshold of modern political
theory. If he has provided what was wanting in Machiavelli—
an interpretation, within the framework of natural law, of the
fact that politics rests in the main on force and selfishness—this
interpretation was indeed rather negative and loose-jointed. If this
objective was to be achieved in a formal manner and put upon
firm intellectual foundations, a revision of the framework itself of

the theory of the family ought to be joined to the theory of the state." (Sabine, *op. cit.*, pp. 410–411.)

natural law was necessary. What was needed was a conception of natural law which would permit whatever happens in nature to be accounted for in terms of the natural agent alone (prescinding from divine causality) and then the projection of this understanding on to the political order.

The modernized theory of natural law—Hugo Grotius (1583–1645)

This revision of the classical natural law teaching was indeed to be made within fifty years of Bodin's death. In the course of the next two centuries it was to receive increasingly explicit formulation under the inspiration of a revived Stoicism which animated the Enlightenment. The ancient Stoic principle of the *autarky* of human reason will be made to have *political* significance. All the renowned thinkers of the seventeenth and eighteenth centuries—Descartes, Spinoza, Hobbes, Leibnitz—adopt a conception of nature that removes "the artificial barriers that had hitherto separated the human world from the rest of nature." [5] These barriers were chiefly the notion of Prime Intellect, on which principle, as Aristotle had said, "depend the heavens and the world of nature," [6] and the notion of human intellect as "separable indeed" although not existing apart from matter.[7] A new sense of "reason" is found in the reduction of "the material and mental spheres to a common denominator; they are composed of the same elements and are combined according to the same laws." [8] Nature is made perfectly accessible to human reason, and thus, indeed, fundamentally "operable," under man's control and direction. This meant that "the autonomy of intellect corresponds to the pure autonomy of nature. . . . Both are recognized as elemental and to be firmly connected with one another. Nature in man, as it were, meets

---

[5] Cassirer, *Essay on Man*, p. 30.
[6] *Metaph.* XII.1072b.13.
[7] *Physics* II.194b.10–15.
[8] Cassirer, *The Philosophy of the Enlightenment*, p. 18.

nature in the cosmos half-way, and finds its own essence there." [9]

All the political philosophers of note will revive a theory of human nature and society whose cardinal principle is the autarky of human reason founded on an autonomous nature whose "reasons" are perfectly accessible to human reason. Professor Sabine, speaking of Grotius, remarks that "the surpassing importance of [his] theory of natural law was not due to the content which Grotius attributed to it. . . . The importance was methodological. . . . It was essentially an appeal to reason, as the ancient versions of natural law had always been, but it gave a precision to the meaning of reason such as it had not had in an equal degree in antiquity." [10] And Professor Cassirer observes that this special character of seventeenth-century political philosophy becomes clear "if, instead of analyzing its first principles, we look at its general method." [11] And what is this method? Cassirer continues:

The doctrine of the state-contract becomes in the seventeenth century a self-evident axiom of political thought . . . this fact marks a great and decisive step. For if we adopt this view, if we reduce the legal and social order to free individual acts, to a voluntary contractual submission of the governed, all mystery is gone. . . . If we can trace the state to such an origin, it becomes a perfectly clear and understandable fact.[12]

[9] *Ibid.*, pp. 44–45.

[10] Sabine, *op. cit.*, p. 425.

[11] Cassirer, *The Myth of the State*, p. 172.

[12] *Ibid.*, pp. 172–173. The physical universe too is at this same time supposedly having all mystery removed from it and is being reduced to "a perfectly clear and understandable fact" through the mathematization of physics: "Both [nature and knowledge] must be understood in terms of their own essence, and this is no dark, mysterious 'something,' impenetrable to intellect; this essence consists rather in principles which are perfectly accessible to the mind since the mind is able to educe them from itself and to enunciate them systematically." (Cassirer, *The Philosophy of the Enlightenment*, p. 45.) We should not forget that Aristotle had shown that the mathematical object is the object most proportionate to the human intellect; he also understood the use of mathematics in physical investigations, but he agreed with Heraclitus that "nature loves to hide," and had properly found nature mysterious. He realized that mathematics cannot lead us directly to

It may seem curious that the idea of contract is employed to express a natural relation. However the secret of its appropriateness is to be found in the fact that the naturalism of this political philosophy demanded an innate social propensity which could be raised to the level of a sufficient explanation of social groupings in such a way as to leave no law to be observed which in any sense is imposed from without, but to leave only a "natural law" which the moral subject gives to himself. And nothing is better designed to express this kind of naturalism than the idea of contract. This is evidently what Professor Sabine intends to express when he says that the importance of Grotius' natural law doctrine was not its content but its "methodology": that it gave a precision to the meaning of reason such as it had not had in an equal degree in antiquity. We shall have to see more fully what this "precision" was.

The theory of autonomous nature was expressed in classical fashion for political philosophy in the celebrated hypothesis of Hugo Grotius. In the *De Jure Belli ac Pacis*[13] he maintained that the natural law would be what it is even if, *per impossible*, there were no God. How much Grotius intended by this "hypothesis" does not matter.[14] What matters is that as it was subsequently interpreted and became the cornerstone of modern political philosophy it meant that nature, hypothetically cut from its dependence on the Prime Intellect, would be considered the sufficient and original formative principle of all that is. The meaning and im-

---

the natural object itself any more than the curved line can express the reality of the snub nose.

[13] There is an English translation, by Francis W. Kelsey and others (Oxford, 1925), which is No. 3 of "The Classics of International Law."

[14] "Grotius was not a philosopher but a jurist; he investigated the foundation of law *à propos* studies of positive legal systems and did not concern himself with either metaphysics or moral science. For him right is founded on the current moral practice, which he takes to be universally admitted; he deems it, then, useless to study morality *ex professo* or to say precisely to what system of morals he adheres. This negligence or weakness on his part his students have made into a doctrine." (Leclercq, *Le Fondement du droit et de la société*, Namur, 1933, vol. I, p. 21.)

plications of this hypothesis for the new science of politics can be grasped only if we see how it meant a truncating of the traditional idea of nature and the law of nature. We shall see that the new "precision" given to the meaning of reason by this modernized version of natural law entailed far more than a mere "methodological" change as Sabine called it; indeed it necessitated a substantial change.

In the classical and medieval conception of natural law, law as an *ordinatio rationis ad bonum commune* (an ordination of reason to the common good) was taken to be an inclination toward the good conceived as consisting essentially in (1) the efficient and material principles presupposed to some form, (2) the form, by which a thing is what it is, and (3) an inclination to action in accordance with the form.[15] Now this whole teleology, resting as it did on the concept of law as *ordinatio rationis*, was essentially dependent on the Prime Intellect. Law being something that pertains to the reason and not to nature (unless it be a rational nature) there can be no natural law for nonrational beings except by way of similitude.[16] If, then, law as an inclination toward the good consisted in material and efficient principles for the sake of some form and form for the sake of action, the elimination of the Prime Intellect upon which the order of things depends leaves the "substitute intelligence" of nature and removes the element of *order to an end as such* from the law of nature. The first consequence of this hypothesis is the removal of the "good," formally taken, as the first principle of politics.[17] Traditionally the good was defined as that which all things desire insofar as they desire their perfection. For while, indeed, as was just noticed, everything is good insofar as

---

[15] *Summa Theol.* I.Q.5 a.5.

[16] *Ibid.*, I.II.Q.91 a.2 ad 3.

[17] The opening sentences of both the *Ethics* and *Politics* of Aristotle announce this first principle: "Every art and every inquiry, and similarly every action and pursuit . . . aim at some good; and for this reason the good has rightly been declared to be that at which all things aim." (*Ethics* I.1094a.) "Every state is a community of some kind, and every community is established with a view to some good; for mankind always act in order to obtain that which they think good." (*Politics* I.1252a.)

it has being, nonetheless "goodness" and "being" are not predicated of a thing in the same way: for a thing is called "good" insofar as it has something added to it which perfects its substantial being: To be a man and to be a good man are not the same thing. With the "good" as such removed, nature's operation is reduced to the action of its efficient and material principles as presupposed merely to the substantial being of things: The goodness of everything in the universe—physical and human—becomes simply identified with the existence itself of things. Since this is precisely the doctrine at the core of the political philosophy of the seventeenth and eighteenth centuries, it becomes imperative at this point to consider more fully the traditional teaching on the good.

St. Thomas sets forth the relation of goodness to being in the following passage:

Although goodness and being are the same really, nevertheless, since they differ in thought, they are not predicated of a thing absolutely in the same way. For since being properly signifies that something actually is, and actuality properly correlates to potentiality, a thing is, in consequence, said absolutely to have being accordingly as it is primarily distinguished from that which is only in potentiality; and this is precisely each thing's substantial being. Hence it is by its substantial being that everything is said to have being absolutely; but by any further actuality it is said to have being relatively. Thus to be white signifies being relatively, for to be white does not take a thing out of absolutely potential being, since it is added to a thing that actually has being. But goodness expresses perfection, which is something desirable, and hence it expresses something final. Hence, that which has ultimate perfection is said to be absolutely good, but that which has not the ultimate perfection it ought to have (although, insofar as it is at all actual, it has some perfection) is not said to be perfect absolutely nor good absolutely, but only relatively. In this way, therefore, viewed in its first (i.e., substantial) being, a thing is said to be absolutely, and to be good relatively (i.e., insofar as it has being); but viewed in its complete actuality a thing is said to be relatively, and to be good absolutely. Hence the saying of Boethius, *that in nature the fact that things are good is one thing, that they are is another,* is to be referred to being good absolutely, and being absolutely. Because, regarded in its first actuality, a thing is a being absolutely; and regarded in its complete actuality, it is good absolutely, though even in its first actuality, it is in some way good, and even in its complete actuality, it is in some way being.[18]

Everything other than God (in whom being and goodness are identical) is said to be good absolutely by reason of something added to its substantial being, and particularly by reason of a thing attaining to something else as an end. This something else is ultimately its right relation to everything else: The final end toward which everything in nature is moved—it was traditionally held—is the common good which is the order of the universe. The reason assigned for this was that because the goodness of God is absolutely one with His being, this goodness can be communicated adequately only by many and diverse creatures.[19] Now "in every effect the ultimate end is the proper intention of the principal agent, as the order of an army is the proper intention of the general. Now that which is best in things is the good of the order of the universe, as the Philosopher clearly teaches in *Metaphysics* XII. Therefore the order of the universe is properly intended by God, and is not the accidental result of a succession of agents. . . ."[20] Now all of nature reflects by its operations this movement toward the common good which is, therefore, a universal final cause drawing all things to itself; for

. . . in natural things, everything which, as such, naturally belongs to another, is principally and more strongly inclined towards that other to which it belongs than towards itself. Such a natural inclination is evidenced from things which are moved according to nature; . . . For we observe that the part naturally exposes itself in order to safeguard the whole; as, for instance, the hand is without deliberation exposed to the blow for the whole body's safety. And since reason imitates nature, we find the same imitation among the political virtues; for it belongs to the virtuous citizen to expose himself to the danger of death for the conservation of the whole body politic; and if man were

[18] *Summa Theol.* I.Q.5 a.1.
[19] *Ibid.* I.Q.47 a.1.
[20] *Ibid.* I.Q.15 a.2.

a natural part of the state, then such an inclination would be natural to him." [21]

Now we must take careful note of the fact that the purely natural and the purely animal "love" of the common good implies a profound participation of nature in intelligence: for it involves a movement toward a universal end. Now universal forms cannot be received by nonrational natures. That is why in the *Commentary* on Aristotle's *Physics* St. Thomas defines nature as a *"ratio indita rebus"*—a reason put into things by the Divine Art so that they may act for an end. And as we have said, the natural law is in irrational nature only by way of similitude: Nature is a "substitute intelligence." We are now in a position to see the profound implications of the principle of the autonomy of nature: If nature is conceived as the original formative principle of all that is, then, since nonrational creatures cannot receive universal forms, the notion of a common end in which all share is removed from nature. The common good for which all of nature indeed acts will henceforth be conceived as sufficiently accounted for in the action of creatures for their singular good, and further, this "common" good will itself not be distinct from the substantial being of things conceived as radically independent wholes. This will be the central doctrine, however differently explained, of the political philosophy of Hobbes, Locke, and Rousseau. Man moves toward the condition of creator by moving toward the condition of substitute intelligence which is nature: Man will be one with nature in not explicitly ordering himself to the common good, and he will distinguish himself in nature (and thus become specifically "human") by ordering the common good of his species in its material and efficient principles to maximize his individual being. The identification of the individual with the species will be done *politically*, i.e., man's nature as specifically human will be coeval with the forming of political society by contract, by "the perfectly clear and understandable fact" of a "voluntary, contractual submission of the governed."

[21] *Ibid.*, I.Q.60 a.5.

Thomas Hobbes (1588–1679)

Thomas Hobbes was the first of the great modern writers in political philosophy to try to establish politics on the foundation of autonomous natural law. Since, in accordance with this principle, the good is defined in relation to the ontological perfection of man's nature, the original condition of man is conceived by Hobbes quite differently from the way it was conceived by the classical and medieval tradition: It is not considered as "formed" as to its substantial being and "unformed" as to the "historical" being of acquired habits, laws, and institutions.[22] On the contrary, the "state of nature" signified for Hobbes precisely the condition of man as it pertains only to the things presupposed to the being of his substantial form, of his specifically human nature, viz., the powers and passions of that nature. As Professor Leo Strauss has shown, Hobbes' task required that the basis of politics be found in man's beginnings—in the *prima naturae:* precisely in those materials and efficient principles that are presupposed to man's form, to his being specifically human. Therefore Hobbes makes the first principle and end of politics not "to be good," but "to be" and the preservation of one's being. When, then, Professor Strauss says that for Hobbes "the individual as such . . . had to be conceived as essentially complete independently of civil society" and "at the same time [Hobbes] holds that this beginning is defective and that the deficiency is remedied by civil society," [23] the meaning is that civil society is not required for the task of perfecting man in that "second nature" of the political virtues; it

[22] Comparing Spinoza with Hobbes on this point, Joseph Maréchal writes: "The good is defined in relation to the 'ontological' perfection of each 'nature'; the moral problem is a problem of maximum being' "; and he adds, "this point of view was already clearly professed by Hobbes, by whom Spinoza was here probably inspired." (*Précis d'histoire de la philosophie moderne*, L'Édition Universelle, Desclée de Brouwer, Brussels and Paris, 1951, vol. I, p. 137, p. 138, n. 77–1.)

[23] Strauss, *Natural Right and History*, pp. 183–184; p. 184, n. 23. Copyright 1953 by The University of Chicago.

is simply required for the formation of man specifically human. Where Machiavelli had begun with man's nature as not presupposed to any given ends, and where Aristotle had said that the State does not make man, but taking him from nature makes him good, Hobbes makes the formation of man specifically human coeval with the founding of political society. It is the production of man himself that is the concern of political science modeling itself on the new physics whose concern is with the material and efficient principles by which the cosmos is made. In practice the substitution of the desire *to be* for the desire *to be good* means that the avoidance of death at any cost takes the place of *telos*, of the good in human life. We must carefully observe the implications of this first principle. Since the good is simply now convertible with being, the desire *to be* is the desire to be that being whose being is identical with its goodness (the Divine Being). Therefore, "self-preservation" in itself is directed toward acquiring a new substantial being lacking to man in the state of nature: The new political science, the heir of the old theology and metaphysics, must erect what Hobbes called "the mortal god," the commonwealth "which . . . is *one person, of whose acts a great multitude . . . have made themselves every one the author.* . . ." (Italics in original.) Carrying out Machiavelli's prescriptions for mastering nature and chance, Hobbes makes a "mighty effort to found a political science that [will] enable men, once and for all, to . . . weather the vicissitudes of politics." [24]

We must inquire a little more closely into this process by which man "produces" himself and observe its precise implications in Hobbes' doctrine. He tells us:

[24] Sheldon S. Wolin, *Politics and Vision*, Little, Brown and Company, Boston, 1960, p. 8. It may be of interest here to take note of Karl Marx's estimate of the seventeenth and eighteenth centuries' political theory of "the fully-developed political state." He writes: "The state is the intermediary between man and the liberty of man. Just as Christ is the intermediary whom man charges with all his [own] divinity, with all of his religious limitation, so the State is the intermediary which man charges with all of his humanity, with all of his human limitation." (Marx, *Die Judenfrage*, p. 583.)

It is true that certain living creatures, as bees and ants, live sociably one with another . . . and yet have no other direction than their particular judgments and appetites . . . ; and therefore some man may perhaps desire to know why mankind cannot do the same. To which I answer: . . . that amongst these creatures, the common good differeth not from the private; and being by nature inclined to their private, they procure the common benefit. But man, whose joy consisteth in comparing himself with other men, can relish nothing but what is eminent.[25]

We must notice two things about these observations of Hobbes: First, he says that among irrational creatures the common good does not differ from the private; and secondly, he alleges a reason for this, namely, that the irrational animal's knowledge does not extend beyond the particular and sensible good. In the nonrational universe where "the common good differeth not from the private" there is no order to a real common good communicable to many. Nor is there, then, a real order to the common good for man, who is one with nature. But man, "whose joy consisteth in comparing himself with other men," knows the universal species, and "can relish nothing but what is eminent." For man there is a "natural right" to do all and take all. And this is the reason—we must carefully notice—why men cannot live sociably one with another. There is indeed no real order to the common good: In other words, man is unlike the irrational creature in that he desires to possess the common good for himself. If to be good absolutely meant—according to traditional political philosophy—to order one's acts to the common good as part to whole, then *to be absolutely as the absolute good* means to order the good of the whole to oneself: This is what distinguishes man in nature, and until it is fully accomplished, man is not yet fully "human." Self-preservation in man is directed to himself considered in some manner the whole species: It is the desire to be the universal man, to be at any cost.[26] And since this principle is operable in each man, "the

---

[25] Thomas Hobbes, *Leviathan*, bk. II, chap. 17.

[26] Even if one had a theoretically sound understanding of the principle of the primacy of the common good (which Hobbes had not), one could none-

war of all against all" is the necessary result of man's original condition. "The individual never ceases to concentrate upon seeking his own good and satisfying his own irreducible, unassimilable endeavor." [27] Man can attain the full intention of his species only by establishing "a common power" upon which all men confer "all their power and strength" so that all their wills may be reduced to one will:

which is to say, to appoint a man, or assembly of men, to bear their person. . . . This is more than consent or concord; it is a real unity of them all, in one and the same person. . . . This done, the multitude so united in one person, is called a *commonwealth.* . . . This is the generation of that great LEVIATHAN, or rather, to speak more reverently, of that *mortal god.* . . . And in him consisteth the essence of the commonwealth; which, to define it, is *one person, of whose acts a great multitude, by mutual covenants one with another, have made themselves every one the author, to the end he may use the strength and means of them all, as he shall think expedient, for their peace and common defense.*[28]

"The basic meaning," says Professor Collins, "of laying down one's right [to all things] is that one should divest oneself of the natural right . . . of man to do all and take all. . . . This right . . . is laid aside not by being renounced, but by a definite transfer to a beneficiary which is not itself the contracting party." [29]

---

theless have a pernicious practical ignorance concerning it (and it is this with which Hobbes appears to have endowed man in "the state of nature"). As Charles DeKoninck points out, "One may refuse the primacy of the common good because, first of all, it is not the singular good of the singular person and because it demands a subordination of the person to a good which is not his by reason of his own personality. By a disordered love of one's private good one rejects . . . the common good as something alien and judges it to be incompatible with one's individual status . . . one freely abdicates the dignity proper to the rational creature in order to establish oneself as a radically independent whole." (DeKoninck, *De la Primauté du bien commun,* pp. 31–32.)

[27] James Collins, *A History of Modern European Philosophy,* The Bruce Publishing Company, Milwaukee, 1954, p. 121.

[28] Hobbes, *Leviathan,* bk. II, chap. 17.

[29] Collins, *op. cit.,* pp. 125–126.

The right of each individual to the potentialities of the whole species is not renounced; it is, rather, guaranteed and made attainable through the intermediary of the "mortal god" which is "charged with all of man's humanity." [30]

But the common good so conceived and established is indeed a good that is alien to the individual who was, strangely, its very principle; for the commonwealth is defined as "one person." Professor Strauss rightly observes that the gist of Hobbes' doctrine of sovereignty is not that it is *expedient* to assign plenitude of power to the ruling authority, but that plenitude of power belongs to the ruling authority *as of right*. The original edition of the *Leviathan* appeared with a quaint frontpiece in which there was pictured a crowned giant whose body was composed of tiny figures of human beings. This representation of the Leviathan suggests the specific nature of the social contract which establishes it: The commonwealth created is "one person" having an integrative unity, which means that the parts of which the body politic is composed have no independence and life of their own. In place of the "unity of order" which the classical and Christian tradition had allowed for the political community, we find a "unity of composition" in which the activity of the parts is principally the same as that of the whole. Indeed Hobbes' citizen is defined in relation to the ruler quite as Aristotle's natural slave was defined in relation to the master: as *"alterius,"* belonging to another as of natural right. But there is an important difference, a difference which is to the advantage of Aristotle's slave: for *he* was described as a "man" and a "separate" instrument, whereas Hobbes' citizen is an integral part of his master, and achieves his humanity in and through the sovereign's power. Indeed, the body politic has so much a "unity of composition" (in which the motion of the parts

---

[30] See above, p. 199, n. 24. "One would not refuse the common good if one were himself its principle. . . . And when one condescends to submit to an ordering of the common good this act of submission emanates from the superabundance of the pure self. . . . This sort of person will even allow himself to be directed by another and recognize a superior, provided that this recognition is the 'fruit' of his own personal choice." (DeKoninck, *De la Primauté du bien commun*, pp. 32–33.)

is principally the same as that of the whole) that it disintegrates not when the laws are "unjust" but when they do not "keep [the citizenry] in such a motion as not to hurt themselves by their own impetuous desires. . . ." [31] The obligation to obedience lasts as long as the power lasts by which the sovereign is able to hold the parts together. The right to revolt is a right not against tyranny but against weakness in the power of the body politic, in the ordering of material and efficient principles to the formation of the "mortal god."

In thus emancipating himself from the old theology and metaphysics, in moving toward the condition of "creator," man has set up a political alienation of himself in the "mortal god"; this, to be sure, is a human rather than a religious form of "alienation." Not until nature itself is "humanized," and (two hundred years later, in Marx's concept of man's "generic being") man's relation to nature is seen to be "directly his relation to man," will "social humanity" achieve its own "aseity." The "conscience of man, in nature, considered as *being*" will be the point of departure for the "science" of society. Then will take place that curious resolution of which Marx boasted—the resolution of the opposition between liberty and necessity that is the hallmark of the totalitarian regime.

John Locke (1632–1704)

If the new principle of the autonomy of nature brings with it a new meaning of "reason" in the reduction of the material and mental spheres to a common denominator, then the ultimate term of the emancipation from a natural law dependent on the Prime Intellect should be—as was observed by Karl Marx—a society representing "the achieved consubstantiality of man with nature." [32] Hobbes considers the relation of nature to man as his own relation to the origin of his own natural determination—man is conceived as producing himself specifically human out of his natural state.

---

[31] Hobbes, *Leviathan*, bk. II, chap. 30.
[32] Marx, *Oekonomische-philosophische Manuskript*, p. 117.

But the causality that is thus exercised by him, although—Hobbes says—unlike that of irrational creatures whose action does not extend beyond "their particular judgments and appetites," operates to separate the universal man (who is actualized in the "mortal god") from the individual. This is why Marx will astutely criticize this "political" emancipation:

> There where the political state has reached its full development, man leads, not only in thought, in conscience, but in reality in life, a double existence, celestial and terrestrial, the existence in the political community where he considers himself as a generic being, and the existence in civil society where he works as a mere part, sees in other men simply means, is himself swallowed up in the role of a simple means, and becomes the plaything of forces extraneous to himself.[33]

With Locke (and still more perfectly with Rousseau) there is an attempt to overcome this double existence, to free man from the political barrier that he has erected between himself and his liberty; there is an effort to free man from the authority of any ruling group. Locke's "limited" government is inspired precisely by this intention; it has no essential relation to the classical and medieval theory of constitutional government.

Although, as Professor Strauss has observed, "Locke's notion of natural law appears much closer to the traditional view . . . than to the revolutionary view of Hobbes, . . . closer inspection would show that this appearance is deceptive and must be traced to Locke's peculiar caution." [34] Strauss has shown that Locke, although ostensibly adhering to the medieval tradition of natural law, did in fact follow "the lead given by Hobbes." [35] "If virtue by itself is ineffectual, civil society must have a foundation other than human perfection or the inclination toward it; it must be based on the strongest desire in man, the desire for self-preservation." [36]

[33] Marx, *Die Judenfrage*, pp. 583–584.

[34] Strauss, "On Locke's Doctrine of Natural Right," *The Philosophical Review*, vol. 70, no. 4, p. 475, October, 1952. See Strauss, *Natural Right and History*, pp. 202–252.

[35] *Ibid.*, p. 478.

[36] *Ibid.*, p. 475, n. 2.

For Locke, as for Hobbes, it is the desire *to be* at any cost that takes the place of *telos,* of the good in human life; and like Hobbes, he seeks to achieve this by referring the common good of the species to the individual himself. But his understanding of how this is to be accomplished is different from that of Hobbes, and it is this difference that will account for Locke proposing a "limited" government in place of Hobbes' absolute government.

We have seen that Hobbes distinguished between man and those irrational creatures which "live sociably one with another." The reason alleged by him why mankind cannot do the same was that "amongst these [irrational] creatures the common good differeth not from the private; and being by nature inclined to their private, they procure the common benefit. But man, whose joy consisteth in comparing himself with other men, can relish nothing but what is eminent." The capacity to compare himself with other men is both the cause of his desiring something eminent, and the reason why man is unable to live sociably. Locke agrees that man's original condition is indeed one of war, for in the state of nature man is equipped with no innate moral principles and "any man may do what he thinks fit." This is why, in pursuing his private good man tends to procure the whole common good for himself. This is the evil of the state of nature. Man must indeed refer the common good to himself (rather than refer himself to the common good), but he must do so not by seeking to procure the common good for himself but by seeing that it is the power of individual well-being that is the cause of the common good, and that this common good is simply the collectivity of private interests. Locke presses the principle of the autonomy of nature further than does Hobbes: Human society must be more closely modeled on the social nature of irrational animals who by pursuing their private good procure the common benefit, which does not differ from the private. Agreeing so far with Hobbes in holding that in the brute animal the common good differeth not from the private, Locke establishes his difference from Hobbes in maintaining that man's difference from the brute consists in this: that thanks to his reason, man becomes aware that the common good is measured by acts which are in pursuit of one's private good—the good that belongs to one insofar as he is an individual (the good which the animal pursues when he desires nourishment for the preservation of his being). Speaking of the role of material causality in political individualism, Professor Yves Simon observes that this individualism "proceeds from the stubborn belief that the best state of affairs is brought about by the independent operation of ultimate units, the independent money-maker, the individual supplier of labor-force, the individual consumer, the individual organizer, and the like, all moved by the power of individual well-being." [37] The pursuit of this private good, when mutually secured, is precisely the public good. It is precisely the *awareness*—of which man alone is capable—of the relation between activity for the private good and the procuring of the common benefit that distinguishes man in nature as specifically human and allows him to relate himself to the species as to his own proper being.

This point of Locke's political doctrine accords perfectly with his empiricist psychology. Locke was of the opinion that it is impossible for the human mind to come to a knowledge of essences. Universal ideas are "nothing but the capacity they are put to, by the understanding, of signifying or representing many particulars. For the signification they have is nothing but a relation that, by the mind of man, is added to them." [38] Now the traditional philosophy had held that because the brute's knowledge is tied to singular sensible objects, the sense appetite of the brute extends only to the singular sensible, to the private good. Nonetheless, it was at the same time maintained, as we have already noted, that "in natural things, everything which, as such, naturally belongs to another, is principally and more strongly inclined toward that other to which it belongs than towards itself. . . . For we observe that the part naturally exposes itself in order to safeguard the whole; as, for instance, the hand is without de-

[37] "Common Good and Common Action," *The Review of Politics*, vol. 22, no. 2, p. 236, April, 1960.

[38] *Essay Concerning Human Understanding*, II. 1. 17; Fraser edition I, Dover Publications, Inc., New York, 1959, p. 136.

liberation exposed to the blow for the whole body's safety." [39]
Thus, while it is not true that the private good "differeth not from
the common benefit" even among irrational creatures, what is
true is that nonrational creatures act *naturally* for the common
good although *knowingly* only for the private benefit. But man,
whose knowledge extends to the universal, can act explicitly for
the common good. Locke, supposing universal ideas to be
"nothing but the capacity they are put to, by the understanding,
of signifying or representing many particulars," makes the difference between the brute animal and man consist in man's awareness that the pursuit of the private good procures the common
benefit conceived as a mere collectivity of private interests.[40] In
the state of nature the individual's pursuit of his private good is
not enlightened to the point of seeing that others have the same
right and that the recognition of this fact alone safeguards one's
own right. This knowledge, made practical by the rules of civil
society, distinguishes man in nature: It is the freedom of constructing rules of mutual security that defines man as specifically
human. His human nature is coeval with society, but it is not—
as it is with Hobbes—alienated on to the "mortal god"; it is retained outside the framework of government. It is this consideration that defines the nature of "limited" government in Locke's
political philosophy.

In Locke's doctrine limits are imposed on government because
the individual remains a radically independent "whole" *vis-à-vis
the political order*. He is conceived neither as a part which is
related by a unity of order to the whole common good (the classical position); nor as alienating his person on to the "one person"

---

[39] *Summa Theol.* I.Q.60 a.5.

[40] The difference between this conception of "common good" and the traditional conception is well expressed by DeKoninck: ". . . the common good
[properly understood] is not a good which is not the good of individual persons and which is only the good of the collectivity envisaged as a kind of
singular entity. In that [latter] case, it would be common only by accident
. . . it would differ from the singular good of the individuals in this—that
it would be the good of *no one*." (DeKoninck, *De la Primauté du bien
commun*, p. 9.)

of the sovereign (as with Hobbes). Natural law as Locke understands it, operates in man as nothing but a series of dictates of
reason in regard to man's mutual security, rules that seek to
guarantee the public good by enabling each individual to pursue
his private good without obstruction from others. The particular
matters with which all action is indeed concerned are not referable to the common good as to a common final cause or end, but
to a common good as a common genus which includes many individuals: Locke's "common good" is common by predication, as
"animal" is common in relation to "brute" and "man." [41] It is not
a common good of the particular individual (as the classical common good was) any more than the common name "animal" is
the name of any animal that *is* (for there is no animal in general).
And this common good is brought about simply by each individual acting for his private good, which—as Hobbes had alleged
of bees and ants—does not differ from the common. The common
good so conceived can be guaranteed only by a constitution so
structured as to eliminate any government in the classical sense
whatsoever. Hence Locke rejects rule in the classical sense of directing men's actions to a common good of which the individual's
action for his private good is not the sufficient measure. He rejects all of the classical forms of government in substance. Government by majority appears to Locke to be less a threat to the individual than either monarchy or oligarchy; but Locke "cannot be
said to have had implicit faith in the majority as a guarantor of
the rights of the individual." [42] Nor are these rights sufficiently

[41] Cf., *Summa Theol.* I.II.Q.90 a.2 ad 2. In answering an objection to
the effect that since law directs man in his actions, and since human actions
are concerned with particular matters, it would seem to follow that law is
directed to some particular good, St. Thomas replies as follows: "Actions are
indeed concerned with particular matters, but those particular matters are
referable to the common good, not as to a common genus or species, but as
to a common final cause, according as the common good is said to be the
common end."

[42] Strauss, *Natural Right and History*, p. 233. Professor Wolin writes: "In
designating the majority as the instrument through which society acts, Locke
dealt still another blow to the distinctive role of the political order. He conceived the majority independently of political processes and institutions; a

guaranteed by the right of resistance to government, for this of itself would put society in continual danger of reverting back to man's natural condition.[43] Neither the form of government, then, nor the right of resistance to government guarantees the right of self-preservation. Upon what principle, then, does this first natural right rest? The solution must be found along the line of Locke's conception of the common good as comprising individuals who by action for their private good cause the preservation of the species. Now the instrument of living, of self-preservation—as Aristotle himself had taught—is property, which man produces by his labor. It is an instrument of economic life and not, formally and properly, of the political life. But it is indeed Locke's doctrine of property that "is almost literally the central part of his political teaching. . . . It distinguishes his political teaching most clearly not only from that of Hobbes, but from the traditional teachings as well." [44] Professor Strauss has shown that if Locke considers labor to be the cause of wealth, he considers, more fundamentally, the spirit of acquisitiveness to be the cause of labor. It is a simple unrectified appetite that is the cause of plenty in society, and, therefore, the equality of all men with regard to the right of self-preservation not only does not hinder the special right of the more skillful acquirers of wealth, but the protection of different and unequal faculties of acquiring wealth is the first object of government.[45] It is, then, the special right of the more

---

force that supplied dynamic direction to society but one that originated outside political processes and institutions." (Wolin, *op. cit.*, p. 309.)

[43] Locke admitted the right of revolution on the part of the people, but this right "does not qualify the subjection of the individual to the community or the society. . . . It is only fair to say that Hobbes stresses more strongly than does Locke the individual's right to resist society or government whenever his self-preservation is endangered." (Strauss, *Natural Right and History*, p. 232.)

[44] *Ibid.*, p. 234.

[45] "In contrast to the Lockean system, which placed the sanctity of private property among the first imperatives of human nature and treated government as a kind of after-thought, mediaeval thought typically regarded both property and government as essential instruments of human needs and pur-

skillful accumulators of wealth that is the central principle of "government" in Locke's philosophy. It is ultimately in regard to this right that government, in Locke's doctrine, must be limited. As Hobbes became the defender of the absolute monarchies of the seventeenth and eighteenth centuries, Locke is the apologist for the laissez-faire democratic individualism of the nineteenth century. The constitution which Locke proposes, of an executive subordinate to and limited by a legislative assembly whose representation is based on numbers and wealth, must not conceal the radical departure from the whole classical idea of government. Locke's limited government is the closest approximation to what he conceives the natural action of animals for the common good to be. Indeed, the limitation on government is essentially a limit put upon the classical virtue of legislative prudence so that unequal talents for acquiring wealth may be uninhibited. As Mrs. Ewart Lewis says, in the Lockean system government was "a kind of afterthought." [46] It does not have even the relative justification that Aristotle allows the claim of the wealthy to rule; for this claim was based not on a purely natural principle but on a prudential judgment (however faulty) concerning the common good of the polis—for the polis is first distinguished from the household association in terms of a full sufficiency of material goods for all. Locke's government is limited in order to ensure, as we have said, the closest modeling of political society on what he conceives the natural action of animals for the "common good" to be—a common good which does not differ from the private and which is brought about by the pursuit of the private benefit. It seeks to guarantee nothing for the individual as such. This is the peculiar paradox of Lockean individualism.

We said earlier that Locke's political philosophy may be under-

---

poses. . . . Both were institutions of human construction; both were rooted in natural law . . . but the specific rights of both were subordinate to, and limited by, the purposes they must serve." (Ewart Lewis, "The Contribution of Mediaeval Thought to the American Political Tradition," *The American Political Science Review*, vol. 50, no. 2, p. 468, June, 1956.)

[46] *Ibid.*

stood as an effort to overcome the separation of man from himself that Hobbes' "mortal god" had effected. Locke was successful to the extent that man is conceived as producing himself specifically human in civil society outside the framework of government. Vis-à-vis the government he is a radically independent whole. This is the familiar laissez-faire individualism of the nineteenth century. But Locke achieves this result by pressing further than did Hobbes the principle of the autonomy of nature, by making man more closely resemble irrational creatures. By so doing, Locke frees man from the domination of the "mortal god," but he loses him in the common species under which the individual is contained indeterminately; the common good when taken to be common in the way "man" is common to "Paul" and "John" entails a confusion of individuals—they exist not for their own sakes but for the sake of the species. We are here indeed at the beginning of the twentieth-century phenomena of the "organization man" and the "other-directed" man. This outcome is in accord with the tendency, of which we have spoken, toward "the consubstantiality of man with nature." For in traditional philosophy it had always been held that nature as such intends no particular individual but intends individuals only that the species may be maintained. The common good that is the object of every purely natural principle is a good that does not have regard for the individual as such, even though it is a natural principle that produces *this* individual, and even though the individual acts naturally for the common good. Aristotle remarks that if nature intended this particular individual, she would be like a man who takes a bath so that the sun might be eclipsed.[47] And St. Thomas makes the same point, saying, "*Natura enim intendit generare hominem, non hunc hominem, nisi inquantum homo non potest esse, nisi sit hic homo.*" [48] (For nature intends the generating of man, but not this man, except inasmuch as man cannot be unless this man be.") The reason assigned by Aristotle and the traditional teaching was as follows: The individual is properly said

[47] *Physics* II.197b.25–27.
[48] *Questio disputata de Anima* a.18.c.

to be *"by nature"* but not to be "nature," a term that is properly applied only to the matter and form of a thing. And this is so because, according to Aristotle's demonstration, the form is the end of generation in natural things, while matter, which is the principle of individuation, is for the sake of the form; and hence the "ultimate intention of nature is towards the species and not the individual. . . ." [49] The intention of the individual as such can be accounted for only through the Prime Intellect which is the cause of the whole being of whatever is. Thus in a natural law hypothetically cut off from the Prime Intellect, no individual is intended as such. But further, in the traditional teaching, the particular individual that is intended (by reference to the Cause of all being) is intended for its own sake only in the case of those creatures who, by reason of moving by a "form understood [which] proceeds from the intellect . . . as a thing conceived, and in a way contrived by it," [50] are masters of themselves—are capable of self-government, of directing themselves explicitly to the common good. It is exactly this capacity that has disappeared and its place taken by the principle of the autonomy of nature and its "substitute intelligence." And with it disappears the care of the rational creature for his own sake—a cardinal point of the traditional natural law teaching. The next step in the direction of the consubstantiality of man with nature will indeed take the form of identifying the species precisely with each individual. The individual who had been alienated from his social being by Hobbes' "mortal god" and by Locke's collectivity of private interests, will in a manner have the fullness of his social nature restored in Jean Jacques Rousseau's "General Will."

Jean Jacques Rousseau (1712–1778)

If with Hobbes and Locke man moves in the direction of his consubstantiality with nature, he nonetheless still distinguishes himself by a certain disengagement of his reason from the rest of

[49] *Summa Theol.* I.Q.85 a.3 ad 4.
[50] *Contra Gentiles* II.chap.47. See chap. II, p. 43.

nature. With Hobbes, man distinguishes himself by explicitly directing to himself a common good which other animals implicitly procure by seeking their private good which does not differ from the common; while with Locke, man distinguishes himself by his awareness (lacking to other animals) that the pursuit of his private good entails the common benefit. Hobbes had called the dictates of reason which establish the political community "conclusions or theorems"; and Locke had allowed a sufficient disengagement of man's reason to have credited it with "universal ideas" in the meager sense of a "capacity they are put to, by the understanding, of signifying or representing many particulars." In both cases—that of Hobbes and Locke—the mind approaches the "substitute intelligence" of nature, but it still remains critical, as it were, from the outside. Man is not yet sufficiently identified with the rest of nature. It was this inadequacy in both Hobbes and Locke that Rousseau criticized and sought to remedy.

Now the difference between the most simple operations of the human soul and those of animals—in which the law of nature for man must be found—cannot, Rousseau maintained, be reason, for indeed "every animal has ideas, since it has senses . . . and it is only in degree that man differs, in this respect, from the brute. . . ." [51] The common denominator between the mental and material spheres means, then, that it is "not so much the understanding that constitutes the specific difference between the man and the brute, as the human quality of free agency." [52] Now since the brute, equally with man, "has ideas," it is man's freedom with respect to ideas that distinguishes him from the brute: "Nature lays her commands on every animal, and the brute obeys her voice. Man receives the same impulsion, but at the same time knows himself at liberty to acquiesce or resist. . . ." [53] However, difficulties attending the question of free

[51] Jean Jacques Rousseau, *Discourse on the Origin of Inequality*, in Robert Maynard Hutchins (ed.), *Great Books of the Western World*, trans. by G. D. H. Cole, Encyclopaedia Britannica, Inc., Chicago, 1952, vol. 38, p. 338.

[52] *Ibid.*, p. 338.

[53] *Ibid.*

will make it unsatisfactory to distinguish man by the quality of
free agency. Rousseau therefore replaces free will with "perfectibility," which "will admit of no dispute." [54] Freedom is replaced, then, by perfectibility as the specific difference between
man and the brute. Since man's perfectibility is made to rest not
on his quality of free agency, it must rest then on some *natural*
principle;[55] and since perfectibility is denied the brute, the natural principle on which man's perfectibility rests must be one
that is not found in the brute. Now we must note that traditional
philosophy had taught that because the natural agent acts by the
form which makes it what it is, and which is only one in one thing,
its effect is one only (from trees come trees, from men come
men); but the voluntary agent acts by an intellectual form which
can extend to many things.[56] Having eliminated the voluntary
and replaced it with a purely natural principle, Rousseau sees in
man's capacity to extend himself to many things the attainment
of his natural being in the simple feeling of existence: Man's
perfectibility consists in *being the things he knows and desires,*
and thus relating himself to himself as a kind of universal being,
and relating himself to the universal man as to his own proper
being. Nature "intends" him, for he *is* the species: Indeed, he is
all things. This is the "perfectibility" that is comprised in the
"simple feeling of existence." [57]

[54] *Ibid.*

[55] Professor Strauss remarks that "Rousseau means to put his doctrine on
the most solid ground; he does not want it dependent on dualistic metaphysics. . . . The argument of the *Second Discourse* is meant to be acceptable to materialists as well as to others. It is meant to be . . . 'scientific' in
the present-day sense of the term." (Strauss, *Natural Right and History,* pp.
265–266.)

[56] Cf. *Summa Theol.* I.Q.47 a.1 ad 1.

[57] It should be instructive to advert here to a passage from St. Thomas in
which he is showing that in men (as in angels) the will is a faculty or power
which is not their nature nor their intellect: "That it is not their nature is
manifest from this, that the nature . . . of a thing is completely comprised
within it: whatever, then, extends to anything beyond it is not its [nature]
or essence. . . . But the inclination towards something extrinsic comes from
something super-added to the essence: e.g., tendency to a place comes from

It is, as we have seen, neither reason nor the quality of free agency that accounts for this perfectibility: It is "conscience," by which Rousseau understands an original vague consciousness of one's identity with the common being of all things: the "science of simple souls." Man is distinguished from the brute by a nature that comprises all things completely within it; if indeed he is subhuman in the state of nature, he is nonetheless infinitely perfectible: It is by the actualizing of this infinite perfectibility that man attains the full measure of his humanity.

But ". . . who does not see . . . that everything seems to remove from savage man both the temptation and the means of changing his condition?"[58] The soul of the natural man "which nothing disturbs is wholly wrapped up in the feeling of its present existence. . . ."[59] This is the enviable condition of those primitive men who possess the "science of simple souls." Since, then, man had neither the temptation nor the means to change

---

gravity or lightness, while the inclination to make something like itself comes from the active qualities.

"Now the will has a natural tendency towards good. Consequently there alone are essence and will identified where the good is wholly contained within the essence of him who wills; that is to say, in God, who wills nothing beyond Himself except because of His goodness. This cannot be said of any creature, because infinite goodness is outside the essence of any created things. Accordingly, neither the will of the angel, nor that of any creature, can be the same as its essence.

"In like manner neither can the will be the same thing as the intellect of angel or man. For knowledge comes about because the thing known is in the angel or man. Consequently the intellect extends itself to what is outside it, according as what is essentially outside it is naturally capable of being somehow within it. On the other hand, the will goes out to what is beyond it, according as by a kind of inclination it tends somehow to what is outside it. Now it belongs to one power to have within itself something which is outside it, and to another power to tend to what is outside it. Consequently, intellect and will must necessarily be different powers in every creature. It is not so with God, for He has within Himself universal being and the universal good. Therefore both intellect and will are His essence." (*Summa Theol.* I.Q.59 a.2.C.)

[58] Rousseau, *Discourse on the Origin of Inequality*, p. 339.
[59] *Ibid.*

his condition, that change must have been imposed accidentally by changes occurring in the physical world. For this reason the nature of man's perfectibility can be known only obscurely and, as it were, obliquely from his history; and indeed recourse to the history of man reveals his perfectibility in the reverse form of his infinite degradation. The discovery, in this form, of man's perfectibility is the purpose of Rousseau's *Discourse on the Origin of Inequality*. Man has become specifically human by a series of natural accidents. In the course of these accidents, which compelled him to invent increasingly elaborate means of survival, man was forced to think. And since his thinking developed in response to actual and varying physical circumstances, it developed unevenly among men and with the admixture of error and uncertainty. It is understandable, then, that as man became specifically human, he should have lost his original happy feeling for simple existence and become narrowly ambitious, grasping and contentious, a more than savage savage.

The first step toward degeneracy occurred when "the first man, who having enclosed a piece of ground, bethought himself of saying *this is mine* and found people simple enough to believe him." [60] Property arose as resources, with the increase in population, became scarcer. Pride and the desire for power accompanied man's differentiating himself from other men as well as from other animals. Conflict arose between rival appropriators of land. Since each man was the judge of his own injuries and insults the conflicts between men became increasingly terrible. And so the most propertied individuals, the group most subject to the depredations of other men, persuaded the population that the only way "to guard the weak from oppression, to restrain the ambitious, and secure to every man the possession of what belongs to him" was to submit to "a supreme power which may govern . . . by wise laws, protect and defend all the members of the association, repulse their common enemies, and maintain . . . harmony. . . ." [61] Thus did man degrade himself, separating

---

[60] *Ibid.*, p. 348.
[61] *Ibid.*, pp. 354–355

himself from himself in that society that Hobbes had held forth as the ideal in *The Leviathan*. Barbarous and weak men accepted "the origin of society and law, which bound new fetters on the poor, and gave new powers to the rich; which irretrievably destroyed natural liberty, eternally fixed the law of property and inequality, converted clever usurpation into unalterable rights, and, for the advantage of a few ambitious individuals subjected all mankind to perpetual labor, slavery, and wretchedness." [62]

But in all the misery of man's history we see as in a glass darkly his true glory: Although the development of reason has alienated man from his original simple feeling of existence by creating different classes and modes of existence, these very inequalities point beyond themselves to an expression, *on the plane of humanity*, of man's original simple feeling of existence, for the wholeness and simplicity of his original condition, in which he will see himself, as it were, face to face. The hidden purpose of the historical process is thus revealed: In the place of the inequalities and distinctions that civil society has historically produced for the good of a few and the ruin of the species, a true public right must effect the union of each with all so that each individual may consciously, on the human plane, refer himself to himself as to a kind of universal. There must be a return to the state of nature, but a "return to the future," on the human plane.

Rousseau cannot, however, see the way to the full restoration of man's original independence. In society man has lost his original independence and has become radically dependent: Not the simple feeling of existence, but the desperate fight for self-preservation, in the interest of which society historically came into being, must always be the root of every civil society, even the best. [63] The distinctions constituted by birth, wealth, position and

[62] *Ibid.*, p. 355.

[63] "Rousseau believed to the end that even the right kind of society is a form of bondage . . . the return to the state of nature remains therefore for him a legitimate possibility. The question is, then, not how he solved the conflict between the individual and society, but rather how he conceived of that insoluble conflict." (Strauss, *Natural Right and History*, pp. 254–255.) The return to the state of nature that Professor Strauss says was a legitimate

education have destroyed man's feeling of simple existence; they have made some men dependent on others and have severed the individual from the simplicity of his natural wholeness; they have made the individual's life have its reason outside himself. But if it is not possible that man return, through civil society, to his original independence, at least the original right of each individual to be the judge of the means necessary for his self-preservation can be restored. If not even the best society can bring about man's absolute emancipation, a "political" emancipation can be achieved, i.e., the emancipation from a ruling class: "For Rousseau, the real 'social bond' consists in the fact that particular individuals and groups are not called upon to rule over others." [64] The political problem is "to find an association which will defend and protect with the whole common force the person and goods of each associate, and in which each one, while uniting himself with all, may obey himself alone, and remain free as before." [65] On the political plane a true public right will effect the union of each with all so that, on this plane, each individual may refer himself to the universal man, to the species, as to his own proper being. This is what the social contract effects. As Professor Jones puts it, ". . . the individual can identify himself with [the general will] because his particular will is an organic part of that larger will." [66] And this is what Marx means when he says that by this "political" form of emancipation (as distinguished from

---

possibility for Rousseau, was a return on the human plane, in the line of Rousseau's teaching concerning man's perfectibility. It was a "return" forward, not back to man's primitive past. As Professor Strauss himself points out, "The feeling for existence as Rousseau experienced and described it has a rich articulation which must have been lacking in the feeling of existence as it was experienced by man in the state of nature." (*Ibid.*, p. 292.)

[64] Cassirer, *Rousseau, Kant, Goethe,* trans. from the German by James Gutmann, Paul Oskar Kristeller, and John Herman Randall, Jr., Princeton University Press, Princeton, N.J., 1947, p. 30.

[65] Rousseau, *Social Contract,* vol. I. p. 6. In *Great Books of the Western World,* vol. 38, p. 391.

[66] Edward McChesney Sait (ed.), *Masters of Political Thought,* vol. II; W. T. Jones, *Machiavelli to Bentham,* Houghton Mifflin Company, Boston, 1949, p. 259.

the complete "human" emancipation which his own doctrine will allegedly accomplish) man leads a "celestial . . . existence *in the political community,* where he considers himself a general being. . . ." [67] This general will is created on the political level by the social contract which reconciles the conflict of civil society's requirement for public judgment with the individual's right to private judgment. By the artifice of each giving himself to all and so giving himself to nobody, the individual remains the judge of the means needed for his self-preservation. Each individual is the author of the law to which all must conform.

The "desperate absurdities of the assumptions of the Social Contract" [68] indeed suggest that Rousseau was groping for a solution to his problem at a deeper level than the "political." That even this best contrived society must be regarded by Rousseau as a form of bondage, is clear both from the fact that the citizen is less free than is man in the state of nature (since the citizen cannot follow unqualifiedly his private desires) and from the fact that Rousseau appeals to a "Legislator" who will instruct the "general will"—a Legislator whose "function . . . has nothing in common with human empire" and who "ought to feel himself capable, so to speak, of changing human nature, of transforming each individual, who is by himself a complete and solitary whole, into a part of a greater whole from which he, in a manner, receives his life and being." [69] It is a generic *being*— not simply a generic will, that Rousseau wants for man. This "greater whole," it should be noted, is not an achievement of the political order, for it is not effected by the general will but is brought about by one whose enterprise is "too difficult for human powers." [70] Man's perfectibility points beyond any civil society: It is the charge of the "Legislator" who will bring man back to the simple feeling of existence—but on the plane of humanity.

[67] Marx, *Die Judenfrage,* pp. 583–584. (Italics added.)

[68] John Morley, *Rousseau,* London, 1873, vol. II, p. 134. Cited by Peter Gay in his Introduction to Ernst Cassirer's *The Question of Jean Jacques Rousseau.*

[69] Rousseau, *Social Contract,* vol. II, p. 7.

[70] *Ibid.*

Rousseau has no prescription for attaining this goal other than the "nation," a much more primordially natural entity than civil society.

"The pre-political nation is more natural than civil society, which is produced by contract. The nation is closer to the original state of nature than is civil society, and therefore it is in important respects superior to civil society. Civil society will approximate the state of nature on the level of humanity to a higher degree, or it will be more healthy, if it rests on the almost natural basis of nationality or if it has a national individuality. . . . National custom and national "philosophy" are the matrix of the general will, just as feeling is the matrix of reason." [71]

This mysterious forming of the free man's life and being out of the depths of race and blood is the work of a "Legislator" whose "divine art" uses the good of civil society as a pure means.

The *mystique* of the nation transcends civil society and goes back beyond self-preservation to the root of self-preservation, namely, the feeling of simple existence, the science of simple souls. But Rousseau does not thereby succeed in raising the science of simple souls to science on the plane of humanity: On the contrary, by appealing to a "Legislator" whose "function has nothing in common with human empire," Rousseau places the principle of social being out of man's self as human. And because the Legislator's enterprise subordinates the good of civil society to the primordially natural nation, to national individuality, man again moves toward the condition of "creator" by moving toward the substitute intelligence of nature.[72] Science on the "human

---

[71] Strauss, *Natural Right and History*, pp. 289–290.

[72] ". . . the nation, understood in the Thomist sense of *Patria* [Fatherland, native country], has indeed rights in regard to the expression of certain of its unique characteristics. The common good of civil society requires that the proper characteristics of the nation be respected—for it is the nation's common good that is sought. . . . However, if the common good of civil society is for the benefit of the nation, it is not directed to the national character as an end; the common good is not a means for the flowering and embellishment of the nation. The good of civil society ought to conform to the nation, ought to be 'its' good. But it does not follow that the good of

plane" can alone pretend to overcome the antagonism between the individual ("who is himself a complete and solitary whole") and the universal being of man; for all the things that man can know and desire (which Rousseau identifies with man's essence, his perfectibility) ought to be wholly comprised within the individual. Nor, then, should the individual be transformed—as Rousseau suggests as the task of the Legislator—from "a complete . . . whole, into a part of a greater whole from which he . . . receives his life and being": rather, the individual life and the general life must be made identical. But this was not possible for Rousseau to achieve, for in his view reason had actually developed unevenly as a result of changes in nature that were accidental in their effect on human perfectibility. Man had irrevocably lost the possibility of attaining, on the human plane, the science of simple souls: the unity of the species had been irrevocably severed in the real life. To put the science of simple souls on the plane of humanity, it was necessary that reason pass into the world itself as a radical critique, that it assume the initiative. The way to the full taking of this step was prepared by David Hume who, standing at "the confluence of the ideas of his epoch . . . opened the way to a new current of ideas which his successors have not neglected to express in their ultimate consequences." [73]

---

civil society be subordinated to the good of the nation. To subordinate the good of civil society to that of the nation is to subordinate reason to nature. This would lead to [an] irrational and voluntarist nationalism. . . . The flowering of the nation is not even itself the proper end of the nation: it remains within the order of means [with respect to the common good of civil society]." (I have made the above translation from DeKoninck, *De la Primauté du bien commun*, pp. 128–129.)

[73] R. J.-M. Marie-de-Lourdes, "Essai de commentaire critique sur l'Enquiry Concerning Human Understanding de David Hume," *Laval Théologique et Philosophique*, vol. 2, no. 1, p. 40, 1946.

VIII

The outcome of autonomous natural law: classical liberalism and conservatism

The political theory of modern liberalism and conservatism represents the second and final step in the progressive realization of the hypothesis of Grotius—the hypothesis according to which we suppose the natural law to be what it is even if there were no Prime Intellect and according to which "the mental and material spheres are reduced to a common denominator, composed of the same elements and combined according to the same laws." We recall that traditionally law as an ordinance of reason for the common good was taken to be an inclination toward the good conceived as consisting essentially in (1) efficient and material principles presupposed to some form, (2) the form by which a thing is what it is, (3) an inclination to action in accordance with the form. With the first stage of the development of the hypothesis of Grotius, the "good"—taken formally, as the perfective principle of nature—was removed, and the concern of politics came to be with human nature's own act of being through political existence: The only "good" that was left was that which is simply convertible with being. With Hobbes, man's making himself specifically human through political existence served to separate him

223

from himself by the abstract alienation of the "mortal god." With Rousseau man is reunited with his universal self on the political plane in the General Will; but Rousseau was unable to restore to man his original "feeling of simple existence" on the plane of humanity. With Locke there is no attempt to identify the individual with the species through the intermediary of state or nation, charged with all the individual's humanity. In Locke's political philosophy the political community has merely the unity found in the manifold of nature by predication and abstraction: It embraces the individuals in the same indeterminate way in which "man" includes "John" and "Paul." Although the goal of Hobbes and Rousseau was more ambitious, the reaching of that goal required first the procedure of Locke: that human reason pass into nature itself as a radical critique. The last vestige of that "artificial barrier" separating man from nature—the human intellect conceived as separable in itself although not existing apart from matter—must be removed: Even the meager awareness that Locke had made the difference between brute and man in the procurement of the common good through the pursuit of private interest must be eliminated. The gap between man and nature must be closed. The full taking of this step was accomplished by David Hume (1711–1776) who perfected the Lockean doctrine and at the same time opened the way to Marx's revolutionary "overthrow" of nature and to the practical attainment for the individual of the abstract ideals of Hobbes and Rousseau. Although indeed Hume's work was not mainly in the field of political philosophy, the general philosophical position that he developed had the profoundest effect on the whole future course of social thought.

David Hume—the attack on causality

Hume pretended to prove what was already implicit in Locke: that there are no universal and necessary reasons in nature, that the universal ideas that Locke had admitted as being "nothing but the capacity they are put to, by the understanding, of signifying or representing many particulars" have no root in reality. The test of utility for any political and moral action, for every law and institution will henceforth not lie in any relation whatsoever to natural and universal necessity. The phase of liberalism that began with the attempt to find in autonomous nature the sufficient, original, and formative principle of human nature, ends by freeing man from the authority of any impersonal, necessary, and universal law of nature. As should be expected, with the elimination of the "ratio" that Aristotle and the medieval tradition had found in nature, law as a *ratio ordinationis* entirely disappears from nature. Thus liberated, politics will find its leading principle in the *mere fact of regularity*—a new conservative (be it noted) blend of the useful and the factual. Regularity in nature will not be recognized for what it had always been taken to be, namely, a *sign* of some determinate reason. The material and efficient principles of nature and of human nature will *not be presupposed to any reason:* They will have no reason beyond themselves. This is the final step in the progressive realization of Grotius' hypothesis. Politics will not now have as its concern human nature's own act of being through political existence: It will be engaged with the manipulability of material and efficient principles, no longer presupposed to any form or essence. This is the root principle of the contemporary phenomena of "social conformity" and the "socialized conscience" on the one hand, and, on the other, of "anomie" and "other-directedness"—of what Lionel Trilling has called liberalism's sense of "variousness and possibility." [1]

Hume will reduce man's knowing powers and, as it were, trace them back from the knowledge of the universal (the prerequisite of all science and art) to experience, memory, and mere sensation. This is not only precisely what he did, but it is the very mode of procedure that he followed, reversing step by step the arguments of the opening chapter of Aristotle's *Metaphysics*. Proceeding henceforth from a concept of nature that reduces it to a merely temporal sense of "that which happens always or

---

[1] Trilling, *The Liberal Imagination*, p. xi.

for the most part," political actions, laws, and institutions will no longer be subject to "understanding" but only to more or less elaborate descriptions. And since, indeed, the intention of this teaching was to show the absence of any necessity in nature, it followed also that—as Hume expressly stated it—"the contrary of every matter of fact is . . . possible; because it can never imply a contradiction, and is conceived by the mind with the same facility and distinctness as if ever so conformable to reality." [2] Thus the conservative side of the coin of classical liberalism was easily turned to the opposite side of doctrinaire liberalism— and indeed of every form of totalitarian destruction. This is why it has been well said that Hume "stands at the confluence of the ideas of his epoch, and opens the way to a current of ideas which his successors have not hesitated to express in their ultimate consequences." [3]

Hume's attack on natural causality is founded on the denial, above alluded to, of nature as the principle of that which happens always or for the most part. Refusing to recognize this principle as the sign of some determinate reason, he cut all communication between the reason that is nature, the reason that is the cause of nature, and the human reason. Since the notions of cause and effect imply order, from which they are inseparable, Hume finds it easier to repudiate natural causality by first repudiating the notion of order. [4] He begins his attack by affirming, indeed, that there is order in thought:

[2] David Hume, *An Enquiry Concerning Human Understanding,* in *The English Philosophers from Bacon to Mill,* Modern Library, Inc., New York, 1939, p. 598.

[3] Marie-De-Lourdes, "Essai de commentaire critique sur l'Enquiry Concerning Human Understanding de David Hume," p. 40. I am fully indebted in the following pages to this excellent critical commentary on Hume's *Enquiry* and have made free use of the material therein, as well as translations of portions thereof.

[4] "Principle" implies a certain order of one thing to another without implying any cause, e.g., window-door; a *terminus a quo* and a *terminus ad quem;* cause implies a certain influx into the being of the caused thing. Cf. *In V Metaph.* lect.1.

It is evident that there is a principle of connection between the different thoughts or ideas of the mind, and that in their appearance to the memory or imagination, they introduce each other with a certain degree of method and regularity.[5]

Since Hume cannot deny the fact of order in our thought, he will deny it in things themselves as the foundation of the order in our thought. Having done this, he will reject both the Intelligence which is the cause of the order of nature and the human intelligence as capable of knowing this order.

Hume enumerates three principles which in his opinion account for the connection between ideas: resemblance, contiguity in time and space, and causality. His method is to identify causality with resemblance and contiguity:

That these principles serve to connect ideas will not, I believe, be much doubted. A picture naturally leads our thoughts to the original [resemblance]: the mention of one apartment in a building naturally introduces an inquiry or discourse concerning the others [contiguity]: and if we think of a wound, we can scarcely forbear reflecting on the pain which follows it [cause and effect]: . . . The more instances we examine, and the more care we employ, the more assurance shall we acquire, that the enumeration, which we form from the whole, is complete and entire.[6]

As an example of resemblance Hume gives us the relation of an image which leads our thought to the original. The example is not apposite: It exceeds altogether the very notion of resemblance. Undoubtedly, an image does suppose resemblance, but an image does not consist properly and formally in the resemblance. As St. Augustine says, an egg is not the image of another egg. (This is not one of St. Augustine's greatest sayings, but it is great right here.) Resemblance is only the generic element of image. Beyond mere resemblance, image adds not only likeness according to the nature of the thing, but an order of origin

---

[5] Hume, *op. cit.*, p. 596.
[6] Hume, *op. cit.*, p. 597.

between the original and the image. Thus, the design of an egg is the image of an egg which is the original of this image. Thus, both by reason of similitude according to the nature of the thing and by relation of origin, image necessarily implies order. Order is not at all implied by resemblance. In short, by the astute intermediary of an evidently bad example, Hume identifies image with resemblance and thus conjures away the order that is essential to imitation. Nor can it be alleged in Hume's behalf that he wanted only to speak of simple resemblance; for if that had been his intention (to deal with pure resemblance—that between two eggs, for example), he would not have been able to establish the connection that was vital for his argument, namely, the connection of order, which he wants to repudiate.

We find the same curious inappositeness in the example that he gives of contiguity. It should first of all be observed that he takes the term "contiguity" in a very general sense of a "pure being-togetherness" (and not in the strict sense, according to which a thing that is in succession and touches is contiguous)[7] which unquestionably includes a relation but abstracts from all consequence and order. "The mention of one apartment in a building naturally introduces an inquiry or discourse concerning the others" precisely indeed because a house is a whole whose parts have a relation of order among them and are also ordered to the whole. Hume avails himself of the order that is evident in his example by relating it to pure contiguity in which there is not necessarily any order. Here again there is the same ruse that he employs in the example of resemblance: He appeals to order for the purpose of denying it through the astute intermediary of a bad example.

Hume's long and labored attack on the principle of causality is replete with the same smooth sophistry that marks the attack on order. The fact that a conclusion, from the point of view of logic, is an effect of the premises is constantly exploited to conceal real causality. The latter, moreover, is identified with re-

[7] Cf. *Physics* V.227a.9.

semblance and contiguity, the vacuity of which he has already put in evidence. The exploitation of logic to conceal real causality is evident in the example Hume gives to show that "the contrary of every matter of fact is . . . possible; because it can never imply a contradiction, and is conceived by the mind with the same facility and distinctness as if ever so conformable to reality." Before considering the example that he offers one should first note that the possibility of *conceiving* the contrary of any proposition whatsoever implies nothing at all of the possible *truth* of this contrary proposition. The propositions that Hume gives—"That the sun will not rise tomorrow" and "that it will rise"—are indeed equally *intelligible:* that is, the term intelligible applies only to the *signification* presupposed to the truth or falsity of the proposition. From the fact, however, that one can conceive that the sun will not rise tomorrow, it does not follow that this hypothesis carries with it a real possibility equal to the contrary hypothesis. Yet this is apparently just what Hume supposes. Further, he has chosen an example which adroitly hides the passage from the possibility of conceiving a proposition to the conception of its real possibility. Thus, for example, I know very well what is *signified* by the propositions "the human soul is immortal" and "the human soul is mortal," but from the knowledge of the signification of these propositions I cannot infer at all that in reality the human soul can be one as well as the other; I cannot deduce from it that "the human soul is mortal" implies no contradiction.

It is, then, not a question of knowing whether the propositions "the sun will not rise tomorrow" and "the sun will rise tomorrow" are equally intelligible as to their signification, but of knowing whether one and the other can be equally true. Now if it is at the same time possible with *real* possibility that the sun will rise tomorrow and that it will not rise tomorrow, this indeed is because the rising of the sun is properly contingent. It is necessary, then, to exclude the possibility of a natural impossibility of the sun not rising tomorrow. In that case Hume would be engaged with propositions concerning future contingents which are neither determinately true nor determinately false; and then all he would be able to say is that he does not see any contradiction in the sun not rising tomorrow, although in reality there may be such a contradiction. But Hume is obliged to suppose as certain that a proposition does not imply a contradiction, for the whole value of his argument turns on *real* possibility. In short, to infer that the contrary of every matter of fact is possible with real possibility, it would be necessary for him to suppose that that of which we do not *see* the contradiction is in fact, in itself, not contradictory. What Hume does is to attribute to things themselves a condition or status that is due solely to the conception of the mind.[8]

When next Hume wishes to put his finger on the relation of cause and effect, he is indeed constrained by the falsity of his preceding analysis to bring forth examples that could not be better suited to conceal real causality:

All reasonings concerning matter of fact seem to be founded on the relation of *cause and effect*. By means of that relation alone we can go beyond the evidence of our memory and senses. If you were to ask a man, why he believes any matter of fact, which is absent; for instance, that his friend is in the country, or in France; he would give you a reason; and this reason would be some other fact; as a letter received from him, or the knowledge of his former resolutions and promises. A man finding a watch or any other machine in a desert island, would conclude that there had once been men in that island. All our reasonings concerning fact are the same nature. *And here it is constantly supposed that there is a connection between the present fact and that which is inferred from it.*[9]

Consider the first example: "If you were to ask," etc. This example puts in evidence not the reason why the friend is in France, but rather the reason why one believes that he is in

[8] "Hume is obliged indeed to base himself upon a knowledge of the real that is infinitely deeper than that to which human science, however perfect one supposes it, can ever attain. No one, in fact, pretends to have a *scientific* certitude of the rising of the sun. Perhaps it is possible that it will not rise, and this possibility can be due to chance, or to nature, who knows? . . . the sun might explode. . . ." (Marie-De-Lourdes, *op. cit.*, p. 39.)

[9] Hume, *op. cit.*, p. 599.

France. But these are two absolutely different things, and it is necessary to insist on it. If one understands the term *cause* of the cause in itself, one must answer by giving the causes of the friend's voyage, e.g., his business affairs, and give the means by which he got where he went. It is true that "the former resolutions" are properly causes, although they do not imply with certainty the stay of the friend in France. To the question posed by Hume one ought to reply simply by giving the reason why one believes that his friend is in France. But this reason is not necessarily a cause. In other words, the "why" absolutely of the presence of the friend in France and the "why" of my knowledge of his presence in France are formally different things, and the notion of causality is in no sense formal in the latter case.

Consider the second example: "A man finding," etc. Here Hume insinuates that the reason why the watch is considered an effect is *because it leads us to the thought of man!* It is very true that the watch is an effect—an effect of the watchmaker's art. The objection to the example is that it relegates to second place the essential point that ought to be brought to light. In order properly to make manifest the relation of causality, Hume ought to have asked the question in the following terms: "How does it happen that from the presence of a watch on a desert island one can infer that there were men on that island?" To which one can reply that the watch and its presence on the desert island can only be effects produced by man. In the example in question it is because the watch is an effect of human art that it leads us to man. It is not considered to be an effect by reason of its leading us to think of man—as Hume wants us to suppose. Here again Hume artfully achieves the disappearance of the notion of causality by identifying it with the mere connection of two facts such that from one the other can be inferred. But this is manifestly not what is required by the notion of causality, for from one fact another can be inferred without the one necessarily being the effect or cause of the other: Do we say that the window is the cause of the door, or night the cause of day? But Hume wants us to suppose that this is all that a causal relation amounts to.

If we come to believe that there exists a relation of causality between two things which experience has always shown to be together, it is never because we have always found them together. It is because of an appearance of causality which in no way consists in the conjunction alone; it is because the case in question resembles other cases where causality has manifestly and incontestably been present. The hidden problem concerns the knowledge that is first of all required before one is able to grasp a thing as the cause or the effect of another thing. The knowledge which permits one to infer suffocation from water— even when one has never experienced this phenomenon—is based, in the last instance, on the sensible appearances of water and on the human physiology. It is not based simply on the experience of preceding cases of suffocation from water. This conjunction indeed is only the point of departure for the investigation into the *determinate* cause of the phenomenon. In the latter case we try to give the reason *per se* why the phenomenon repeats itself, the "why" of the occurrence concerning which pure experience only indeterminately gives us knowledge that there *is some* reason. Hume indeed denies in advance the very possibility of science which has always been a knowledge *approaching* the true causes in their proper determination. Does not the physicist seek to know why there is a constant relation between volume, pressure, and temperature of a gas? The constancy of this relation through many experiences is only the reason for seeking the determinate reason of this constancy. Is it not because the physicist knows that there ought to be a reason for this regularity that he looks for this reason?

If indeed, as Aristotle says, "experience seems pretty much like science and art," there is, as he carefully points out, an essential difference:

. . . but really science and art come to men *through* experience; for "experience made art," as Polus says, "but inexperience luck." Now art arises when from many notions gained by experience one universal judgment about a class of objects is produced. For to have a judgment that when Callias was ill of this disease this did him good, and similarly in the case of Socrates and in many individual cases, is a matter of experience; but to judge that it has done good to all persons of a certain constitution, marked off in one class, when they were ill of this disease, e.g., to phlegmatic or bilious people when burning with fever —this is a matter of art.

With a view to action experience seems in no respect inferior to art, and men of experience succeed even better than those who have theory without experience. (The reason is that experience is knowledge of individuals, art of universals, and actions and productions are all concerned with the individual for the physician does not cure *man*, except in an incidental way, but Callias or Socrates or some other called by some such individual name, who happens to be a man. If, then, a man has the theory without the experience, and recognizes the universal but does not know the individual included in this, he will often fail to cure; for it is the individual that is to be cured.) But yet we think that *knowledge* and *understanding* belong to art rather than to experience, and we suppose artists to be wiser than men of experience (which implies that Wisdom depends in all cases rather on knowledge); and this because the former know the cause, but the latter do not. For men of experience know that the thing is so, but do not know why, while the others know the "why" and the cause. Hence we think also that the master-workers in each craft are more honourable and know in a truer sense and are wiser than the manual workers, because they know the causes of the things that are done (we think the manual workers are like certain lifeless things which act indeed, but act without knowing what they do, as fire burns—but while the lifeless things perform each of their functions by a natural tendency, the labourers perform them through habit); thus we view them as being wiser not in virtue of being able to act, but of having the theory for themselves and knowing the causes. And in general, it is a sign of the man who knows and of the man who does not know, that the former can teach, and therefore we think art more truly knowledge than experience is; for artists can teach, and men of mere experience cannot.[10]

Confounding experience, universal, and cause by constantly introducing as examples of causality various illusions concerning knowledge of the determinate causes, Hume "proves" that the

[10] *Metaph.* I.981a.1–981b.10.

idea of causality is itself identical with these illusions. Holding all along to a confusion between, on the one hand, reason and real cause, and on the other hand, reason and the cause of knowledge, Hume has an easy time of it making loose use of this ambiguity. The marvelous order of the first chapter of Aristotle's *Metaphysics* is reversed so that human art and science are reduced to the mere experience by which indeed—as Hume says —brute beasts, ignorant and stupid peasants—nay infants—improve.[11]

It is, then, not to be wondered that, as Professor Sabine says, after Hume's critique of natural causality, values came to be nothing but "the reaction of human preference to some state of social and physical fact; in the concrete they [were] too complicated to be generally described even with so loose a word as utility." [12] The first effect in the order of morals and politics was the abandonment of the meaning of "government" even in the reduced sense in which Hobbes, Locke, and Rousseau had understood it. The place of "government" was taken by "society" which was conceived as having intrinsic principles of natural operation presupposed to no intelligible form. Professor Sheldon Wolin expresses very well the general effect of Hume's critique:

The offspring of this kind of theorizing was a non-political model of a society which, by virtue of being a closed system of interacting

[11] Commenting on Hume's claim to originality in the treatment of "the nature of that evidence which assures us of any real existence and matter of fact, beyond the present testimony of our senses, and the records of our memory," Marie-De-Lourdes observes that this precisely was one of the principal occupations of philosophers since ancient times: "Let us merely mention Parmenides, Plato, and Aristotle. But one will perhaps be less astonished at this singular remark of Hume's if the peculiar manner in which he poses the problem be taken into account. He appears as an innovator indeed if one considers the terms and the context of the problem without even mentioning all the false presuppositions of which they are the fruit. He is original indeed in this, that with a hardihood and a truly exceptional lack of information he has opened the way to a new current of ideas, which his successors have not failed to express in their ultimate consequences." (Marie-De-Lourdes, *op. cit.*, p. 40.)

[12] Sabine, *A History of Political Theory*, p. viii.

forces, seemed able to sustain its own existence without the aid of an "outside" political agency. . . . The effect . . . was to accept existing society as a datum, susceptible to minor modifications but always with the frame of reference supplied by the *status quo*. . . . The unique aspect of [the liberal] theory was the contention that purposive activity could be undertaken successfully without reference to any supporting principles excepting that of "nature." . . . The teachings associated with the traditional authorities of church, class, and political order were held to be unnatural. Hence what was truly radical in liberalism was its conception of society as a network of activities carried on by actors who know no principle of authority. Society represented not only a spontaneous and self-adjusting order, but a condition untroubled by the presence of authority.[13]

The reduction of nature to the mere fact of regularity in the operation of its material and efficient principles left man not only without proper first principles for a science of politics— these had already been lost by Machiavelli, Hobbes, Locke, and Rousseau—it left him without any clear and consistent idea of the human nature itself. As Professor Wolin observes, ". . . no longer able to communicate on the basis of a common interior life [men] were reduced to knowing each other solely from the outside; that is, on the basis of socially acquired responses and values." [14] Had not Hume himself had the public intervene: "The discovery of defects in the common philosophy . . . will . . . be . . . an incitement, as is usual, to attempt something more full and satisfactory than has yet been proposed to the public." [15] The "socialized conscience" begins to make its appearance: A conscience that develops by a whole series of "tropisms" in response to outside stimuli. This new concept of the socialized conscience was given classic formulation in Adam Smith's *Theory of Moral Sentiments*.

[13] From *Politics and Vision* by Sheldon Wolin, by permission of Little, Brown and Company, Boston. Copyright © 1960, by Little, Brown and Company, Boston, pp. 292, 298, 301.

[14] *Ibid.*, p. 340.

[15] Hume, *op. cit.*, p. 599.

Adam Smith—the Theory of Moral Sentiments

All virtue, according to Smith (1723–1790) must have its roots in sympathy. The whole basis of morality lies in participation in the feelings of others; but to have ethical value this participation must be considered to be that of an *impartial and well-informed spectator*. From what source does this impartial spectator derive his judgments? It is the imagination alone that enables us to put ourselves in another person's situation; it is by this same faculty that we can divide ourselves, as it were, into two persons and attain an impartial judgment on the morality of our own actions. Since Smith's moral system

demands a constant changing of places and balancing of judgments insofar as we must continually place ourselves in other people's situations to judge their conduct as well as our own, Smith is quite emphatic about the necessity of man living in society if his actions are to be provided with a norm or standard by which they can be classified as proper or improper. Society is the mirror in which we see ourselves as other human beings see us and therefore it enables us to regulate our conduct in conformity with the general judgment. If a man could grow up to maturity in complete isolation in some solitary place, with no means of communication whatsoever with the members of his own species, he would be absolutely incapable of thinking of merit or demerit in reference to his own character; he could no more think of the beauty or deformity of his mind or conduct than he could judge of the beauty or deformity of his own face. Man needs his fellow creatures as reflectors and models by which he can measure his own perfection or imperfection. In this way we can always have a means of testing to see if our actions are such that other people can sympathize with them and use them as a standard for themselves. Our interest in beauty and morals consists wholly and solely in the effect that will be produced upon those around us; "Virtue is not said to be amiable, or to be meritorious, because it is the object of its own love or of its own gratitude, but *because it excites those sentiments in other men.*" [16]

[16] Mother Marie de Jesus, "Adam Smith's Theory of Moral Sentiments," *Laval Théologique et Philosophique*, vol. 17, no. 1, p. 116, 1961.

This notion of social conformity carries implications much beyond the obvious fact that society cannot exist for long if its members do not observe some common ways of behavior. In the first place, the moral self is alienated on to the otherness of society which becomes the common denominator by which the individual must measure his tastes, actions, and whole manner of life. Secondly, because the self is objectively alienated, projected into detached otherness, the sense of emancipation comes from the fact that one can place the burden of responsibility for one's actions upon the self's otherness, upon society. Thirdly, and perhaps most significantly in the light of the development of the thesis I have been maintaining throughout this book, the individual is induced to overcome the external quality of the social norms and to form his interior conscience by them. We must appreciate the curious outcome here of moving toward the condition of "creator" by moving toward the condition of the substitute intelligence which is nature. It is not only that we are back to the ant and the spider of Aristotle's second book of the *Physics;* we are there without the "wisdom" even of these creatures, for there is here no longer the intelligence that Aristotle had found indicated by the repeated success of an operation: There is left only the stupidity that he had found indicated by the uniformity of pattern. It is precisely the *stupidity* of it that we are asked to embrace. Thus the correspondence of the pure autonomy of intellect with the pure autonomy of nature—the essence of rationalism—turns out to be irrationalism raised to a power.

Jeremy Bentham (1748–1832)

The moral theory we have been examining was first put to use by Jeremy Bentham in his celebrated Panopticon project for prison reform. As the name suggests, the prison was to be a circular structure which would make possible a simultaneous scrutiny by the warden of all the prisoners. Under the totally watchful eye of the prison warden the inmates would be under compulsion to follow the required behavior pattern. As Professor

Wolin keenly observes: "Obviously this was too illiberal a notion to apply unaltered to normal existence, but with a slight change, say, substitute society for the warden, would not the social nonconformist feel the same pressure for compliance as the prisoners, *but with the added advantage of having no identifiable overseer?*" [17] This estimate is confirmed indeed by Bentham's final blueprint for a future society:

A whole kingdom, the great globe itself, will become a gymnasium, in which every man exercises himself before the eyes of every other man. Every gesture, every turn of limb or feature, in those whose motions have a visible influence on the general happiness, will be noticed and marked down.[18]

The extreme empiricism of the whole liberal heritage led Bentham to recommend so monstrous a caricature of a free society. The liberal philosophy had made it impossible to understand the "good" in reference to any supporting principle other than "nature" in the purely temporal aspect of its regularity, this latter no longer taken as a sign of some determinate reason. We must see how Bentham drew these dreary and ominous consequences from the way he conceived the good—how his caricature of a free society derives from conceiving the good simply as the useful, itself determined by the regularity of response to pleasure and pain. To do this we must consider the fact that according to traditional political philosophy, the good, as desirable, was called an end or term of movement of desire; and this movement was said to terminate absolutely in the end and relatively in the means through which we come to the end. Now the ultimate term of movement was taken in two ways: either as the thing itself toward which the desire tends, or as a state of rest in that thing. Therefore, in the movement of desire or appetite, the thing that terminates the movement *relatively*, as a means tending toward something else, was called *the useful;* that sought after as the last thing absolutely terminating the

---

[17] Wolin, *op. cit.*, p. 348. (Italics added.)
[18] John Bowring (ed.), *Deontology*, London, 1834, p. 101.

movement of desire as a thing toward which for its own sake the desire tends, was called *the befitting* (for the befitting is that which is desired for its own sake); but that which terminates the movement of desire in the form of repose in the thing desired, was called *the pleasant*.[19] It should be observed, then, that as St. Thomas points out, "those things [that] are properly called pleasing have no other formality under which they are desirable except the pleasant, although at times they are harmful or unbefitting. Whereas the useful applies to such as are undesirable in themselves, but are desired . . . as helpful to something further, e.g., the taking of bitter medicine." [20] Now the Humean critique of nature had eliminated the *rationes* from nature in such fashion as to leave natural operation presupposed to nothing properly "befitting": The consequence was that the good as pleasant is unspecified by any good as befitting, and therefore the useful good can only be what will increase pleasure quantitatively since the things that are called pleasing have no other formality under which they are desired except the pleasant. Thus it was that Bentham was led to make pleasure the simple criterion of the useful, and to make no distinction among pleasures other than a quantitative one. As he unabashedly put it, given the equal quantity of pleasure, push-pin is as good as poetry. Now then, since each individual pursues the maximum quantity of pleasure for himself, and since the quantity of each individual's pleasure is increased by the growing productive capacity of other individuals, the useful is specified by the power of social organization. Society becomes highly complex and individuals increasingly interdependent:

But the more society spreads and the more complicated it becomes, "the more men live in public, the more amenable they are to the moral sanction." Thus they become "every day more virtuous than on the former day," and "they will continue to do so, till, if ever, their nature shall have arrived at its perfection. Shall they stop? Shall they turn

---

[19] See *Summa Theol.* I.Q.5 a.6.C.
[20] *Ibid.* ad 2.

back? The rivers shall as soon make a wall, or roll up the mountains to their source." [21]

As Halévy puts it, ". . . as social relations increase and tighten, the individual will find himself more and more tightly bound, by the force of things, to the accomplishment of his social task, until the day when it will no longer be possible . . . not to act morally." [22] This can easily enough be accomplished since "the mischiefs of disobedience are greater than the mischiefs of obedience": "Every gesture, every turn of limb or feature, in those whose motions have a visible influence on the general happiness, will be noticed and marked down." Where there is no longer anything "befitting," we all become prisoners of all, and the Panopticon project is extended to "the great globe itself." The Big Brothers, like the great whales of Matthew Arnold's poem,

> . . . come sailing by,
> Sail and sail, with unshut eye,
> Round the world forever and aye. . . .

John Stuart Mill (1806–1873)

John Stuart Mill's modification of Benthamite liberalism did nothing to restore the idea of self-government. Although he substituted "qualitative superiority" in pleasures for quantitative superiority as a test of utility, he maintained that the qualitatively superior pleasures would be agreed upon if all had the same experience of different kinds of pleasure. He thus abandoned— as A. D. Lindsay has pointed out[23]—the traditional Aristotelian

[21] Élie Halévy, *The Growth of Philosophic Radicalism*, Beacon Press, Boston, 1955, p. 471. The citations made by Halévy are from Bentham's *Deontology*, vol. I, p. 101.

[22] *Ibid.*

[23] In the introduction to J. S. Mill, *Utilitarianism, Liberty, and Representative Government*, Everyman Library, E. P. Dutton & Co., New York, 1950.

notion of the wise or prudent man as a remote but proper measure
of the true human good. The *raison d'être* of Mill's eloquent
appeal for liberty was the emancipation from the prudence of
the prudent man as a proper if remote measure and rule: In its
place he substituted what he supposed would be the agreed-
upon-by-all judgment of a society of men experienced in different pleasures. In doing so he destroyed the root meaning of
"moral action" which depends not on a natural power determined
to one act, but on a rational power that is indifferently disposed
to many different things contained under the notion of the
good, whether true good or having the appearance of good.
For we must carefully note that in traditional political philosophy pleasure was indeed considered to have the requisite
uniformity of a measure by which to judge moral good and evil
insofar as all pleasure is repose of the appetite in something
good.[24] But the "something good" for man is the activity that is
befitting his nature: As Aristotle had put it, "appropriate pleasures
increase activity . . . whereas pleasures arising from other
sources are impediments to activity." [25] And therefore a man is
recognized as good or bad chiefly according to the pleasures
that he takes: He is a good man who takes pleasure in the things
that ought to please him, and he is an evil man who is pleased
with the things that ought to displease him. Pleasure, then, is a
measure of moral good and evil in the sense that it is the
pleasures that a man takes that give us his measure. Now then,
the prudent man was said to be a *proper* measure for others
because of the conformity of his appetite with an end known to
be truly good. (He was said to be a *remote* measure—and not
an immediate rule and measure for others—because he is to be
imitated by each one doing what each one's own particular contingent circumstances require. The proximate rule for every individual in his own circumstances is ineluctable and incommunicable in purely rational terms.) But for Mill the good is defined

[24] See St. Thomas, *Summa Theol.* I.II.Q.34. a.4: "Whether Pleasure is the
Measure or Rule by which to Judge of Moral Good or Evil?"
[25] *Ethics* X.1175a.29–1175b.30.

in terms of a pleasure that is specified by the fact that it pleases a society of men experienced in different pleasures; by a kind of intrinsic natural principle of operation society itself will be the measure and rule of the useful. For Mill, as for Adam Smith, there is no possibility of man knowing, apart from the mirror of society, what is meritorious and what is not, what is useful, and what is not, in reference to the character. The "socialized conscience" is wholly formed by society as by its proximate measure and rule. What Halévy says of Bentham holds true for Mill: As social relations increase and tighten, the individual finds himself more tightly bound, by the force of things, to the accomplishment of his social task, until the day when it will no longer be possible not to act morally.

However eloquent, Mill's appeal to liberty was thus a specious one. Professor Wolin is right in observing that "there remained a hopelessly unreal quality about Mill's principles of liberty, one which has the effect of reducing them to mere preaching. . . ." [26] In repudiating the intellectual virtue of prudence, Mill was forced to fall back on "mere preaching"—indeed on the very power of society that he had sought to expel in his essay *On Liberty*. How proximate a rule for the individual society was conceived to be will become clear from consideration of the fact that Mill:

. . . proposed that the tyranny of opinion be invoked in order to promote . . . his own pet causes. First, his personal *bête noir*, the old problem of overpopulation, could be alleviated, Mill argued, if there were sufficiently intense social disapproval of large families. . . . Secondly, Mill's argument in *Representative Government* for an "open" rather than a secret ballot was founded on the proposition that voting was a public trust and hence "should be performed under the eye and criticism of the public. . . ." It is less dangerous, Mill concluded, for the individual to be influenced by "others" than by "the sinister interests and discreditable feelings which belong to himself, either individually or as a member of a class." Finally, Mill's sympathies with moderate socialism were derived in part from a belief that

[26] Wolin, *op. cit.*, p. 349.

a society based on communal ownership had superior methods at its disposal for compelling the lazy members to produce.[27]

This is more than preaching; it is indeed more than "utility." For utility derives—as we have noticed—from the necessity of the end, which necessity is not repugnant to liberty when the end cannot be attained except in one way. But apart from the coercion of society, "ends" do not exist for Mill and Bentham: That which *must be* (which is the necessary) is no longer anything that belongs to man by virtue of an intrinsic principle (for Hume had removed the *"rationes"* from nature); nor does it belong to him by virtue of any knowable end that follows upon his nature. It is, therefore, simply the necessity that is imposed by the agent, by the mere power of society, and this had traditionally been defined as "the necessity of coercion," which, St. Thomas says, "is altogether repugnant to the will." [28] In fact, it is violence. How little indeed Mill and his confreres knew— and how disdainful they were—of the ancient philosophy! It is an extraordinary and terrifying thing. For this naïveté—joined with a confidence that would be touching were it not so presumptuous—brought these men to undermine the whole structure of philosophic wisdom, both speculative and practical.

Edmund Burke (1729–1797) and modern conservatism

Modern conservatism as it has developed on the foundation of Burke's thought retains the basic liberal position. Whatever his intentions, Burke was powerless intellectually to restore the classical sense of the "practical" and of "government." The man-

---

[27] From *Politics and Vision* by Sheldon Wolin, by permission of Little, Brown and Company, Copyright © 1960, by Little, Brown and Company, Inc., Boston, pp. 349–350. We may see now that Professor Sabine was more right than he knew when he said that after Hume's critique of natural causality, values came to be "too complicated to be generally described with so *loose* a word as utility." (Above, p. 234. Italics added.) As social relations increase and tighten, it becomes impossible not to act morally!

[28] *Summa Theol.* I.Q.82 a.1.

ner of his opposing "abstract theory" and "abstract rights" and giving primary place to history and experience, shows that Burke misconceived the very character of the autonomy of human reason that he hoped to repudiate; he failed to see that it was precisely by moving toward the condition of the substitute intelligence of nature that man sought to emancipate himself in terms of the condition of "creator." Burke's warm approval of Adam Smith's *Theory of Moral Sentiments* clarifies for us his view on the question of what the measure of truth is in practical matters.[29] For the Greek-Medieval tradition, truth in practical matters is measured primarily by conformity of the appetite with what is known to be truly good, whereas according to this same tradition, speculative truth is measured by mere conformity of the reason with what is.[30] Smith's theory—which Burke proclaimed to be "in all essential parts just"—had indeed held "that virtue consists in conformity to reason . . . in some respect," but this respect had nothing to do with the first principles of right and wrong. "These first perceptions as well as all other experiments upon which any general rules are founded, cannot be the object of reason, but of the immediate sense and feeling."[31] In the same vein Burke observed that "When we go but one step beyond the immediate sensible qualities of things, we go out of our depth. All we do after is but a faint struggle, that shows we are in an element which does not belong to us."[32] This is the ele-

---

[29] "We conceive that here the theory is in all its essential parts just, and founded on truth and nature. The author seeks for the foundation of the just, the fit, the proper, the decent, in our most common and most allowed passions; and making approbation and disapprobation the tests of virtue and vice, and showing that those are founded on sympathy, he raises from this simple truth, one of the most beautiful fabrics of moral theory, that has perhaps ever appeared." (*Annual Register*, II, 1759, p. 485. Cited in Francis P. Canavan, S.J., *The Political Reason of Edmund Burke*, The Duke University Press, Durham, N.C., 1960, p. 56.)

[30] *Ethics* VI.1139a.22ff. Cf. *In VI Ethics* lect.2.

[31] Smith, *Essays*, London, 1869, p. 283.

[32] *A Philosophical Inquiry into the Origin of Our Ideas of the Sublime and the Beautiful*, in *The Works of Edmund Burke*, Bohn's Standard Library I, George Bell & Sons, London, 1889, p. 143.

nent of "abstract rights" and "immutable principles" which (because—as will become evident—Burke understands them in the
Hobbesian sense) "in proportion as they are metaphysically
true, they are morally and politically false." [33] They are not,
then, for Burke, as they were for the classical tradition, universal
common notions from which conclusions are drawn and determinations made by political prudence; rather, these "metaphysic
rights entering into common life, like rays of light which pierce
a dense medium, are, by the laws of nature, refracted from their
straight line. Indeed, in the gross and complicated mass of human
passions and concerns, the primitive rights of men undergo such
a variety of refractions and reflections, that it becomes absurd
to talk of them as if they continued in the simplicity of their
original direction." [34] What Burke has in mind is not, then, the
work of political prudence classically understood: for prudence
makes varying determinations of common first principles in such
fashion that these principles are said to be "changed" only "by
way of addition," or according to their original direction.[35] What
Burke has in mind—as indeed he says—is rather the "abatement"
of "anything from the full rights of man"; it is the "abatement" of
these rights that defines the "convenience" of society.[36] Burke's
rhetoric, acceptable on that level, is based on faulty understanding of the principles of political philosophy. What has been said
of Adam Smith may with equal justice be said of Burke:

The moral judgment is based, not upon inner intuition of rational
truth . . . but upon the reflected sentiments of other individuals; and
the moral sentiments of himself and of those of his fellowmen, mutually supporting and influencing one another, produces the objective
order of moral standards. At the same time this objective moral order
is not a transcendent rational order, like the order of immutable truth

[33] Edmund Burke, *Reflections on the Revolution in France,* William B.
Todd (ed.), Rinehart & Co., Inc., New York, 1959, p. 74.

[34] *Ibid.,* p. 73.

[35] *Summa Theol.* I.II.Q.94 a.5.

[36] Burke, *Reflections on the Revolution in France,* p. 72.

to which the intellectualist moralist appealed, but an order immanent in human experience, and varying with the conditions of experience.[37]

In short, moral truth finds its measure in conformity of the reason with what *is,* and not in conformity of the desires with what is known to be truly good. And "what *is*" is what is refracted and reflected by the mirror of society.

It is Burke's agreement with the Hobbesian view of natural rights that explains his insistence on the need "to abate anything from the full rights of men" and his conviction that these rights, as first principles, are defective in proportion to their degree of abstract perfection. Burke adheres closely to the Hobbesian account of natural rights:

Government is not made in virtue of natural rights, which may and do exist in total independence of it; and exist in much greater clearness, and in a much greater degree of abstract perfection; but their abstract perfection is their practical defect. *By having a right to everything, they want everything.* . . . Society requires not only that the passions of individuals should be subjected, but that even in the mass and body, as well as in the individuals, the inclinations of men should frequently be thwarted, their will controlled, and their passions brought into subjection. This can only be done *by a power out of themselves;* and not, in the exercise of its function, subject to that will and to those passions which it is its office to bridle and subdue. . . .

The moment you abate anything from the full rights of men, each to govern himself, and suffer any artificial, positive limitation upon those rights, from that moment the whole organization of government becomes a consideration of convenience.[38]

The "metaphysic rights" of man are, for Burke, politically irrelevant. Indeed, they enter the cultural life of man only under pain of chaos entering. Nor does it help Burke's position to say that because he misunderstood the nature of the first principles he did well to pronounce them "politically false": For the con-

[37] Glenn Morrow, *The Ethical and Economic Theories of Adam Smith,* Cornell University Press, Ithaca, N.Y., 1923, p. 33.

[38] Burke, *Reflections on the Revolution in France,* pp. 71–72.

sequence was that the political art by which the chaos of "abstract rights," with all their alleged speculative rectitude, is kept from breaking through and destroying men's "organization . . . of convenience" must needs be accomplished by *a power out of themselves.*"

What is this "power out of themselves?" It cannot be "reason" or "will," for these indeed in their "abstract perfection" and in the "simplicity of their original direction" lead to "[the] right to everything." We get a clue to the answer in Burke's comparison of the art of politics with the sciences of medicine and physiology. The "political system is placed in a just correspondence . . . with the mode of existence decreed to a permanent body composed of transitory parts." [39] The political order is to be accepted very much as an individual accepts his physical nature —as indeed not subject to his will. Now in the first *Lectio* of Book I of his Commentary on the *Ethics* of Aristotle, St. Thomas had clarified Aristotle's distinction between physics and politics by observing the following:

So the task of social philosophy, with which we are here dealing, is the study of human actions insofar as they are related to one another and have some end in view. It must be noted that we are dealing only with human actions, that is to say, with actions that proceed from human volition according to the ordinance of reason. For there are certain actions found in man which are not so subject to the will and reason, and these are not properly said to be human; such, for instance, are the purely vegetative processes of the body. Such actions cannot strictly be called human and do not enter in any way into the considerations of political philosophy. [40]

The power that Burke alludes to as "out of themselves," and "in the exercise of its function [not] subject to [the will]," is first and radically the "political system . . . with the mode of existence decreed to a permanent body composed of transitory parts"; and secondly, the "physicians" of this body, whose "con-

[39] *Ibid.*, p. 38.
[40] *In I Ethics* lect.1.

stitutional policy [works] after the pattern of nature." [41] Now medicine is of course an "operable" science, but it is classed under physics in the sense that the principle of its operation derives from properties of natural powers. St. Thomas explains the matter as follows:

. . . the subject of medicine [the human body] is not a part of the subject of natural science in the same way as it is a part of medical science. Although the curable body is a natural body, it is not, however, the subject of medicine inasmuch as it is curable by nature, but as it is curable by art. Since, however, in the healing which is effected by art, art is the minister of nature [because some natural power, aided by art, is the cause of healing] the principle or reason of the operation of art ought to derive from the properties of natural things. And thus medicine is subordinate to physics; and in the same way . . . the science of agriculture, and all other sciences of the same order. [42]

Now classical political philosophy had held that it is not any natural power that is first and properly the concern of the political art, but on the contrary, rational powers that are not determined to one particular action but are inclined indifferently to many. It is precisely their specification by free action—which cannot rely upon or imitate a principle of natural operation— that constitutes the proper art of politics. [43] It is true that Aristotle also compares medicine and politics as arts, [44] but not, of course, in the decisive respect which distinguishes medicine as an operable science under physics from politics as a practical science whose principles of operation do not derive from the properties of natural things. But it is precisely in respect of this difference that Burke likens them. With Aristotle the comparison is made on the basis of the element of "possibility" that both the physician and the politician must consider: The "possibility" that the politician must consider is basically rooted in the customs and

[41] Burke, *Reflections on the Revolution in France*, p. 39.

[42] *In de Trinitate*, Q.5 a.1 ad 5.

[43] Cf. *Summa Theol.* I.II.Q.55 a.1.

[44] See above, Chap. V, pp. 136–137.

habits of a people—customs and habits which, be it noted, not only have a rational root (and are thus based on a free principle) but are precisely taken as most efficaciously and clearly expressing the people's freedom.

Finding the principle or reason of the political art in some natural power of "a permanent body composed of transitory parts," Burke placed the ends of human life out of man's self as human. Practical truth for Burke is measured, as indeed it was for Hume and Smith, by conformity with what *is*—society's standards—not by conformity with what is known to be the true human good. The result was to leave political matters free from the scrutiny of human reason as ordering and directing to an end known to be good and realized through good acts, habits, laws, institutions; and to turn them over to "a power out of themselves." Indeed the ultimate outcome of this line of thought was to put the ends of human life on the same plane with the final causes in nature—something Aristotle had explicitly warned against: The explanation of which is that since the *rationes* in nature have no necessity in them except *ex hypothesi* (for they depend ultimately on the simple will of God),[45] it follows *a pari* that the ends of human life come to depend on the inscrutable will of the political artist—of Carlyle's "Able-Hero," of Nietzsche's superman, of the Duce and the Fuehrer. The facet of autonomous nature emphasized by Burke's conservatism has its natural issue in the sort of obscurantist spiritualism of Hitler's "community homogeneous in nature and feeling"—*die Einheit Deutscher Seelen*—based on the primordial nature of race and blood; it may equally well be considered to have its natural issue in Marx's statement that "the human essence is no abstraction in each single individual [but rather], the *ensemble* of . . . social relations." One's "species-life," one's "social humanity" is one's "real" life and one's life in its individuality is not one's "real" life.[46] It becomes, in either kind of totalitarianism, impossible

---

[45] *Physics* II. See Chap. II, pp. 35–36.

[46] Burke could subscribe to Marx's statement that when consciousness supposes that it is really conceiving "something other than . . . existing prac-

not to act morally. We are confronted with the entrance of magic and myth into the secular world.

The dilemma of liberalism

It is the considerations that we have been examining in this chapter that serve to explain the matter that was so great a puzzle to Cassirer in *The Myth of the State*: How is it that in the twentieth century, the age of man's highest technical competence, the elements of magic and myth for the first time in the history of civilization should have entered into the purely secular sphere? [47] Our whole preceding inquiry has turned on the question of this paradox of modern political theory—of the general loss of "vision of a general enlargement and freedom and rational direction of human life." [48] It is a question that may well be, as Professor Trilling suggests, "the most important, the most fully challenging question in culture that at this moment we can ask." It is indeed the most important political question, for "it is no longer possible to think of politics except as the politics of culture, the organization of human life toward some end or other, toward the modification of sentiments, which is to say, the quality of human life." [49]

It was the Humean expulsion of the divine *rationes* from nature that opened the way to the entrance of myth and magic into our secular culture and made it possible for the politicians of the great totalitarian systems to act, at the same time, as political craftsmen and magicians, to be priests "of a new, entirely irrational and mysterious religion." [50] The order whereby the teleological character of human life had formerly been "projected,"

---

tice, . . . conceiving something without conceiving something real," it flatters itself. See Marx and Engels, *The German Ideology*, International Publishers Company, Inc., New York, p. 20.

[47] Cassirer, *The Myth of the State*, pp. 281–282.

[48] Trilling, *The Liberal Imagination*, p. xi.

[49] *Ibid.*

[50] Cassirer, *The Myth of the State*, p. 282.

if you will, upon the whole realm of natural phenomena is, in modern theory, reversed. "Aristotle's final causes are characterized as a mere *'asylum ignorantiae.'*" [51] Asylum of ignorance indeed, because if we accept nature as the original formative principle of all that is, then the "aberrations" in nature become just as "intelligent" as its apparent "intentions." This is why Mr. Trilling can observe that the democratic virtues require the acceptance of all social facts "in the sense that no judgment must be passed on them, that any conclusion drawn from them which perceives values and consequences will turn out to be 'undemocratic.'" [52]

How "free" and "democratic" is nature may indeed best be seen by recalling Eddington's picture of its status in modern physics, where the exigencies of the experimental method justify its special view of nature. The world of "scientific nature" is "mostly emptiness" in which, "sparsely scattered, . . . electric charges [rush] about with great speed . . . modern physics has by delicate test and remorseless logic assured me that my [scientific world] is the only one which is really there—wherever 'there' may be." [53] This is what the teleology of nature looks like when, in the line of its hypothetical autonomy, it is cut from dependence on the Prime Intellect. The physical universe appears to be bereft of specific natures and recognized "intentions": it is no longer "familiar," "given," or "governed." Liberty of contrariety seems to be the very essence of liberty.

This certainly appears to be the meaning of liberty outlined for us by the late Judge Learned Hand in an address entitled "A Fanfare for Prometheus." [54] Judge Hand begins his inquiry

---

[51] Cassirer, *Essay on Man*, p. 36.

[52] Trilling, *op. cit.*, p. 234.

[53] Eddington, *The Nature of the Physical World*, pp. ix–xvi.

[54] Judge Hand's address has been printed by the American Jewish Committee. A major portion of it appears in Edwin S. Newman (ed.), *The Freedom Reader*, Oceana Publications, New York, 1955, pp. 22–26. The citations hereinafter made are to this edition. The essay is also contained in Irving Dillard (ed.), *The Spirit of Liberty Papers and Addresses of Learned Hand*, Alfred A. Knopf, Inc., New York, 1959, pp. 219–225.

into the notion of liberty by remarking indeed that it is "a naïve opinion" that holds "that [liberty] means no more than that each individual shall be allowed to pursue his own desires without let or hindrance." [55] For this—he says somewhat surprisingly—is what characterizes those who believe in "indefectible principles": "Human nature is malleable *especially* if you can indoctrinate the disciple with indefectible principles." [56] What Judge Hand apparently means in these obscure and cryptic passages is that if there were some definite shape to human nature itself (human nature would be especially malleable), one could then without "let or hindrance" pursue the work of its formation. But there is no such definite shape at all, Hand thinks. Human nature is indeed malleable, but it is properly such, Hand tells us, not because of the infinite variability of prudential judgments in attaining the mean of reason which is the appointed end of the natural reason, but rather because of the absence of any end appointed by the natural reason. Disciples of indefectible principles are compared to the bee or the ant who "appears to be, and no doubt in fact, is, accomplishing his own purpose." [57] Judge Hand sees in the regularity of the bee's and the ant's action for an end a rudimentary "liberty" the perfection of which is in proportion to the possibilities of deflecting from any fixed end. Since the possibility of deflection from a "natural intention" is notably greater in the case of human behavior, Judge Hand seems to think that the specific difference between human liberty and animal "liberty" lies in the absence in human affairs of any indefectible principles. The traditional idea of a free nature, namely, one that moves itself by an idea "conceived and in a way contrived by it" [58] gives way to a concept of liberty based on the element of indetermination in nature. And indeed, if we accept the hypothesis of the autonomy of nature, then not only —as I have said—do the "aberrations" in nature become just as

[55] *Ibid.*, p. 22.
[56] *Ibid.*, p. 23. (Italics added.)
[57] *Ibid.*, pp. 22–23.
[58] *Contra Gentiles* II.chap.47.

intelligent as its apparent "intentions," but—by the law that reduces the material and mental spheres to a common denominator —they become *the exemplar of freedom* in the world of culture and civilization. As Judge Hand says, human nature is malleable *especially* if you can indoctrinate the disciple with indefectible principles; it is freer and not so malleable if it cannot be definitely shaped. But what human nature is if it has no recognizable shape at all is something for which it is hard to find a word: It is like Eddington's "scientific table"—it is "there—wherever 'there' may be." This is why, when the world of culture and civilization finds its prototype in the "scientific world" of physics, the modern politician can act as both *homo faber* and *homo magus.* There is here a freedom greater than even Machiavelli had conceived for human nature; for he had brought the ends of human life under the rules of an art operating on man's original indetermination to good and evil as upon uniform and homogeneous matter: He had advised the prince to know how not to be good; but the theory of human nature in modern liberalism does not know what "not to be good" is. Man is part of that world of "shadows" of which Eddington speaks, and finds himself by "radar," as Mr. Riesman says. And Mr. Trilling, to refer to him again, says that the American critic in his liberal and progressive character, prefers Theodore Dreiser to Henry James because Dreiser's books "have the awkwardness, the chaos . . . which we associate with 'reality.' In the American metaphysic, reality is always material reality . . . unformed, impenetrable. . . ." [59] No more than does physics have anything to say about the "familiar table" that "lies visible to my eyes and tangible to my grasp," does liberalism have anything to say about the familiar world of moral, aesthetic, and political ends. This is not the cynicism of Machiavelli; this is "truth" and "science." By delicate test and remorseless logic the social scientist has shown that "facts" are the only things that are really there: Curiously the "facts" make up indeed a shadow-world comparable to the world of shadows with which experimental physics rightly

[59] Trilling, *op. cit.*, pp. 10–11.

deals—the "frank realization of which is one of the most significant of recent advances"—in physics!

For we must notice what is the character of the facts that prevent man, in Judge Hand's view, from pursuing his desires without let or hindrance. They are, he tells us "at war" with "indefectible principles." [60] Now in regard to them, we must again take notice of the important difference between the physical world and the world of human culture and civilization. After telling us that modern physics has assured us that the "scientific table" is the only one which is really "there," Eddington quickly adds:

> . . . I need not tell you that modern physics will never succeed in exorcising that first [familiar] table . . . which lies visible to my eyes and tangible to my grasp. . . . No doubt they are ultimately to be identified in some fashion. But the process by which the external world of physics is transformed into a world of familiar acquaintance . . . is outside the scope of physics. . . . The frank realization that physical science is concerned with a world of shadows is one of the most significant of recent advances.[61]

The physicist is not disturbed by his inability to account for the "familiar world": It is there, "without let or hindrance." It is something "given" and something "governed." And because this is so the hypotheses employed by physicists to "save the appearances" are not unlimited in number: They must increasingly explain the domain understood by the sensible impressions. But the world of human culture and civilization is, on the contrary, as we have had occasion to point out, a world that has to be constructed—not from nothing, but, unlike the familiar world of physics, there is nothing there that cannot be exorcised. The politician can indeed be both *homo faber* and *homo magus,* "the priest of a new, entirely irrational and mysterious religion." (We see two of these "priests" in the cartoon which precedes the epilogue to this book.) What can be exorcised are the ends

---

[60] *The Freedom Reader,* p. 24.
[61] Eddington, *The Nature of the Physical World,* p. xvi.

of human life appointed by the natural reason (including truth, which is the end of the theoretic intellect) and the natural associations (the family, the State) that help to guarantee the ends of living. These can indeed be exorcised:[62] They were said, in the traditional philosophy, to be indefectible principles because the liberty of contrariety whereby they can be exorcised is not a mark of the perfection of human nature. Indeed, as Aristotle says, it is vice that exorcises them. The self-liberation envisaged by liberalism is precisely that man may experience very tangibly the material infinity experienced theoretically by the modern physicist, and free himself from the world of common experience—the world from which the physicist never succeeds in freeing himself. If modern physics were taken to mean, indeed, that the human intellect by becoming aware of its own infinity through measuring its powers by the infinite universe, reaches things as they really are in nature so that nature be considered "operable" in itself,[63] modern social science means that in the world produced by human effort, man is freed from the imaginary boundaries of "indefectible principles" and "natural associations" so that he may experience practically and not merely theoretically the generic nature of his being: a shadow world of facts that have about them indeed the quality of myth and magic. As Mr. Nehru, in the cartoon preceding our epilogue, is telling the U.S. and the U.N.: "You don't understand that we alone can say what is right and what is wrong." For the facts which liberalism recognizes as providing the "only truthworthy way of living" must never be thought of as "explaining" the domain of that common

---

[62] The common principles of the natural law cannot, in the abstract, be blotted out of the conscience; but these can be blotted out "in the case of a particular action, insofar as reason is hindered from applying the general principle to a particular point of practice, on account of concupiscence or some other passion; . . .—But as to the secondary precepts, the natural law can be blotted out from the human heart, either by evil persuasions, just as in speculative matters errors occur in respect of necessary conclusions; or by vicious customs and corrupt habits. . . ." (*Summa Theol.* I.II.Q.94 a.6.)

[63] See Cassirer, *Essay on Man,* p. 15; *The Philosophy of the Enlightenment,* p. 37.

moral experience which holds the same relation to the field of human behavior as common sensible experience holds in relation to physics. Pornography; *Confidential* (which Mr. Riesman says the Bill of Rights guarantees);[64] a democratic pluralism of sexuality; the radar-controlled, other-directed society of peers; the disappearance, not of a ruling class, but of what Mr. Walter Lippmann calls "the functional [arrangement] of the relationships between the mass of people and the government" (the substitution of veto-groups, Gallup-pollsters, and inside-dopesters for genuine rule)—these things mean that the threads by which in former generations the State was fastened to the organic whole of human existence have—all of them—been cut: Machiavelli was, after all, sharp enough. Fortune-teller that he was, he foretold the disappearance of the "familiar world," and with it the appearance of myth and magic in the secular sphere. Indefectible principles are not among the facts in accord with which we must live if we want to be free. The only facts are material and efficient principles, "manipulable" indeed, but no longer presupposed to any intelligible end. As Mr. Trilling says, ideas perceptive of values and consequences "are held to be mere 'details,' and what is more, to be details which, if attended to, have the effect of diminishing reality." [65] They have less relation to the world of morals and politics than does the "familiar table" to the world of physics; for the "scientific table" saves the appearances of the familiar one.

The growing awareness of liberalism that such ideas are not among the facts in accord with which we must live marks the transition of liberalism from what Mr. Riesman calls the phase of "other-direction" to what he calls "autonomy." It marks also its dilemma. For if liberalism's phase of anomie and other-direction is characterized by the "facts" arising from indetermination of material and efficient principles in human behavior, its phase

---

[64] David Riesman, "The Supreme Court and Its New Critics," *The New Republic*, n. 6, p. 12, July 29, 1957.

[65] Trilling, *op. cit.*, p. 19.

of autonomy calls for the conscious overthrow of that common experience of moral ends and purposes that opposes its "free constructs." This is liberalism's necessary direction. But although Judge Hand observes that "[indefectible principles] are at *war* with our only truthworthy way of living in accord with the facts," he is hesitant before the step which is necessary if he is to overcome the self-doubt of liberalism and fully prove its position and existence.

Liberalism's path from anomie to autonomy can only be what it is indeed for Marx—the destruction of every hitherto-existing social form so that man himself may become "the totality . . . the subjective existence of society thought and felt for itself." [66] There is more than a striking parallel between Mr. Riesman's description of autonomy as implying "a heightened self-consciousness" by which man realizes "increased possibilities of being and becoming" and Marx's final emancipation of man's "generic being" —a "being which relates itself to the species as to his own proper being or relates itself to itself as a generic being." [67] Is this not the meaning of Riesman's "heightened self-consciousness" which, he tells us, "is not a quantitative matter but in part an awareness of the problem of self-consciousness itself, *an achievement of a higher order of abstraction?*" [68] The separating of man's individual self from his generic self is expressly attributed by Erich Fromm, the distinguished defender of liberal humanism, to the institution of the family; man can be returned to himself (obviously by a "higher order of abstraction") only when the primordial relationship of the family community is rationalized and exorcised. [69] The title of Mr. Fromm's book on humanistic ethics—*Man for Himself*—epitomizes this demand and is curiously reminiscent of Marx's italicized emphasis on a "complete, conscious return, ac-

[66] Marx, *Oekonomische-philosophische Manuskript,* p. 117.

[67] *Ibid.,* pp. 113–114.

[68] David Riesman, *The Lonely Crowd,* Doubleday & Company, Inc., 1955, p. 143. (Italics added.)

[69] Fromm, *Man for Himself,* Rinehart & Company, Inc., New York, 1947, chap. I, pp. 10–13.

complished within the interior of the whole wealth of past development, of *man for himself.* . . ." [70]

In short, liberalism's primal act of imagination whereby it established its essence and existence in the enhanced sense of freedom consequent upon the Humean principle that the aberrations in nature are ever so conformable to reality as its apparent intentions issued in anomie and other-direction. This condition is overcome by the profounder insight that, as we have noted, by the law that reduces the material and mental spheres to a common denominator, the aberrations in nature become the exemplar for freedom in the world of culture and civilization. The way to autonomy then must lie, as Marx most clearly perceived, in destroying all the "intentions" of nature—the "forms and products of consciousness" represented by "'pure' theory, theology, philosophy, ethics, etc." These are the presuppositions of Riesman's "tradition directed" and "inner directed" societies and of Fromm's authoritarian ethics—"religion, the family, state, law, morals, science, spirit, etc." [71] These are the indefectible principles and natural associations, and they are not among the facts in accord with which we must live—in a people's democracy. But they are precisely the things upon which, in the classical tradition of the West, all free government has depended. And the reason for this is that the very notion of a free nature is derived from seeing the human intellect as separable of itself (although not existing apart from matter) and thus as capable of sharing through "religion, the family, state, law, morals, science, spirit, etc." in the activity of that Prime Intellect by whose perfect freedom all things both are and are governed. The affinity, as Aristotle says, of all human activity with God's activity, the capacity to share in the Divine activity by way of proportion in the political life and by way of union and informing in the life of science and wisdom—it was precisely this capacity that guaranteed man's independence both from any blind necessity

[70] Marx, *Oekonomische-philosophische Manuskript*, p. 114. (Italics in the original.)

[71] *Ibid.*, pp. 114–115.

of nature and from any political "art." It is the Marxist revolutionary idea that completes the introduction of the elements of myth and magic into the purely secular sphere, bringing to full perfection the notion of political "art" by transposing into practice—into unassailable "facts"—the whole order of things that Aristotle, by reserving to the speculative intellect, had made the bastion of human freedom.

IX

The Marxist revolutionary idea: the enlightenment in Germany

It is of profound interest that the modernized theory of natural law, in which the new sense of "reason" is found in the reduction of the mental and material spheres to a common denominator, is hailed by both the chroniclers of Western democratic ideas and the Father of Communism as a great step in the direction of freedom. But Marx's appreciation of this development is incomparably astute. Marx saw that the notion of autonomous natural law had effectively repudiated the "essentiality" of God but that it had not affirmed the "essentiality" of man: Indeed, "All the suppositions of [the] egoistic life (the life that does not consider the individual to be a "generic being") continue to subsist in civil society outside the political sphere . . . as properties of bourgeois society." [1] These are the suppositions of that consciousness that separates itself from the real world and proceeds "to the formation of 'pure' theory, theology, philosophy, ethics, etc." [2] These are permitted to subsist as properties of bourgeois society because the liberal phi-

[1] Marx, *Die Judenfrage*, pp. 583–584.
[2] Mark and Engels, *The German Ideology*, p. 20.

261

losopher is hesitant about taking the needed step of destruction; he fails to affirm man's "essentiality"; he leaves him, in the real life if not in theory, just where he was: an individual, separated from the generic life, folded back on himself, uniquely occupied with his own private, egoistic interests. The conflict between "the theoretical mind and the mundane reality which exists independently of it" is only partially resolved by the repudiation of the Divine Mover, by the principle of autonomous nature; what remains to be won for man is the general or universal being of nature.[3] In order that the universal being of nature be won for man "really" and "practically," not merely in the abstract, indecisively and hesitantly, *all* the forces extraneous to man must be overcome and nature itself be submitted to the will of man. Man has been "naturalized"; nature must now be "humanized": In producing himself specifically human, man must at the same time be shown to be a universal being, to produce, in some fashion, the whole of nature. Precisely that "perfectibility" that Rousseau sought—the simple feeling of existence—as something completely comprised within man's essence, must be attained on "the human plane" and in the "real life." It is only on this condition that the conflict between the theoretical mind and mundane reality will be overcome. Communism must take "its departure from the . . . conscience of man in nature, considered as *being*." This means that the theoretical declarations of the seventeenth- and eighteenth-century philosophers asserting the autonomy of nature must advance by transposing into *practice* an attitude toward the whole of nature that hitherto had been reserved to the speculative intellect, whose object was the truth of what is. It becomes necessary to see that "the relation of man to nature is directly his relation to man," i.e., that man is "a conscious generic being . . . which relates itself to the species

---

[3] "Communism begins as soon as atheism begins; atheism is, at the beginning, still very far from being communism, all atheism holding . . . at the beginning a preference for the abstract. The philanthropy of atheism is only, then, at first an abstract philosophical philanthropy, while that of communism is immediately *real* and leads to action at once." (Marx, *Oekonomische-philosophische Manuskript*, p. 115.)

as to his own proper being [and] which relates itself to itself as a generic being." [4] Man must come to see that he *is* all that he knows and that he is the act whereby all things are made—all things humanly significant, which becomes the totality of significance. This is what Marx called "the generic natural relation." This is the revolutionary idea that claims to bring to final solution the "antagonism between man and nature, . . . between origin and being . . . between liberty and necessity, between the individual and the species";[5] all the great thinkers of the past had striven, consciously or unconsciously, to resolve these antagonisms. For this extraordinary conception of man as a universal being, Marx was indebted to the nineteenth-century German philosophical revolution and particularly to Ludwig Feuerbach (1804–1872).

The German philosophical revolution

In a passage of strongly prophetic color, the nineteenth-century German poet Heinrich Heine described the general import of the philosophical revolution that was worked in Germany in the course of his century. The passage must be read with the understanding that Marx and Russia are the heirs of the German philosophical revolution:

. . . when it was observed that young Germany, absorbed in metaphysical abstractions, had become unfit for practical life, well might patriots and friends of liberty feel a righteous indignation against philosophy, whilst some of them went the length of utterly condemning it as a vain and profitless pursuit of shadows.

We shall not commit the folly of confuting these malcontents. German philosophy is an important fact; it concerns the whole human race, and only our latest descendants will be in a position to decide whether we are to be praised or blamed for having first worked out our philosophy and afterwards our revolution. . . . Give yourselves no

---

[4] Marx, *Oekonomische-philosophische Manuskript,* p. 114.
[5] *Ibid.*

anxiety however, ye German Republicans; the German revolution will not prove any milder or gentler because it was preceded by the "Critique" of Kant, by the "Transcendental Idealism" of Fichte, or even by the Philosophy of Nature. These doctrines served to develop revolutionary forces that only await their time to break forth and to fill the world with terror and with admiration. Then will appear Kantians as little tolerant of piety in the world of deeds as in the world of ideas, who will mercilessly upturn with sword and axe the soil of our European life in order to extirpate the last remnants of the past. There will come upon the scene armed Fichteans whose fanaticism of will is to be restrained neither by fear nor by self-interest; for they live in the spirit; . . . But most of all to be feared would be the philosophers of nature were they actively to mingle in a German revolution, and to identify themselves with the work of destruction. For if the hand of the Kantian strikes with strong unerring blow, his heart being stirred by no feeling of traditional awe; if the Fichtean courageously defies every danger, since for him danger has in reality no existence;—the Philosopher of Nature will be terrible in this, that he has allied himself with the primitive powers of nature. . . . Smile not at my counsel, at the counsel of a dreamer, who warns you against Kantians, Fichteans, Philosophers of Nature. Smile not at the fantasy of one who foresees in the region of reality the same outburst of revolution that has taken place in the region of intellect. The thought precedes the deed as the lightning the thunder. German thunder is of true German character; it is not very nimble, but rumbles along somewhat slowly. But come it will, and when ye hear a crashing such as never before has been heard in the world's history, then know that at last the German thunderbolt has fallen. At this commotion the eagles will drop dead from the skies and the lions in the farthest wastes of Africa will bite their tails and creep into their royal lairs. There will be played in Germany a drama compared to which the French Revolution will seem but an innocent idyl. . . . And the hour will come. As on the steps of an amphitheatre, the nations will group themselves around Germany to witness the terrible combat. I counsel you, ye French, keep very quiet, and, above all, see that ye do not applaud. We might readily misunderstand such applause, and, in our rude fashion, somewhat roughly put you to silence. For, if formerly in our servile, listless mood we could often times overpower you, much easier were it for us to do so in the arrogance of our newborn enthusiasm for liberty. Ye yourselves know what, in such a case, men can do; and ye are no longer in such a case. Take heed, then! I mean it well with you; therefore it is I tell you the bitter truth.

As ye are, despite your present romantic tendency, a born classical people, ye know Olympus. Among the joyous gods and goddesses, quaffing and feasting of nectar and ambrosia, ye may behold one goddess, who, amidst such gaiety and pastime, wears ever a coat of mail, the helm on her head and the spear in her hand. She is the goddess of Wisdom.[6]

The first "outburst of revolution . . . in the region of intellect" came when Immanuel Kant (1724–1804) was, as he tells us, awakened from his "dogmatic slumber" by "the suggestion of David Hume." [7] Accepting Hume's critique of causality as valid, Kant saw that scientific knowledge would be simply impossible unless its principles were now taken as originating not in experience but rather in the pure understanding. The mistake of Aristotle—that "acute thinker" who unfortunately had not had the advantage of Hume's "devastating" critique—had been to derive the highest genera from an analysis of being rather than from an analysis of thought. According to Kant, indeed, the intellect does not *apprehend* anything in nature: Thought is entirely confined to judgment—the "making" that is involved in such logical operations of the mind as the syllogism and proposition; and judgment is possible because the understanding is equipped with "a priori forms" or categories by which it is able to make its judgments.[8] Further, if apprehension is not an act of the intellect (as traditional philosophy had held), it is obvious that

---

[6] Heinrich Heine, *Religion and Philosophy in Germany*, London, 1891, pp. 158–162.

[7] *Prolegomena to Any Future Metaphysic*, trans. by P. Carus, revised by L. W. Beck, The Liberal Arts Press, Inc., New York, 1950, p. 8.

[8] Speaking of Kant, Charles DeKoninck has observed that "the critical spirit" is indeed one of the great deceptions of philosophical history. Never have philosophers, more than those informed by the so-called "critical spirit," posed more assumptions and postulated more "evident" truths. And among them, none more than Kant so well succeeded in imposing the acceptance of his impossible "evidences," carefully couched in intuitions. (DeKoninck, *De la Primauté du bien commun*, pp. 103–104.)

the judgments made by the intellect are not only a priori, but of themselves state relations of empty forms: To be filled with content, to be productive of intellectual knowledge they must be made to apply to the sensuous world. The old traditional metaphysics was nothing indeed but these empty forms, the bare structure of the *understanding*.[9] There is no *transcendent knowledge;* the element of transcendence in our knowledge of the sensuous world—in mathematics and physics—comes wholly from ourselves—from the a priori sensible forms of space and time, and from the categories of the *understanding*.

In banishing metaphysics to the area of "formal" logic, Kant was not—it should be noted—repeating the position of Plato. His error was quite the contrary. Plato had supposed the ma-

[9] We may note that in the classical and medieval philosophy, the subject of metaphysics was considered to be real being. It is not grasped by abstraction (as, for example, we do *abstract* "rational animal" from the individual men who alone exist). The being with which metaphysics deals is grasped, rather, by a judgment which affirms that certain beings do exist apart from matter and motion. Because such beings actually do exist apart from all matter and motion, the intellectual act whereby we know of such things was called "separation" rather than "abstraction." Now logic is an instrument of thought which guides us in the attainment of true science—whether that science be mathematics (whose definitions abstract from sensible matter), or physics (whose definitions abstract from individual matter), or metaphysics (whose definitions are of beings that can and do exist apart from matter). Logic, then, extends to all being, but, unlike the being which is the subject of metaphysics, the being with which logic is concerned is wholly in the mind. That is why, as we noted in Chapter I, Aristotle remarks that the procedure of some of the early natural philosophers in treating questions of logic was understandable enough because, thinking that they were inquiring into the whole of nature and of being, they needed to inquire into the rules of thought, which are applicable in every science. Thus, while logic has universal being as an object and is as extensive as metaphysics itself, the formal aspect under which it studies being is different from that of metaphysics. St. Thomas makes this difference clear. ". . . since reason must negotiate concerning all that is in things, logic will be of those things which are common to all. . . . Not that logic is of common things themselves as subjects. For logic considers as its subjects: syllogism, enunciation, predicate and things of that sort." (Commentary on the *Posterior* is simply dualism." (*Ibid.*)

terial world to have its real existence in an immaterial fashion, the supersensible world itself bearing the imprint of purely logical being. Kant, on the other hand, regarded metaphysics as *only* a science of the *structure of* the understanding, its concepts being merely regulative and constructive of the phenomenal world. Indeed it was precisely this that was the decisive first step in reclaiming the universe of being for man. For, as Hegel was to show, by confining metaphysics to the order of logic, Kant was in effect identifying the two in such fashion as to concede to the human mind a causal knowledge of reality—something Plato would never have dreamed of. Indeed it was exactly this that, in Kant's view, Hume's critique of causality in nature had necessitated. According to Kant it is solely from the principles of our understanding that the world of experience receives intelligibility. Thus Kant's categories, taken in their aspect of pure concepts and empty forms (Kant's "formal logic") do themselves advance beyond this condition to a "transcendental logic" which is constitutive of the empirical world. And since, as Hegel observed, the mind is quite aware of the limits of scientific understanding, it is by this very fact shown to be *anterior* to these limits and may be identified with absolute and infinite being. Insofar as the understanding thus reflects upon itself and enjoys self-consciousness, it is identical with absolute being. Thus it was Hegel who took the second decisive step in reclaiming the universe of being for man: Where Kant had confined metaphysics to logic, Hegel converted logic into metaphysics. As Professor Collins puts it:

The implication of this Hegelian criticism of Kant is that logic must take another step forward. Kant recognized the first two stages of logical development: *formal* and *transcendental* logic. . . . But Hegel now seeks to complete the advance of logic, by adding the third and ultimate phase: *speculative*.or *metaphysical logic*. This logic embraces the entire content of reality and hence is identical with metaphysics. Hegel brings to its culmination the process of ontologizing logic: "*Logic therefore coincides with Metaphysics, the science of things set and held in thoughts.*" In his speculative logic, the movements of thought are also interpreted as the pulsations of real being. The dualism between thought and being is overthrown. In reason's purview, they manifest a fundamental identity.[10]

Marx points out that the *Encyclopedia* of Hegel had begun with logic and ended with pure speculative thought and absolute knowledge. It had ended with the philosophic spirit conscious of itself as the absolute spirit: Man has reappropriated his substantial forces, forces that in the whole past history of philosophy had become foreign objects. And in this conception, Marx goes on to observe, there were present all the elements of a critique of political economy and philosophy—but hidden, quite indistinct, and bearing a "mystical allure." For while Hegel had reclaimed the whole of nature for men, this reclamation operated only in the conscience, in "pure thought" and in abstraction, "the appropriation of these objects insofar as they are thoughts, and movements of thoughts." [11] In Marx's estimate, Hegel had in a measure grasped the notion of human alienation—"that religion, wealth, etc. are only the reality of Man's objectification alienated"; but the reclamation of the material world is, "with Hegel, under this form that materiality, religion, the power of the state are spiritual beings. . . ." For Hegel "the *human* character of nature and of nature produced by history, the products of man, appear in this, that they are products of the abstract spirit, and therefore *spiritual* elements, *ideal* beings." [12] That Hegel's absolute spirit was only a "mystical allure" and that Hegel had in effect objectified the divine idea in the concrete world of nature "and of nature produced by history, the products of man . . ." is well brought out by Professor Stace:

It appears that a certain Herr Krug, supposing Hegel to be attempting in the philosophy of nature to deduce all actual existent objects from the pure Idea, enquired whether Hegel could deduce the pen with which he, Herr Krug, was writing. Hegel demolishes the unfortunate Krug in a contemptuous and sarcastic footnote, in which he

[10] Collins, *A History of Modern European Philosophy*, pp. 605–606.
[11] Marx, *Oekonomische-philosophische Manuskript*, p. 155.
[12] *Ibid.*

states that philosophy has more important matters to concern itself with than Krug's pen. And the general position he takes up is that the philosophy of nature cannot and should not attempt to deduce particular facts and things, but only universals. It cannot deduce *this* plant, but only plant in general; and so on. The details of nature, he says, are governed by contingency and caprice, not by reason. They are irrational. And the irrational is just what cannot be deduced. It is most improper, he tells us, to demand of philosophy that it should deduce *this* particular thing, *this* particular man, and so forth.[13]

Ludwig Feuerbach and the humanist critique of philosophy

The elements of a true critique of political economy and philosophy would have to penetrate Hegel's "mystical allure" and resolve "the absolute metaphysical spirit into the real man standing on the foundation of nature." This was the contribution of Ludwig Feuerbach to whom must be credited the third great "outburst of revolution in the region of intellect." It is "to the discoveries of Feuerbach" that, Marx acknowledges in his essay on Political Economy and Philosophy, "the positive and general critique [of political economy and philosophy] owes its true foundation . . . It is Feuerbach alone who has provided the positive humanist and naturalist critique." [14] And Friedrich Engels, in his *Ludwig*

[13] W. T. Stace, *The Philosophy of Hegel*, Macmillan & Co., Ltd., London, 1924, pars. 425, 426, p. 308. Professor Stace very rightly adds that in his own opinion "Hegel was wrong, and Krug right, as regards the question of the pen. And Hegel's ill-tempered petulance is possibly the outcome of an uneasy feeling that Krug's attack was not without reason. If we are to have an idealistic monism it must explain everything from its first principle, thought. And that means that it must deduce everything. To leave anything outside the network of deduction, to declare anything utterly undeducible, is simply dualism." (*Ibid.*)

[14] Marx, *Oekonomische-philosophische Manuskript*, p. 34. "Who has annihilated the dialectic of concepts, the war of the gods which the philosophers alone knew? Feuerbach. Who has put man in place of the old lumber, and in place of the infinite consciousness as well? Feuerbach, and no one else. Feuerbach, who completed and criticized Hegel from a Hegelian standpoint,

Feuerbach expresses this indebtedness with the greatest enthusiasm:

> Then came Feuerbach's *Essence of Christianity* . . . The spell was broken, . . . and the contradiction, shown to exist only in our imagination was dissolved. One must himself have experienced the liberating effect of this book, to get an idea of it. Enthusiasm was general; we all became at once Feuerbachians.[15]

Feuerbach alone discovered the elements of a true critique because he was able "to furnish proof" that the alienation with which Hegel begins (religion, theology) is first suppressed by him when he poses "the real, sensible, finite and the particular," and then afterwards revived by the assertion that the *human* character of nature and of nature produced by man, are spiritual elements, ideal beings. Thus Hegel first negates religion by reducing it to philosophy (the real, sensible, finite) and then negates the negation by affirming abstract thought, spirit, the infinite. The contribution of Feuerbach was to have seen that the negation of the negation is *philosophy negating itself*, that is to say, philosophy affirming itself as "nothing else than religion put into thoughts and developed by thought." [16] Feuerbach thus made it clear that it is just as necessary to condemn philosophy (which turns out to be simply another form and another mode of the alienation of man's being) as it is necessary to condemn religion. The affirmation of the self and the manifestation of the self are indeed in a measure implied by Hegel's negation of the negation (that is why Marx will allow that in Hegel there are present all

---

resolving the metaphysical absolute spirit into the real man standing on the foundation of nature, was the first to complete the criticism of religion—inasmuch as, at the same time he undertook a critique of Hegelian speculation, and thereby sketched the great and masterly outlines of all metaphysics." (Quoted by Otto Ruhle, *Karl Marx, His Life and Work*, trans. by Eden and Cedar Paul, The Viking Press, Inc., New York, 1929, p. 33.)

[15] Engels, *Ludwig Feuerbach and the Outcome of German Classical Philosophy*, International Publishers Company, Inc., New York, 1941, p. 18.

[16] Marx, *Oekonomische-philosophische Manuskript*, p. 155.

the elements of a true critique of political economy and philosophy); but with Hegel this position "is considered as a position not yet certain of one's proper self, and consequently still afflicted by its contrary, doubtful of itself, and therefore incomplete, not yet proving its existence. . . ." [17] With "unobtrusive simplicity" Feuerbach opposes to this hesitant position "the position materially certain and founded on itself," establishing "*true materialism* in *real* science by making theory take its fundamental principle from the social relation of 'man with man.'" [18]

Now to reclaim the material world not merely speculatively (as Hegel had done) but really and practically, required some return to a theoretical mind that recognized the independent reality of the material world. We may recall Marx's estimate of the post-Aristotelian philosophies of conduct: that they were a natural outcome of the Aristotelian system which "closes itself into a completed, total world" and forces its heirs to turn against their age in revolt and escape. And Marx observes that "it is a psychological law that the theoretical mind, when it becomes free in itself, is transformed into practical energy, and as *will* turns against the mundane reality which exists independently of it." [19] If then Aristotle "freed" the theoretical mind, it makes little difference that he closed himself in it and devoted himself to the formation of "pure" theory, theology, philosophy, ethics, etc. (and from Marx's standpoint it is understandable enough because the alienation of the true substantial forces of man arises precisely out of the fecundity of the intellect). The really important thing to observe is that a certain disengagement of "mundane reality" from "mind" and "spirit" is necessary before the material world can be reclaimed for man. We find this "disengagement" in Aristotle but not in Hegel; Marx had to avail himself of this difference between Hegel and Aristotle by a special indebtedness to each. The difference between Aristotle

---

[17] *Ibid.*, p. 152.

[18] *Ibid.*

[19] Marx–Engels, *Über die Differenzen der demokritischen und epikureischen Naturphilosophie, Gesamtausgabe,* vol. I, sec. I, p. 1.

and Hegel was that Aristotle's "pure" theory, theology, philosophy, etc. had not reclaimed the material world for man; the material world existed indeed, but independently of the theoretical mind; Hegel's "pure" theory, theology, philosophy, etc. had reclaimed the material world for man, but this reclamation operated only in "pure thought" and in abstraction, so that mundane reality was in effect negated. There remained, therefore, the need to reclaim the material world for man practically and not merely speculatively. And this required a return to a theoretical mind that recognized the independent reality of the material world. It is therefore not surprising to find Feuerbach entering into a "serious and critical" relationship with the Aristotelian order of ideas as well as with the Hegelian. The fact is that Feuerbach presents his thesis on the generic being of man as the natural outcome of the great doctrines of the past and depends fully and explicitly on the doctrines of both Aristotle and St. Thomas Aquinas.

Feuerbach saw that Hegel's speculative derivation of all things from the *understanding* conscious of itself as absolute being, was indeed—as Herr Krug was implying—nothing more than a speculative game.[20] We must begin—as indeed Aristotle had begun—with the "pen of Herr Krug." But we must now be made to see what Feuerbach tried to establish: that (in Marx's para-

---

[20] It is very true, Prof. Charles DeKoninck points out, that from the universal or common notions (intentions) of the reason one can descend to reality and can treat of the subject of the natural sciences. It is not in this regard that the Hegelian dialecticians are at fault. They are at fault in supposing that the use of logic can of itself adequately attain reality; if this were the case, if the logical and the real were identical, then contradiction would be possible. But this is precisely what Hegel maintained. And this is indeed why the Hegelian dialectic had hidden its practical mode under "a mystical allure": for it pretended to derive all things in their differences from that common being which is a universal only in the logical order. Hegel's dialectic remained sterile, a speculative game. Marx will identify the dialectical procedure of Hegel with things envisaged in their ultimate concretion. But of the things that surround us, it is matter that is the proper principle of their ultimate concretion. Matter will itself become the primordial principle, the Prime Intellect. (DeKoninck, *De la Primauté du bien commun*, pp. 106–107, 111.)

phrase) "the activity of the general conscience is the theoretical form of that of which real common being is the living form." [21] Man's existence indeed, as Hegel affirmed, "centers in his head, i.e., in Thought, inspired by which he builds up the world of reality"; but henceforth that head flatters itself if it thinks "that it is something other than consciousness of existing practise, that it is really conceiving something without conceiving something real." The "absolute being" that man conceives is conceived *by him*, that is, by a material individual whose real being is of the same material, individual nature as Herr Krug's pen, except— except that man, capable of knowing the universal (as "the theoretical form of that of which real common being is the living form"), is a generic or universal being: The "absolute metaphysical spirit" is the "real man standing on the foundation of nature." And because the conscience is the theoretical form of that of which material reality is the "living form," it will not be confined—Marx will point out—to the purely speculative game of deriving all things in their differences from "absolute being": It will actually change the world by seizing hold of the revolutionary principle of contradiction that is now taken to operate as the fecund principle in matter.

Absorption in metaphysical abstractions may, as Heinrich Heine observed, provoke practical men to righteous indignation, but following Heine's sage advice, we will not commit the folly of being among the malcontents if we see how these philosophic doctrines "served to develop revolutionary forces" that today indeed "fill the world with terror and with admiration" as they threaten "mercilessly to upturn . . . the soil of our . . . life in order to extirpate the last remnants of the past." We must, then, examine with care and at some length the thought of Feuerbach. This is all the more necessary because, although there is increasing recognition of his great formative influence, there is a fairly understandable reluctance to attempt the unraveling of his thickly twisted thought.[22]

[21] Marx, *Oekonomische-philosophische Manuskript*, pp. 125–126.
[22] Erich Fromm's writings are greatly indebted to Feuerbach, particularly

Feuerbach begins his task by a very bad but clever allusion (it is scarcely an analysis) to the self-awareness which reveals to man certain activities which set him apart from all other things surrounding him. *The Essence of Christianity*[23] opens abruptly with the observation that brutes have no religion; and, with that unobtrusive simplicity of which Mark speaks, Feuerbach immediately gives as the reason for this absence of religion the fact that the brute has no consciousness of itself as a species; consciousness of oneself as a species is the very ground of religion, Feuerbach argues, inasmuch as religion is the consciousness of the infinite, and the consciousness that man has of him-

---

The Art of Loving and *Man for Himself*, but there is nowhere in Fromm an exposition of Feuerbach's philosophy. Similarly, in *The Quest for Being*, Sidney Hook is said to enter the lists on the side of Feuerbach, but he doesn't stay by his side long enough for us to get so much as a glimpse of him. Nor in his *From Hegel to Marx* does he do more than give an extended cursory presentation of Feuerbach's thought. Years ago Santayana observed that "One of the peculiarities of recent speculation, especially in America, is that ideas are [taken or] abandoned in virtue of a mere change of feeling, without any new evidence or new arguments. We do not nowadays refute our predecessors, we pleasantly bid them goodbye . . . people refused to be encumbered with any system, even one of their own; they were content to imbibe more or less of the spirit of a philosophy and to let it play on such facts as happened to attract their attention . . . they found new approaches to old beliefs or new expedients in old dilemmas. They were not in a scholastic sense pupils of anybody or masters in anything. They hated the scholastic way of saying what they meant, if they had heard it; they insisted on a personal freshness of style, refusing to make their thought more precise than it happened to be spontaneously, and they lisped their logic, when the logic came." (George Santayana, *Character and Opinion in the United States*, Charles Scribner's Sons, New York, 1920, pp. 9–10.)

[23] *Das Wesen des Christentums*, Ludwig Feuerbach's principal work, first appeared in 1841. In 1849 (in Leipzig) Feuerbach published a revised and augmented edition, in the body of which as well as in the appendices, he attempted to show the Christian origins of his anthropotheism by numerous citations from St. Thomas Aquinas. The final German edition is the Stuttgart edition of 1903. The work was translated into English from the second German edition by Marian Evans (pseudonym: George Eliot, 1819–1880) as *The Essence of Christianity*. The references hereinafter made are to the third edition, Kegan Paul, Trench, Trubner & Co., Ltd., London, 1893.

self as a species is a consciousness of the infinity of his own nature. Feuerbach's statement on this point is as follows:

> But what is this essential difference between man and the brute? The most simple, general, and also the most popular answer to this question is—consciousness: but consciousness in the strict sense; for the consciousness implied in the feeling of self as an individual, in discrimination by the senses, in the perception and even judgment of outward things according to definite sensible signs, cannot be denied to the brutes. Consciousness in the strictest sense is present only in a being to whom his species, his essential nature, is an object of thought. The brute is indeed conscious of himself as an individual—and he has accordingly the feeling of self as the common center of successive sensations—but not as a species; hence, he is without that consciousness which in its nature, as in its name, is akin to science. Where there is this higher consciousness there is capability of science. Science is the cognizance of species. In practical life we have to do with individuals; in science, with species. But only a being to whom his own species, his own nature, is an object of thought, can make the essential nature of other things or beings an object of thought.
>
> Consciousness, in the strict or proper sense, is identical with consciousness of the infinite; . . . in the consciousness of the infinite, the infinity of one's own nature is the object of consciousness.[24]

Feuerbach's "authority" for the many difficult points that he has thus rapidly set forth is the following text of St. Thomas Aquinas, which appears on the second page of Feuerbach's appendix:

> . . . Knowing beings are distinguished from non-knowing beings in that the latter process only their own form; whereas the knowing being is naturally adapted to have also the form of some other thing, for the species of the thing known is in the knower. Hence it is manifest that the nature of a non-knowing being is more contracted and limited; whereas the nature of knowing beings has a greater amplitude and extension. That is why the Philosopher (Aristotle) says that *the soul is in a sense all things*. Now the contraction of a form comes through

[24] *Ibid.*, pp. 1–3.

the matter. Hence, as we have said above, according as they are the more immaterial, forms approach more clearly to a kind of infinity.[25]

The first requisite of a criticism of Feuerbach is to examine carefully what he says and what he neglects to say on the matter of "consciousness of species." This becomes at once a task of clearing up the ambiguity in Feuerbach's use of the terms "consciousness" and "species"; for what has to be done is to distinguish the doctrines he draws upon from the misunderstanding that Feuerbach has of these doctrines.

Feuerbach says that where there is consciousness in the strict sense there is capability of science, and that science is the consciousness of species. The translator of the English edition of *Das Wesen des Christentums* translates "consciousness" (*Bewusstsein*) here by "cognizance." Presumably Feuerbach means that science is about universals, universals being understood in opposition to the mere individual. This understanding is justified by the fact that Feuerbach opposes the brute, who is conscious merely of the individual, to man, who is conscious of the species. It is also plain from what he says later on, that man is both an individual and the species to which he belongs. All this is confirmed by what he says in the above paragraph: "In practical life we have to do with individuals; in science, with species": This verifies our interpretation of individual and species, for whether speculative or practical, the object of science remains universal. It is in the practical virtues, art and prudence, that we reach the individual.

Feuerbach goes on to say, however, that it is precisely man's consciousness of himself as a universal that makes him capable of science. This is what he calls "consciousness in the strict sense." We must note the meaning that Feuerbach gives to what he calls "consciousness in the strict sense" by referring to the etymology. What he says of the German is also true of the Latin: *Cum* and *scientia* compose the word. Now, if he takes *scientia*

---

[25] This citation will be found in the Stuttgart edition (1903) of the *Sämmtliche Werke*, vol. VI, *Das Wesen des Christentums*, p. 337. The quotation is from *Summa Theol.* I.Q.14 a.1.C.

in the strict sense, it does of course require intellect and the capacity for reflection. And so we may say that Feuerbach speaks of intellectual consciousness, something the brutes do not have. But when Feuerbach goes on to say that the brute does not have its own species for an object, whereas man is conscious of himself as a species, the ambiguity of the term "species" is exploited here, along with the ambiguity of the term "consciousness" to suggest that man is conscious of himself as a universal in concretion. The ambiguity of the proposition that the brute does not have its own species for an object (and that man does) may be made clear from the following consideration: No man identifies himself with the human species. What he may well know is that he is a man, but not that he is *man*. It is true that the species has no existence except in individuals, in Socrates, or in Plato etc. But Socrates is not the species (any more than is dog the species brute); he belongs to the species, he is of the species. It is only when we consider the abstract species that we have a "one toward many." This "one" is universal in the sense that it is predicable of many: "man" can be said of Socrates, of Plato, etc. But we cannot say that man is Socrates, nor that man is Plato. A man may know the species to which he belongs, but he does not know himself as the species itself. When Feuerbach goes on to say that "only a being to whom his own species is an object of thought can make the essential nature of other things or beings an object of thought," he has made use of the ambiguity of the terms "species" and "consciousness" in such a way as to suggest that man's capacity to grasp the universal proceeds from an intuition of himself as a universal.

We must try to see what is the nature of the experience by which man allegedly perceives himself as a universal in concretion. The experience, Feuerbach points out, is not a direct one; indeed, it is precisely the indirectness of the experience that misleads the ordinary man into supposing himself only an individual and not at the same time the species.

Man is nothing without an object . . . But the object to which a subject essentially, necessarily relates, is nothing else than this subject's own, but objective nature. The *absolute* to man is his own nature. The power of the object over him is the power of his own nature. Thus the power of the object of feeling is the power of feeling itself; the power of the object of the intellect is the power of the intellect itself.[26]

We shall have to observe in some detail this process by which "the absolute metaphysical being is reduced to the real man standing on the foundation of nature." In the following sequence Feuerbach adduces feeling as an example of what he says is applicable to all human activities; and since he says in another passage that what is true of feeling is "infinitely more" true of intellect, we shall substitute "thinking" for "feeling" in the following passage.[27] Feuerbach observes that if "thinking" is taken as the "essential organ" of religion, then it follows that "the *object* of religious thinking is a matter of indifference, only because when once thinking has been pronounced to be the subjective essence of religion, it in fact is also the objective essence of religion, though it may not be declared, at least directly, to be such." Hence the first step is this: "Thinking is pronounced to be religious, simply because it is thinking. The ground of its religiousness is its own nature—lies in itself. But is not thinking thereby declared to be itself the absolute, the divine?" Feuerbach continues:

But suppose, that notwithstanding, thou wilt posit an object of thought, but at the same time seekest to express thy thinking truly

---

[26] *Ibid.*, p. 4. The indirect nature of this experience is what accounts for the way in which religion has historically developed, Feuerbach tells us: "But when religion—consciousness of God—is designated as the self-consciousness of man, this is not to be understood as affirming that the religious man is directly aware of this identity; for, on the contrary, ignorance of it is fundamental to the peculiar nature of religion. To preclude this misconception, it is better to say, religion is man's earliest and also indirect form of self-knowledge. Hence religion everywhere precedes philosophy . . . Man first of all sees his nature as if out of himself before he finds it in himself." (*Ibid.*, p. 13.)

[27] *Ibid.*, pp. 9–10, 15. Cf. "feeling is only acted on by . . . itself, its own nature. Thus also . . . and infinitely more, the intellect." (*Ibid.*, p. 6.)

. . . without introducing by thy reflection any foreign element, what remains to thee but to distinguish between thy individual thinking and the general nature of thought: to separate the universal in thinking from the . . . influences with which thinking is bound up in thee under thy individual conditions? Hence what thou canst alone contemplate, declare to be the infinite . . . is merely the nature of thought.

To understand this passage we must ask what is that "foreign element" which we are told not to introduce if we wish to express our thinking truly and without which there remains nothing to distinguish except "thy individual thinking and the general nature of thought." This "foreign element" is not, of course, "thy individual thinking"—for thy individual thinking "remains" to be distinguished from the general nature of thought; nor is it simply the object of thought—for that is posited. The "foreign element" is the object *as object*, for as Feuerbach says, "man first of all sees his nature as if *out* of himself before he finds it in himself." [28] So we are asked to exclude the object *as object* if we wish to express our thinking truly. Hence it becomes evident that the foreign element that must be excluded is simply whatever would contract one's individual thinking in such fashion that it would prevent objects of thought (and of feeling and willing) from being wholly comprised in man's nature. One's individuality— with the influences with which thinking is bound up under the conditions of individuality—must not, then, be considered to contract thought to a mode of knowing that is not identical with the plenitude of being: For Feuerbach immediately adds, ". . . does not the subject precede the predicate? The predicate is nothing without a subject; the subject is a human being, a sensate nature. Hence the antithesis of the divine and human is altogether illusory [and] is nothing else than the antithesis between the human nature in general and the human individual." [29] Thus in that plenitude of being which is identical with thought, it is general human nature that the individual has for object. And thus

[28] *Ibid.*, p. 13. (Italics added.)
[29] *Ibid.*, p. 15.

are joined the man who is conscious of his infinite self and the man who is "put in the place of the old lumber and of the infinite consciousness as well"; this is "the real man standing on the foundation of nature," a generic being, a universal in concretion.

But now, by what device do we manage to exclude the object of thought *as object* and to identify it with the thinking subject? The confusions here are as incredible as they are clever. They can be cleared only by a consideration of the correct doctrine on the points of which Feuerbach has very breezily availed himself.

It is quite true that man does not have a direct experience of his nature. "The science of the soul is very certain," says St. Thomas, "insofar as each one experiences in himself that he has a soul and that the operations of the soul are in him. But as to knowing what the soul is—that is very difficult." [30]

This experience is described by St. Thomas in the following fashion:

One perceives that one has a soul, that one lives and that one is because one perceives that one thinks or that one exercises vital operations of this kind; this is why the Philosopher says, in the IXth book of the *Ethics:* . . . he who sees perceives that he sees, and he who hears, that he hears, and he who walks, that he walks, and in the case of all other activities similarly. So that we perceive that we perceive, or we know that we know. And by that very knowing that we know and perceiving that we perceive, we perceive and we know that we are. For to be is, for man, to sense and to think. But no one perceives that he thinks except by thinking something, for one thinks something before knowing that one thinks; this is why the soul arrives at the actual perception that it is by means of the thing that it thinks or that it senses. [31]

Those things which are in the soul by their essence are known through experimental knowledge, insofar as through his acts man has experience of his inward principles. For example, we perceive our will

---

[30] *In I de Anima* lect.1.

[31] *QQ. DD. de Veritate* Q.10 a.8C.

by willing, and by exercising the functions of life, we observe that there is life in us.[32]

We must notice that this internal experience does not have a direct object given: The act which we experience in ourselves is undoubtedly the object of this experience, but it is not an object *au même titre* with the object that allows us to perceive this act. The same is true of every knowledge which we have of ourselves in self-conscious activities. It is one thing to see "this white" or to understand that "the diagonal is incommensurable with the side of the square," and quite another thing to perceive that "I see this white" or that "I understand that the diagonal is incommensurable with the side of the square." It is only in perceiving such an object that one perceives that very act itself by which one is brought to attain it. And when we reflect deliberately upon the act by which we know this white, when in this act of reflection we know, as object, the act of knowing this white, the object of this act of reflection continues no less to be *the act by which we see this white*. It is certainly true that we return to this act of knowing in order to fix upon the act itself and not upon the object of this act, but it remains nevertheless the case that the act which makes the object of this return upon itself is never, itself, directly given as an object all by itself. Thus, too, the internal experience that we have of knowing the universal (I am aware that I know what it is to know—*intellectus meus intelligit se intelligere simpliciter*—as opposed to *intellectus meus intelligit se intelligere*) does not have for its object the universal itself, *but my singular act of knowing the universal*. It is thus useless to look for a pure consciousness without an object other than itself. Now up to a point Feuerbach agrees: "Man is nothing without an object." We must here remember that Hegel's reclamation of the material world had operated in "pure thought," in abstraction; it was the "negation of the negation," in which mundane reality was the thing negated. In order to reclaim the material world for man so that the "human character of nature"

---

[32] *Summa Theol.*, I.II.Q.112 a.5 ad 1.

appears as a material element, a certain disengagement of mundane reality is, as we have pointed out, necessary. Hence "man is nothing without an object"—and, as St. Thomas and Aristotle say, the human intellect derives its knowledge from a material nature. But now, continues Feuerbach, is not the power of the object of the intellect the power of the intellect itself? And is not "the power of the object over man the power of his own nature?" The object *as object* must be overcome (its power over man must be shown to be the power of his own nature) in such fashion that it be wholly comprised in man's nature. Thus, while assuredly dependent on an object, man will have his own nature for object and, in a manner, pre-exist other objects. Since notwithstanding the positing of an object there remains nothing further "to thee to distinguish except thy individual thinking . . . and the general nature of thought," it follows that man by his nature is "being thinking for itself": the singular, material individual man distinguishes himself from all other things by an awareness of his own individual universality. As we have seen Erich Fromm express this Feuerbachian doctrine, "the realm of love, reason and justice" must be taken to exist as a reality "only because and inasmuch as man has developed these powers in himself." Once this Feuerbachian doctrine is understood, then, as Marx puts it, all the religion, law, science, morals, spirit that arose out of "pure theory, theology, philosophy, ethics, etc." will disappear, giving way to the fiat of "socialized humanity." Man will have overcome every object foreign or extraneous to himself.

The tour de force by which Feuerbach overcomes the "foreign element" and has all objects completely comprised in man's nature is accomplished by a misuse of St. Thomas' doctrine on universals.[33] There are three kinds of universal, and Feuerbach confuses them: (1) the universal *in re*, (2) the universal *a re acceptum per abstractionem*, and (3) the universal *ad rem*. (1)

---

[33] Feuerbach cites relevant passages from both the *Summa Contra Gentiles* and the *Summa Theologica*. The citation of the *Summa Contra Gentiles* (I.chap.21) and the *Summa Theologica* (I.Q.3 a.3) will be found in the Stuttgart edition (1903) of the *Sämmtliche Werke*, vol. VI, *Das Wesen des Christentums*, pp. 341–342.

We oppose the individual man, Socrates, to the universal "man." But "man" is not something besides Socrates, Plato, etc. The universal *in re* (in the thing) refers to the individuals in which the nature is found, although it is not actually in these particulars as a universal; the universal *in re* constitutes the formal principle of the singular (that which makes Socrates and Plato to be *the same animal,* namely, *man*) and has no separate existence as a universal. (2) Insofar as a universal is predicable of many—as man is predicable of Socrates and Plato—it belongs to the logical order and has no being outside of the reason; for *taken with the intention of universality* it is neither a principle of existence nor a substance: this is the universal *a re* (abstracted from the thing). No man identifies himself with human nature itself, the species which is the object of science. What he may well know is that he is *a* man, but not that he is *man*. It is true that the species has no existence except in individuals—in Socrates, Plato, etc. But Socrates is not the species; he is of the species; he belongs to the species. It is only when we consider the abstract species that we have a "one toward many." This "one" is universal in the sense that it is one and predicable of many: Man can be said of Socrates, Plato, etc. But we cannot say that man is Socrates, nor that man is Plato. Indeed if we could, then Socrates and Plato would have to be specifically different natures, and in this respect they would cease to have the kind of universality that Feuerbach insists is distinctive of man. The universal *a re* is also called universal *in praedicando* because it can be said of many and predicated as "being in"—"*inessendo.*" [34] As "*inessendo,*" as *in* the things of which it is predicated, it functions as the formal constituent in relation to individuating matter: It makes Socrates and Plato to be the *same animal,* namely *man*. As predicable of many, then, "man" is a universal *a re acceptum per abstractionem;* in the order of causality, that is, as the formal constituent principle of the individual, it is a universal *in re*. But this universal *in re* does not exist as a universal, it is not

---

[34] "*Inessendo*" is written as one word to distinguish it from the universal *ad rem,* which is called universal "in *essendo.*" See pp. 284–285.

a universal *in act*—it is not a universal *ad rem*. Only in a being not composed of matter and form—a separated substance—does the essence (*Wesenheit*), the species (*Gattung*) have singular existence. For essence and species actually mean the same thing; but no being that is composed of matter and form is its own essence, this being true only of separated substances.[35] The reason for this that the definition of a thing is not assigned to individuals but to species, and therefore individual matter, which is the principle of individuation, is outside the essence: For if the species is communicated to many, no individual of the many can be identified with the species. And therefore every natural thing, although it comprises matter which is part of the species, e.g. bones, flesh, but not *these* bones and *this* flesh, and which pertains to the essence, has also individual matter which does not belong to the definition. Therefore no natural thing is its own essence, and is not, in its individual existence, the species itself, but belongs in the species. Now Feuerbach wishes us to believe that not only does individuating matter (which in the philosophy of St. Thomas and Aristotle had been held to prevent Socrates and Plato from being the *same man*) not prevent human essence from having singular existence in Plato and in Socrates so that there would not be in Socrates and in Plato any parts that are not parts of humanity; he wishes us also to believe that man's essence is the same as his existence: In short, he wishes us to suppose that man belongs to the third of the three kinds of universal, (3) the universal *ad rem*.

Now this latter kind of universal is called a universal not because it has its being in many, but because it exists singularly as a universal and because its power extends to many kinds of

---

[35] *In VII Metaph.* lect.11. "In anything that is not its own species but is a determinate individual in a species, there must be some material parts that are not parts of the species. Socrates, because he is not himself his humanity but has humanity (or is human) must have in him material parts that are not parts of the species but part of this material individual, whose principle of individuation is matter, for example *these* bones and *this* flesh. . . . But if there were any individual that were itself its species—as if, for example Socrates were humanity itself—there would not be in Socrates any parts that were not parts of humanity." Cf. *Ibid.* lect.10; *In VIII Metaph.* lect.6.

effects. This universal belongs to the real order; it is a real "one toward many," a universal *in essendo*. If in addition to being a universal *in essendo*, such a form were also not contracted under a common genus, such a form would be infinite and perfect; for if we consider that form is not made perfect by matter but is contracted by matter, that form which is not contracted to any specific nature is its own being and is both infinite and perfect: Such a form is the universal cause of everything that is: God's causality extends to all that is and to whatever anything is. Not only is God His own essence, but in Him there is no distinction between essence and existence. It is to this universal *ad rem* that Feuerbach, using the texts of St. Thomas, wishes to assimilate the individual man. For indeed, as St. Thomas points out, since it is by their forms that all things are either intelligible or capable of being made intelligible, that form which is not only the essence but the existence as well is also the same as its intelligence: He is that plenitude of Being where thought is identical with being.[36] Objects of his knowledge other than Himself are seen not in themselves (the object is not a "foreign element," to use Feuerbach's phrase) but in Himself inasmuch as His essence contains the likeness of things other than Himself. Now Feuerbach cites this very doctrine from the texts of St. Thomas. In suggesting, then, that we exclude the object *as object* in order "to express thy thinking truly," how does he manage his gross confusion of the universal *in praedicando* with a material individual who will at the same time be the universal cause of all being? For the form of man, while separable of itself, does not exist apart from matter, and for that reason is not actual by its own essence; it cannot even know itself through itself, but only as it is made actual through understanding things other than itself. It is obviously not entirely easy to say how Feuerbach identifies the individual man with a universal *in causando*. His procedure appears to be as follows.

The universal of predication has no existence apart from the reason; on the other hand, understood with the intention of universality, this universal is a principle of knowledge insofar as

[36] *Summa Theol.* I.Q.7 a.1.

the intention of universality results from the mode of understanding by way of abstraction. But now, it is accidental to the universal to be abstracted from particulars; the universal could be knowable either according to the order of causality or according to the order of nature; and, in fact, since the specific nature as existing in the singular has the character of a formal principle in regard to the singular (making it to be *what* it is) there would *have* to be an intellect which knows this universal according to the order of causality, and there *could* be an intellect which would know this universal according to the order of nature. But such an intellect would have to be a self-subsisting universal. Now the universal, "man," which, as a universal *in praedicando* is opposed to the singular but not to matter, can be "converted" into a universal *ad rem* (which is not opposed to the singular, but is opposed to matter) on the supposition that matter is the principle of formal division of individual forms; on this supposition, which is made by Feuerbach, the universal *in praedicando* becomes a universal *ad rem* in all the things of which it is predicated. Thus, when Feuerbach says that existence in general —humanity, for example—is an absurdity, an insipidity, he thinks that the absurdity is removed by predicating humanity of Socrates, Plato, etc. He quotes St. Thomas to the effect that "forms that are not predicated of subsistent things . . . are not single *per se* subsistent forms individualized in themselves—" meaning, of course, that Socrates is not himself humanity—and therefore Feuerbach takes this to mean, no less, that *unless* humanity is predicated of Socrates, Plato, etc., it is merely an "empty predicate"; but when humanity is predicated of Socrates, Plato, etc., it is then individualized in itself. He thus makes matter the principle of formal division, and makes each individual to be at once both individual and species. Now if man were a subsisting species of this kind, he would be a universal *ad rem*— he would be not merely a univocal cause, but like every separated substance, a universal cause.[37]

[37] It may be helpful in understanding Feuerbach's procedure to advert to the Platonic confusion of the logical and the real order. Plato too, as we saw

We have finally to grasp the sense of this impossible perversion. To do so we must first notice that, as St. Thomas makes clear, the first object of the human intellect is a material essence under a predicate most indeterminate and confused—the being of common predication, a universal *in praedicando*. This being of common predication has no existence, no formal term, apart from the specific natures to which it is attached. When we were treating of Plato's doctrine that the State is the individual writ large, we cited the following clarifying text of St. Thomas:

That which is common to many is not something besides those many except . . . logically: thus animal is not something besides Socrates and Plato and other animals except as considered by the mind, which apprehends the form of animal as divested of all that specifies and individualizes it: for man is that which is truly animal, else it would follow that in Socrates and Plato there are several animals, namely animal in general, man in general, and Plato himself.[38]

---

in Chap. I, confused the universal *in praedicando* with the third kind of universality of which we have spoken: He gave to this universal a separate existence; the universal "man" exists, and the individual men whom we know through our senses are merely weak participations of the idea Man. Plato's mistake was to suppose that the universal, understood with the intention of universality—which is indeed a principle of knowledge insofar as this intention results from the mode of understanding by way of abstraction— is also a principle of existence. The universal, understood with the intention of universality, belongs, as we have seen, to the logical order and is neither a principle of existence nor a substance. Now Feuerbach confuses the logical and the real in a different way: He identifies the properties of Plato's separate idea with the singular material individual, and then goes on to say that man is distinguished from all other things in that he is aware of this universality; he makes the singular, material individual a universal in act, a universal *ad rem*.

[38] *Contra Gentiles* I.chap.26. See *De Ente et Essentia* chap. 4. Nor is this common being the cause of the distinction of things, for a thing is not placed in a genus according to its being, because then being would be a genus signifying being itself; and clearly the being of anything contained in a genus must be something beside the *whatness* of the genus, otherwise man and brute animal would be identical species. Further, if being were a genus, it would be necessary to find a difference in order to contract it to a species.

Therefore that being which is predicable of all things is, as such, indeterminate and confused, and is infinite by pure potentiality only; and because, apart from the specific natures to which it is attached, it has no formal term, it is said to exist outside of any genus and to be the being to which no addition is made. It was because of defective reason, St. Thomas says, that some, realizing that the Divine Being is also called the Being to which nothing is added, supposed the Divine Being to be the common being of all things, not perceiving that being-in-general cannot be without some addition.[39] Those who were guilty of this error "gave the incommunicable name, i.e. God, to wood and stones." [40] But Feuerbach, appreciating the fact that the Divine Being is common not by predication but as a real "one toward many," whose causality extends to all that is and to whatever anything is, gives the incommunicable name to Man. Now it is necessary to recall what we have just said concerning the first object of the human intellect: It is under the being of common predication that man first apprehends some material quiddity. Thus indeed there is a certain adequation between

---

Now no difference participates in the genus so that the genus is contained in the notion of the difference; for in that case the genus would be placed twice in the definition of the species; but the difference must be something besides that which is contained in the notion of the genus. Now there can be nothing besides that which is understood by being, if being belongs to the notion of those things of which it is predicated—for all things that are are said to be. And thus by no difference can being be contracted. See *Contra Gentiles* I.chap.25.

[39] "A thing-that-has-nothing-added-to-it can be understood in two ways. Either its essence precludes any addition (thus, for example, it is of the essence of irrational animal to be without reason), or we may understand a thing to have nothing added to it, inasmuch as its essence does not require that anything should be added to it (thus the genus animal is without reason, because it is not of the essence of animal in general to have reason; but neither is it of the essence of animal to lack reason). And so the divine being has nothing added to it in the first sense; whereas being-in-general has nothing added to it in the second sense." (*Summa Theol.* I.Q.3 a.4 ad 1.)

[40] *Contra Gentiles* I.chap.26.

this most indeterminate and confused universal and the human intellect; it is the most purely potential concept which best reflects the pure potentiality of the most imperfect of intelligences. This, then, is the ground for Feuerbach's saying that in the object, man has his own nature—his "objective," "infinite" nature—for object. If by negative abstraction we wish to consider this being apart from all determinate existence, and to consider it as if it were itself determinate existence and formally infinite, then because this being (actually most confused and indeterminate) is the first object of the human intellect, it would follow that the human intellect derives all specific differences from this indeterminate being; and thus the intellect of man becomes that plenitude of being where thought is identical with being. Feuerbach thus reduces the Being which is properly and formally infinite to the being of common predication, that "real common being" of which Marx speaks, and of which man's general conscience is, Marx says, the "theoretical form." For Feuerbach—as for Marx—the generic being of man as manifesting itself in the generic conscience is "being thinking for itself." [41] We have just seen in what sense it is indeed true that man's "generic conscience" may be said to be the "theoretical form" of "real common being": In the sense precisely that the pure potentiality of the most imperfect of intellectual natures may be regarded as the "theoretical form" of the most indeterminate and confused universal—the being of common predication ("real common being"). This most purely potential concept best reflects the pure potentiality of the least perfect of intellectual natures. It is in this way that Feuerbach resolves, as Marx puts it, "the metaphysical absolute spirit into the real man standing on the foundation of nature."

There is a certain irony in Feuerbach's thesis: He is forced to take that which is least in human intellectual existence and to crown it with the fullness of intellectual existence. But the development of his argument shows a certain genius in the light

---

[41] Marx, *Oekonomische-philosophische Manuskript*, p. 117.

X

The Marxist revolutionary idea: philosophy passes into practice

Feuerbach had resolved the "religious essence" into "human essence" and had proposed the idea of religious self-alienation and the duplication of the world into a "theoretical" (religious) and a mundane ("real") world. Hegel's overcoming of the religious form of alienation had operated only in pure thought and the movement of thought. With Feuerbach this abstract form of alienation is overcome in such fashion that man's conscience is seen to be a theoretically *sensible* conscience, that is to say, the theoretical form of real sensible being which is the "living form." "Feuerbach, not satisfied with *abstract thinking*, appeals to *sensuous contemplation*, but he does not conceive sensuousness as a practical, human-sensuous activity." [1] Not satisfied with "abstract thinking," the "philanthropy" of Feuerbach does indeed go beyond the "philanthropy" of atheism, for that philanthropy "is at first only an abstract philosophical philanthropy." The philanthropy of Feuerbach, like that of true communism, is "immediately real"; it is unlike that of true communism

---

[1] Marx, "Theses on Feuerbach," no. V, in Engels, *Ludwig Feuerbach and the Outcome of Classical German Philosophy*, p. 83.

because it does not "lead to action at once," but offers "sensuous contemplation," a kind of passive practice.[2]

Sensuous activity remained, with Feuerbach, a passive activity because, Marx tells us, he failed to see that man's absolute being is an *historical* being: Feuerbach sees the total philosophical activity of the individual to be nothing but the theoretical form of the sensuous world, but he doesn't see that man's conscience is not only a theoretically sensible conscience but also a *practically* sensible conscience. Feuerbach "never manages to conceive the sensuous world as the total living sensuous activity of the individuals composing it." [3] Feuerbach had indeed understood that the relation of man to nature is directly his relation to man; but he had been unable to complete the generic natural relation because he did not comprehend its other component element: that "the relation of nature to man is his own relation to the origin of his natural determination." That is, he did not understand that man's absolute being is not "an abstract essence" but is, rather, "the ensemble of social relations." [4]

---

[2] It was, Engels tells us, precisely Feuerbach's "extravagant deification of love to which 'true socialism' . . . in Germany after 1844 became linked, putting . . . the liberation of mankind by means of 'love' in place of the emancipation of the proletariat through the economic transformation of production . . ." (*Ibid.*, p. 19.)

[3] Marx and Engels, *The German Ideology*, pp. 37–38.

[4] Marx, *Theses on Feuerbach*, no. V, in Engels, *Ludwig Feuerbach and the Outcome of Classical German Philosophy*, pp. 83–84. "Feuerbach, who does not attempt the criticism of this real essence, is consequently compelled: 1. To abstract from the historical process and to fix the religious sentiment as something for itself and to presuppose an abstract—*isolated*—human individual. 2. The human essence, therefore, can with him be comprehended only as 'genus,' as a dumb internal generality which merely *naturally* unites the many individuals." (*Ibid.*) Again: "He does not see how the sensuous world around him is, not a thing given direct from all eternity, ever the same, but the product of industry and of the state of society; and, indeed, in the sense that it is an historical product, the result of the activity of a whole succession of generations, each standing on the shoulders of the preceding one, developing its industry and its intercourse, modifying its social organization according to the changed needs." (Marx and Engels, *The German Ideology*, p. 35.)

. . . since for the socialist man, all the pretended history of the world is nothing but the production of man by human work, . . . the development of nature for man is the . . . evident and irrefutable proof of the *birth* of himself, *of his origin.* From the fact of the *substantiality* of man, from the fact that man becomes practically sensible . . . in nature. . . it becomes impossible practically to ask if there exists a being outside of man, a being placed above that of nature and man. This question implies the non-essentiality of man. . . . Socialism . . . takes its departure from the *theoretically and practically sensible conscience* of man in nature, considered as *being.*" [5]

If indeed matter is the principle of all fecundity (see Chapter IX, p. 272, n. 20; p. 273.) *values* make their appearance out of human, social interaction with mundane reality. Man works in the face of natural matter as a natural force (man is nothing without an object, as Feuerbach had said), but we must see that his own "natural forces" are put in movement by him in order that he may "appropriate for himself natural matter under a form which can serve his own life," that is to say, under a form by which he is made specifically human. He thus exercises his proper causality.

Labour is, in the first place, a process in which both men and Nature participate, and in which man of his own accord starts, regulates, and controls the material re-actions between himself and Nature. He opposes himself to Nature as one of her own forces, setting in motion arms and legs, head and hands, the natural forces of his body, in order to appropriate Nature's productions in a form adapted to his own wants. By thus acting on the external world and changing it, he at the same time changes his own nature. He develops his slumbering powers and compels them to act in obedience to his sway. We are not now dealing with those primitive instinctive forms of labour that remind us of the mere animal. An immeasurable interval of time separates the state of things in which a man brings his labour-power to market for sale as a commodity, from that state in which human labour was still in its first instinctive stage. We presuppose labour in a form that stamps it as exclusively human. A spider conducts operations that

---

[5] Marx, *Oekonomische-philosophische Manuskript,* p. 125.

resemble those of a weaver, and a bee puts to shame many an architect in the construction of her cells. But what distinguishes the worst architect from the best of bees is this, that the architect raises his structure in imagination before he erects it in reality. At the end of every labour-process, we get a result that already existed in the imagination of the labourer at its commencement. He not only effects a change of form in the material on which he works, but he also realises a purpose of his own that gives the law to his modus operandi, and to which he must subordinate his will. And this subordination is no mere momentary act. Besides the exertion of the bodily organs, the process demands that, during the whole operation, the workman's will be steadily in consonance with his purpose. This means close attention.[6]

From these considerations the root difference between man and brute becomes evident: human work is superior to that of the animal because by his intelligence and will (even though these are only products of matter) man is more profoundly the cause of his work: Indeed he is the cause of the being of his own species and of the perfection of every natural species. It is precisely in these profound differences between human work and that of the animal—differences which define "historical materialism"—that there arises the fundamental conflict to which we have adverted—the conflict between the theoretical mind and the mundane reality which exists independently of it. This conflict—which defines "dialectical materialism"—arises indeed out of the fecundity of thought in work and in organizing work: Man is exposed to the "delusion" that spirit (or mind) is the primordial reality. The primordial reality, rather, is to be found in matter and its fecund principle of contradiction—of which the human conscience is the theoretical form. And since, as Feuerbach had allegedly shown, the conscience overcomes the object as object, man comprises in himself the fecund principle: "the relation of man to nature is directly his relation to man, just as the relation of nature to man is directly his own relation to the origin of his own natural determination."[7] Man thus exercises

---

[6] Marx, *Capital*, pt. III, chap. 7, Eng. trans., Modern Library, Inc., New York, pp. 197–198.

[7] Marx, *Oekonomische-philosophische Manuskript*, p. 113.

his causality in understanding and changing the world by the destruction of every "intention" or "*ratio*" in nature—for these stand as "foreign objects," as contradictions to the absolute unity of the individual's "generic being."

But it is precisely the fecundity of thought that leads man to cut himself off from the "real" world, to "manufacture" "pure" theory, theology, philosophy, and every ideology. He "emancipates" himself from the world, and this emancipation begins with the division of work into material and mental.

Division of labor only becomes truly such from the moment when a division of material and mental labor appears. From this moment onward, consciousness *can* really flatter itself that it is something other than consciousness of existing practice, that it is really conceiving something without conceiving something real; from now on consciousness is in a position to emancipate itself from the world, and to proceed to the formation of "pure" theory, theology, philosophy, ethics, etc. But even if this theory, theology, ethics, etc. comes into contradiction with the existing relations, this can only occur as a result of the fact that existing social relations have come into contradiction with existing forces of production. . . .[8]

When Marx speaks of "pure" theory, theology, etc., as efforts of man to emancipate himself from the world, he implies an alienation of man's generic being; and this will be understood if we recall that "by social we understand the cooperation of several individuals, no matter under what conditions, in what manner, and to what end," so that even forms of alienation such as religion, the state, law, morals, science, spirit, are particular modes of social life, for they are modes of production and fall under its general laws.[9] It is the fecundity of intellect in organizing work that produces "theology" and every other form of "abstract alienation"—the state, law, morals, science, spirit, all dependent on the initial alienation of self represented by the God-creature relation. Hence it is that the unity of the species

---

[8] Marx and Engels, *The German Ideology*, p. 20.
[9] Marx, *Oekonomische-philosophische Manuskript*, p. 117.

cannot be restored even by "the fully-developed political state" —where those who lack the means of mental production are no longer subject to the ideas of a ruling class. For these "alienations" continue to subsist in civil life outside the political sphere. Rousseau's "General Will" was a mirage.

[Although] the perfect political state, according to its essence, is the generic life of man by opposition to his material life [nonetheless all] the suppositions of [the] egoistic life continue to subsist in civil society outside of the political sphere . . . as properties of bourgeois society. There, where the political state has reached its full development, man leads not only in thought, in conscience, but in reality, in life, a double existence, celestial and terrestrial, the existence in the political community, where he considers himself as a generic being, and the existence in civil society, where he works as a mere part, sees in other men simply means, is himself swallowed up in the role of a simple means, and becomes the plaything of forces extraneous to himself.[10]

It is easy to see that if "the ideas of the ruling class are in every epoch the ruling ideas," the last form of human emancipation *within the framework of the actual social order* will be the above described political emancipation: The precise understanding of which is the emancipation not absolutely of man, but of the *State* from the ideas of a ruling class. This is the situation in the fully developed political State. "Political" emancipation is accomplished by the "theoretical" and "political" suppression of religion and private property and of all the distinctions constituted by talent and education. These are suppressed in the State which affirms itself purely and simply *State* by ignoring these "illusions" for purposes of voting and holding office. In this kind of emancipation man achieves his liberty only through the *intermediary* of the State.

The state is the intermediary between man and the liberty of man. Just as Christ is the intermediary whom man charges with all of his [own] divinity, with all of his religious limitation, so the State is the

[10] Marx, *Die Judenfrage,* p. 583.

intermediary which man charges with all of his humanity, with all of his human limitation.[11]

There must be no "intermediary" between man and the liberty of man; he must be his own master, find the independence which resolves the old antagonisms between origin and being, freedom and necessity, man and nature, individual and species. The "political emancipation" of man constitutes a great progress, but it is not the final form of human emancipation. For in the fully developed State every man is equally considered as an isolated monad, not as a generic being. "Quite the contrary, the generic life itself, Society, appears as a frame external to the individual, as a limitation on his initial independence." [12] The "perfection" of the State, then, is in no way opposed to all the suppositions of the egoistic life which continue to subsist in civil society outside the political sphere. Speaking of the Declaration of the Rights of Man and of the Citizen (1791) and of the Declaration of the Rights of Man (1793), Marx observes that "none of the pretended rights of man goes beyond the egoistic man, man such as he is, that is to say, an individual separated from society, fallen back upon himself, uniquely preoccupied with his own personal interests and obedient to his own *privé arbitraire.*" [13]

If political emancipation is the last form within the actual social order, there is required for the complete return of man to his generic being the destruction of that civil society wherein all the suppositions of the egoistic life continue to separate the individual from his social being. At the other extreme from Plato, by an obverse Platonic confusion of the logical and the real, Marx declares the individual man to be the whole of society: "Man—to whatever degree . . . that he may be a particular individual . . . is as much at the same time the totality, the ideal totality, the subjective existence of society thought and felt for itself." [14] Had not Feuerbach shown that man is con-

[11] *Ibid.,* p. 583.
[12] *Ibid.,* p. 595.
[13] *Ibid.*
[14] Marx, *Oekonomische-philosophische Manuskript,* p. 117.

scious of himself as being both individual *and* species? Feuer-bach's fault was to have taken this species for "abstract essence" and not for "the ensemble of social relations." What Aristotle had suggested by way of irony in criticizing Plato—that if he wanted the simplest possible unity he ought to have reduced the state to the family and the family to the individual—is true of Marx without irony.

The generic being of man asserts, as we have seen, the *"theo-retically and practically* sensible conscience of man in nature con-sidered as *being"*; true social existence is not achieved until the sensible expression of human life alienated is also overcome; for this alone brings with it "the return of the man of religion, of the family, of the state, etc., to his human existence, that is to say, his social existence." [15] "The complete, conscious return, accomplished within the interior of the whole wealth of past development, of *man for himself,* as a social being," requires the suppression not only of those alienations that operate in the domain of conscience—religion, the family, morals, science, spirit, the state, but it requires the suppression of the material and sensible expression of human life alienated. The material and sensible expression of human life alienated (private prop-erty) and its movement (production and consumption) are the sensible manifestations of the movement of all anterior produc-tion, namely, of religion, the family, state, law, morals, science, spirit, etc. which are only particular modes of production and fall under its general laws. Hence:

> The positive suppression of private property, as an appropriation of *human* life is therefore the positive suppression of every alienation, and thus the return of the man of religion, of the family, of the state, etc. to his *human* existence, that is to say, his social existence. . . . Eco-nomic alienation is that of the *real* life—its suppression, therefore, em-braces both [the theoretical and practical] sides.[16]

The reason for this is that in private property "all the physical and intellectual senses have . . . been replaced by the simple

[15] *Ibid.,* p. 115.
[16] *Ibid.*

alienation of all the senses, the sense of *having*." And this is so because "private property has rendered us so foolish and inactive that an object is [considered to be] ours only when we have it . . . exists for us only when it is immediately possessed, eaten, drunk by us, carried by us, worn by us, etc., in short, used by us." [17] With the suppression of private property the senses . . . become directly, in practice, *theoreticians*.

They relate themselves to the thing for love of the thing, but the thing is itself an *objective human* relation with itself and with man and vice versa. The need of the spirit has lost its egoistic nature, and nature has lost its simple utility from the fact that the utility has become a *human utility*.

From the fact that everywhere in Society the objective reality becomes for man the reality of human forces, human reality, and consequently the reality of his own forces, all *objects* become for him the objectification of himself, objects which manifest and realize his individuality, *his* objects, that is to say, the object of himself. [18]

The division of labor, which began with the division of work into material and mental, is brought to an end with the suppression of private property, and the unity of the species is achieved both theoretically and practically. It is achieved first, on the theoretical side, by the overcoming of the alienations that operate in the conscience (state, religion, law, morals, science, spirit); man is brought beyond atheism to his own "essentiality" (man "in nature is considered as *being*"): The religion, state, law, morals, science, and spirit that took their rise from "pure theory, theology, philosophy, ethics, etc." *are at an end*. An instance of this in the seizure of Goa in December, 1961, is so apposite and so appositely put by Mr. R. H. Shackford that it deserves to be quoted in full:

United Nations, Dec. 20—India's new "dictum of international law" amounts to legalization of aggression when colonial areas are involved.

India's delegate to the UN, C. S. Jha, junked all of what he called

[17] *Ibid.*, p. 118.
[18] *Ibid.*, p. 119.

"narrow-minded" concepts of international law under which India's invasion of Goa can be nothing but aggression.

He did this at the Monday night session of the UN Security Council during debate on a resolution calling for a cease-fire in Goa and the withdrawal of Indian troops. The Soviets vetoed the resolution, which got seven of the council's 11 votes.

If the Indian ideas were accepted, it would mean that:

The use of force to liquidate "the remnants of colonialism" would be approved and encouraged.

All remaining colonial and dependent areas would be denied the legal status they have had for many years.

The nations with responsibility for dependent areas would be stripped of all legal rights in those areas.

A UN General Assembly resolution, which is only a recommendation with no mandatory power, would supersede the charter of the UN which is a formal, ratified treaty among nations.

The essence of Jha's argument was that any principles of international law which deny a nation like India the right to take Goa by force are old-fashioned.

Although Portugal has held Goa as a colony for 451 years, Jha argued there was no frontier between Goa and India because Portugal never has had sovereign rights there.

Portugal's "occupation" of Goa, he insisted, has been illegal since the 16th century and is "even more illegal" today. And then he set forth this incredible idea:

"If any narrow-minded, legalistic considerations—considerations arising from international law as written by European law writers—should arise, those writers were, after all, brought up in the atmosphere of colonialism.

"I pay all respect due to Hugo Grotius, who is supposed to be the father of international law and we accept many tenets of international law. . . .

"But the tenet . . . quoted in support of colonial powers having sovereign rights over territories they won by conquest in Asia and Africa is no longer acceptable.

"It is the European concept and it must die. It is time, in the 20th century, that it died."

Jha's principal supporter in this new theory of world law was Ceylon's G. P. Malalasekera who argued that India couldn't possibly be accused of using force because of its deliberate policy of not being a member of a military alliance.[19]

Granted that there is an urgent need for a reconsideration of the status of "dependent" peoples, we have here certainly a frightening confirmation of Heinrich Heine's prophecy that "then will appear Kantians as little tolerant of piety in the world of deeds as in the world of ideas, who will mercilessly upturn with sword and axe the soil of our European life in order to extirpate the last remnants of the past." Here indeed is the ultimate issue of the Enlightenment's principle of the autarky of human reason: the legal and social order reduced to wholly voluntary acts, to "a clear and understandable fact" (as we saw Cassirer praise that principle); a "precision"—indeed!—is given to the meaning of reason such as it had not had in an equal degree in antiquity (as we saw Professor Sabine describe its special character). At last we are to live in accord with "the facts"—which, we will recall, Judge Learned Hand had told us was our only "truth-worthy" way of living. By "delicate test and remorseless logic" the new "scientific world" is there—wherever "there" may be (to use Sir Arthur Eddington's words once more). For indeed, magic and myth, as Cassirer himself said, have entered into the world of culture and civilization: that world which, as Aristotle warned, can be exorcised.[20]

On the "practical side," the unity of the species is achieved by the overcoming of the material alienation of human life: This takes man beyond the need for "having," that is, work ceases to be a mere means to existence. It has lost its "simple utility" be-cause objects have become "the objectification of [man], objects which manifest and realize his individuality, *his* objects, that is to say, the object of himself."

The suppression of private property, as much as the suppression of religion, is a negation which communism poses as a

[19] "India Turning World Law Topsy-Turvy," a report by Mr. R. H. Shack-ford of the Scripps-Howard Staff, *The Rocky Mountain News*, Denver, Thursday, Dec. 21, 1961, p. 46.

[20] Consult the cartoon facing p. 311, which shows two exorcists at work.

negation. We will recall that there can be no intermediary between man and his liberty. As we have observed, the "theoretical" and "political" suppression of human alienation left the State as an intermediary charged with all of man's humanity, with all his human limitation. We must now see that the *real* suppression of all these alienations in the destruction of private property is not, *as a mere negation,* the true fulfillment of man's generic being. The real life of man is no more the reality of man based on the suppression of private property than is "the theoretically and practically sensible conscience of man in nature, considered as *being*" a conscience which has need, as an intermediary, of the suppression of religion:

> Socialism, insofar as it is socialism, has no more need of [the mediation of atheism]; it takes its departure from . . . the *conscience* that man has of himself, a *positive* conscience which no longer has need, as an intermediary, of the suppression of religion, *just as the real life is no more the reality of man based on the suppression of private property.* Communism poses the negation as a negation; it is consequently the *real* element, and indispensable to the historic development of the future, to human emancipation, and the recovery of human dignity. Communism is the necessary form and organic principle of the immediate future, but communism is not in itself the goal of human education,—the form of human society.[21]

The *real* life of man is the life of sensible activity as opposed to the *theoretical* life, which is the "activity of the generic conscience." Just as the activity of the generic conscience, by affirming the "essentiality" of man, has no further need of atheism (which does not go beyond the nonessentiality of God) so the *real* life has no need for suppressing private property, for this would imply the need for suppressing *the need for having*—a need which implies the poverty of man's own substantial forces, the interior riches of his infinite being. Thus in the last phase of social development work will be not only a means to existence, but—in accordance with the principle that man is most properly

---

[21] Marx, *Oekonomische-philosophische Manuskript*, pp. 125–126.

a producer when he is free from physical need and sets himself up freely in the face of his production—work will itself be the first need of life, the activity by which man transforms nature and produces *himself*.

As an achieved naturalism, this form of communism is true humanism, and as an achieved humanism it is true naturalism. It is the true solution to the antagonisms between man and nature, between man and man, the true solution of the struggle between origin and being, between objectification and subjectification, between liberty and necessity, between the individual and the species. . . . Society is the achieved consubstantiality of man with nature, the veritable resurrection of nature, the realization of the naturalism of man and the humanism of nature.[22]

But we must now carefully follow through with Marx to see indeed the disaster that overtakes the individual at the very point of attaining his apotheosis: Man, we recall, is not an "abstract essence"—he is the result of the activity of a whole succession of generations, of the total sensuous activity of all individuals composing the sensuous world. "The highest point attained by contemplative materialism, i.e., materialism which does not understand sensuousness as practical activity, is the outlook of single individuals in 'civil society.' . . . The standpoint of the old materialism is 'civil society'; the standpoint of the new is *human* society or socialized humanity."[23] The "unity of the species" is achieved *in the individual* only in the "universal consciousness": "Man is the totality, the *ideal* totality, the *subjective* existence of society thought and felt for itself."[24] It is only in the activity of the generic *conscience* that the individual realizes the "general mode" of the generic life; and this "general mode" in him is "the theoretical form of that of which the living form is the real community." In his species-conscience, then, the

[22] *Ibid.*, pp. 116–117.

[23] Marx, "Theses on Feuerbach," nos. IX and X, in Engels, *Ludwig Feuerbach and the Outcome of Classical German Philosophy*, p. 84.

[24] Marx, *Oekonomische-philosophische Manuskript*, p. 11. (Italics added.)

individual *reproduces* his *real* existence in thought: the real existence, in its living form, is the "ensemble of social relations." In its "living form" then—as distinguished from its "theoretical form"—the unity of the species is achieved in the community, in "socialized humanity." Therefore, in what Marx calls the "real life" the individual is only "a determinate generic being"—a "more particular mode of the generic life." As he says:

> Death appears as a hard victory of the species over the individual, and seems to contradict the unity of the species; but the determinate individual is only a determinate generic being, and as such he is mortal. . . . Each of his human relationships . . . are in their objective relationship . . . the appropriation of [the] object, the appropriation of human reality. This manifestation is as multiple as are *human determinations and activities,* human *activity* and human *suffering,* for suffering, taken in the human sense, is a pleasure proper to man.[25]

Thus indeed not only is the individual's mortality quite indifferent to his real species-being, his social humanity; his life in its individuality is not his "real" life: *This* flesh, *these* bones have only the life of the flesh, the bones of the total sensuous activity of all generations. When treating Feuerbach, I alluded to St. Thomas' statement that ". . . if there were any individual that were itself its species—as if, for example Socrates were humanity itself—there would not be in Socrates any parts that were not parts of humanity." It is precisely in this way that we are to understand Marx's statement that society is "not an abstraction confronting the individual—the individual life and the species-life are not different." [26] This is the sense of the individual no longer being "a mere part . . . swallowed up in the role of a simple means . . . the plaything of forces extraneous to himself." This is that apotheosis and transfiguration of the "withdrawal" and "protest" of the early post-Aristotelian philosophies of conduct of which we have spoken; it is the realization at once of the political significance of the early philosophies

[25] *Ibid.,* pp. 117–118. (Italics in the original.)
[26] *Ibid.,* p. 116.

of conduct and the "human" significance of the political philosophy of the revolutions of the seventeenth and eighteenth centuries. The "intolerable attitude" of "half-contemplation and half-action" —as Marx described the position of the post-Aristotelian philosophies of conduct—is overcome by the absolute "aseity" of "socialized humanity." This is the perfecting state of the liberal "socialized conscience": the external quality of social norms need no longer be overcome and "appropriated" into the inner life of the individual, for "the individual life and the species-life *are not different*." "The objective reality [has become] for man the reality of human forces . . . the reality of his forces . . . *his* objects, that is to say, the object of himself." We have achieved in a practical way Rousseau's feeling of simple existence; a more simple feeling for existence there could not be. With a vengeance has man overcome the need for "having": his liquidation itself is carried out by his own "substantial forces." These are "the armed Fichteans," of whom we have heard Heine speak, "[who] live in the spirit," "Kantians as little tolerant of piety in the world of deeds as in the world of ideas."

In describing a play by the German poet, Bertold Brecht, Arthur Koestler shows us the dread spirit of the "armed Fichteans":

The play takes the form of a trial. Three Comintern agents return from a secret mission in China, and explain before a Party tribunal, in the form of flashbacks, why they had been obliged to kill their fourth, young comrade and to throw his body into a lime pit. The tribunal is represented by an anonymous, Greek 'Controlchorus.' The three agents are equally anonymous—they wear masks on their mission, having effaced their personality, their will and feeling, by order of the Party:

'You are no longer yourselves. No longer are you Karl Schmitt of Berlin. You are no longer Anna Kyersk of Kazan, and you are no longer Peter Savich of Moscow. You are without a name, without a mother, blank sheets on which the Revolution will write its orders.

'He who fights for Communism must be able to fight and to renounce fighting, to say the truth and not to say the truth, to be helpful and unhelpful, to keep a promise and to break a promise, to go into danger and to avoid danger, to be known and to be unknown. He who fights for Communism has of all the virtues only one: that he fights for Communism.'

The 'young comrade' however, was unable to live up to this ethical code. He was guilty of four crimes, having successively fallen into the traps of pity, of loyalty, of dignity and of righteous indignation. In the first episode he is described as one of a gang of coolies pulling a boat up the river. He tries to help some exhausted comrades, thereby attracts attention, and the agents have to decamp. In the second episode he comes to the defence of a workman beaten up by the police, with the same result.

In the third, he is sent to negotiate with a representative of the Chinese bourgeoisie, who is willing to arm the revolutionary coolies to get rid of his British competitors. All goes well until the fat bourgeois sings a song in praise of business profits; the young comrade is so disgusted that he refuses to accept food from the bourgeois, and the deal falls through. The moral is driven home by the Controlchorus, who asks the rhetorical question:

Controlchorus: But is it not right to place honour above all?
The three agents: No.
Controlchorus: What vileness would you not commit to exterminate vileness? . . . Sink into the mud, embrace the butcher, but change the world: it needs it.

The climax of the play is the fourth episode, in which the young comrade deviates from the Party Line. The line, it should be remembered, was the Stalin-Chiang pact of 1927, one of the most terrible episodes of Comintern history, which led to the wholesale massacre of Chinese Communists by Chiang, and with Stalin's passive complicity . . . . The young comrade in the play refuses to implement that line. He tears up 'the scriptures of the Party classics,' and cries out:

'All this no longer has any bearing. At the moment when the fight is on, I reject all that was valid yesterday and do my human duty. My heart bleeds for the Revolution."

He tears his mask off and shouts to the coolies:

"We have come to help you. We come from Moscow."

So the agents, who "in the dusk saw his naked face, human, open, guileless," have to shoot him. But before they do that, they ask the young comrade whether he agrees to be shot. He answers:

> "Yes. I see that I have always acted incorrectly. Now it would be better if I were not."
> *The three agents:* "Then we shot him and threw him into the lime pit and when the lime had absorbed him we returned to our work."
> *Controlchorus:* "Your work has been blest. You have propagated the Principles of the Classics, the ABC of Communism . . ." [27]

The comment of Halévy, to which we earlier alluded, on the principles of classical liberalism is fulfilled in Marxism: ". . . as social relations increase and tighten the individual will find himself more and more tightly bound, by the force of things, to the accomplishment of his social task, until the day when it will no longer be possible to draw a line between the egoistic and the sympathetic feelings, and he will no longer be able not to act morally." [28] And thus too, an observation which we made concerning Hobbes is fulfilled: The good is defined in relation to the ontological "perfection" of each nature; the moral problem has become a problem of the maximization of being. By a "heightened self-consciousness," an achievement of "a higher order of abstraction"—to use the phrases that Mr. Riesman uses to describe autonomy—the comrade *is* socialized humanity. So that indeed his mortality is not only quite indifferent to his real species-life; it contributes to it! Had not Feuerbach already called death the supreme act of liberty, coming to man not from any defect in him but from the excess of his interior riches which are too great for his mortal frame? [29] And we have seen Marx's statement that death only *appears* to contradict the unity of the species: For as a "determinate generic being" the individual's death is itself "the appropriation of human reality," for "suffering, taken in the human sense, is a pleasure proper to man." The fecundity

---

[27] *The Invisible Writing*, The Beacon Press, Boston, 1954, pp. 41–42.

[28] Halévy, *The Growth of Philosophic Radicalism*, p. 471.

[29] *Gedanken über Tod und Unsterblichkeit, Sämmtliche Werke*, Stuttgart, 1903, vol. I, pp. 17ff.

of nonbeing has taken the place of the Prime Intellect as the primordial principle upon which depend the heavens and the world of nature. And thus there is fulfilled, in a surprising way, the aspiration of ancient Stoicism—to see the Socratic injunction "Know thyself" as having not merely "a moral but . . . a universal and metaphysical background." [30] When there "exists no spiritual realm outside of man or transcending him," when "the realm of love, reason and justice exists as a reality only because . . . man has been able to develop these powers in himself," when "there is no meaning to life, except the meaning man himself gives to it," when "man is utterly alone except inasmuch as he helps another," [31] then indeed the help a comrade gets is that of helping himself to the lime pit. Since his "real" life is his "species-life," since he *is*, in his *real* life, "socialized humanity," any other attitude would imply the "nonessentiality" of man! As Lenin says, in the higher phase of communism "the necessity of observing the simple and fundamental rules of human society will pass very rapidly into a state of habitude." Very rapidly. In fact by magic, under a "Controlchorus" which directs an "entirely irrational and mysterious religion": The "aseity" of social humanity means indeed that the fiat of social humanity precedes whatever and whoever is or may come to be; while man, as a determinate individual ("a determinate generic being"), is as pure potentiality to an infinite number of—yes —uses; just indeed as nature, precisely in the line of its pure autonomy is, as St. Thomas points out, reducible to pure potentiality to an infinite number of forms. The Comintern agents are all of them anonymous; they wear masks on their mission, having effaced their personality, their will and feeling by order of the Party. They have overcome the age-long "antagonism between man and nature . . . between origin and being . . . between liberty and necessity, between the individual and the species." [32]

[30] Cassirer, *Essay on Man,* p. 22.

[31] The phrases in quotation marks are from Fromm, *The Art of Loving,* p. 72.

[32] Marx, *Oekonomische-philosophische Manuskript,* pp. 116–117.

"You Don't Understand That We Alone Can Say What Is Right And What Is Wrong!"

Epilogue

The cartoon facing this page provides a suitable commentary on the outcome of the modern theory of politics. It brings home to us the several prophetic warnings of Heinrich Heine: It shows us how the most abstract and difficult philosophical conceptions "only await their time to break forth and to fill the world with terror and with admiration." It teaches us, therefore, not to grow unduly impatient at "metaphysical abstractions" which appear to render one unfit for practical life. It suggests, indeed, the truth of Heine's remark that "only our latest descendants will be in a position to decide whether we are to be praised or blamed for having first worked out our philosophy and afterwards our revolution. . . ."

Now if we look closely, we shall see that in Mr. Menon, Rousseau's "noble savage" seems to have fulfilled Rousseau's hope for his "perfectibility" on the "human plane," while Mr. Nehru appears as "the priest of a new, entirely irrational and mysterious religion." (Ernst Cassirer, *The Myth of the State*). It is entirely irrational and mysterious because in the twentieth century, the age of man's highest technical competence, the elements of magic and myth have for the first time in the history of civilization taken possession of the purely secular sphere. And this has happened because "the realm of love, reason and justice exists as a reality *only because, and inasmuch as,* man has been able to develop these powers in himself. . . ." [1] And therefore the legal and social order fulfills at last the hopes of the Enlightenment by being taken into hand, reduced "to free individual acts," to "a clear and understandable fact"—e.g., Goa and Kashmir. It is "truth" and "science" that Messrs. Nehru and Menon are drumming into the befuddled heads of two innocent heirs of the Enlightenment. These innocents *don't* seem to understand that the human mind is prior to "the truth of things" (*rerum veritas*)!

Recall what was said in the beginning of this study: that the modern theory of man can recover the loss of its intellectual center on condition that the human intellect is seen to occupy a center position between the condition of creator and the condition of nature, and that the very notion of self-government derives from seeing the human intellect as separable of itself (although not existing apart from matter) and thus as capable of knowing the good proper and natural to man. It was this capacity to know this good that was the guarantee at once of man's independence from any blind necessity of nature and from any political "art." In the Classical-Christian tradition, the state, law, morals, science, spirit, were participations of the human intellect in the life of that Prime Intellect upon whose perfect freedom depend the heavens and the world of nature: All human activities, Aristotle had pointed out, are akin to God's activity. [2] The likeness of the speculative intellect, in science and wisdom, was said to be one of "union" and "informing," while that of the practical intellect, in the civilizing arts, was said to be one of "proportion." And of the virtues that pertain to human affairs —the political virtues—St. Thomas observed that their exemplars must preexist in God, just as in Him preexist the types of all things. [3] The great lacuna in the development of political thought

---

[1] Fromm, *The Art of Loving*. (Italics added.)

[2] *Ethics* X.1178b.22–24.

[3] *Summa Theol.* I.II.Q.61 a.5c.

and practice has been the failure to combine the wisdom that knows that here we have no everlasting city, with the wisdom that knows the need to put the political virtues under some degree of pressure, as it were, from their exemplars in the Divine Mind: The failure to act on St. Augustine's insight that social justice should take its initial movement from its Divine exemplar in "the most Just Disposer . . . of all the adjuncts of [temporal peace]—the visible light, the breathable air, the potable water, and all the other necessaries of meat, drink, and clothing." [4] This is the true liberalism.

If it was hard to understand St. Augustine's statement that virtue sought on its own account and not referred to the true God is a vice issuing in "ambition," "proud sovereignty," and "suicide," his meaning today lies under a magnifying glass. The "variable impiety" of which—he said—that kind of virtue is the source, is palpably around us: The "Controlchorus," the voice of "social humanity," contemns the good of human nature itself —"loyalty," "dignity," "pity," and "righteous indignation." It contemns the good of civil society itself: "the honesty of virtue, the love of country, the faith of friendship, just dealing, and all the things belonging to good manners." The Earthly City has become—if not indeed visible—certainly palpable; and all the more palpable because in the liberalism of the West it finds only its own, weak impalpable counterpart: the very source of its own variable impiety. In Marxism, by a long linear development, the state, law, morals, science, spirit have disappeared and their place taken by the fiat of "social humanity." Philosophy has passed into practice.

It is remarkable that in the twentieth century the force of these ideas rather than of others is moving civilization toward the goal of one world; yet it is probable that never before in history

[4] In *The 20th Century Capitalist Revolution,* Harcourt, Brace and Company, Inc., New York, 1954, Mr. Adolf A. Berle, Jr., seems indeed to have an adumbration of this, and it is all the more remarkable because it seems not to have occurred to the commentators (and he is not a commentator) on the great social encyclicals of the Popes. See especially chap. V, "Corporate Capitalism and 'The City of God.'"

has life itself seemed so random a thing and existence so marginal and insecure. We recall Aristotle's saying that the slave lives on the margin of society, enjoying a random freedom. What Aristotle held to be true of the "natural slave" appears to be true today for the whole of human nature, concerning which we must not forget Aristotle's observation that it is itself "in many ways in bondage." And the whole world itself, subject to man for the first time for its very existence, takes on the aspect of the margin of civilization, its denizens moving toward the condition of Rousseau's noble savage—on the plane—of course!—of "humanity."

index